# GCSE Religious Studies

## Complete Revision and Practice

Covering Christianity, Roman Catholic Christianity, Mark's Gospel, Judaism and Islam

# Contents

# Contents

## Section Seven — Religion and Revelation



## Section Eight — Worship and Symbolism



## Key to Symbols:

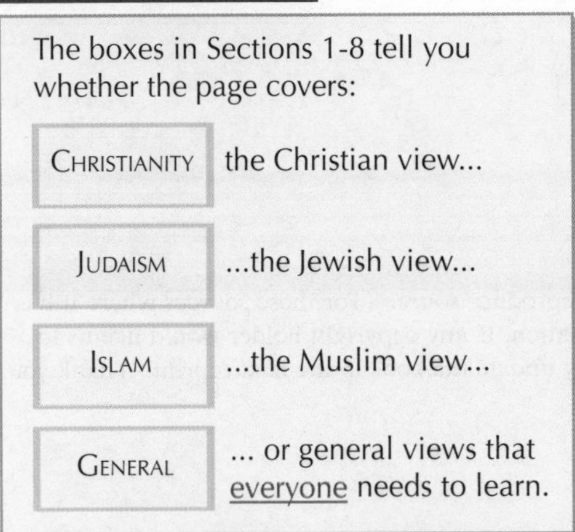


## Section Nine — Roman Catholic Christianity



## Section Ten — St Mark's Gospel



## Bible/Qur'an References:

References from the Bible always go in the order: *Book Chapter:Verse(s)*. So whenever you see something like: **Mark 3:5-6**, it means it's from the book of **Mark**, **Chapter 3**, **verses 5-6**.
Similarly, references from the Qur'an are shown with the ***Surah*** (***Chapter***) followed by the ***Ayat*** (***Verse***).

Published by CGP

*Editors:*
David Hickinson, Sharon Keeley, Luke von Kotze, Andy Park, Julie Wakeling

*Contributors:*
Maria Amayuelas-Tann, Jill Hudson, Duncan Raynor, Paul D. Smith, Nigel Thomas

ISBN: 978 1 84762 406 2

With thanks to Mary Falkner and Karen Gascoigne for the proofreading.
With thanks to Laura Jakubowski for the copyright research.



**With thanks to Enid Thompson for the church photos on page 92.**



Groovy website: www.cgpbooks.co.uk

Jolly bits of clipart from CorelDRAW®
Printed by Elanders Ltd, Newcastle upon Tyne

Based on the classic CGP style created by Richard Parsons.

# Reasons for Belief

GENERAL

Millions of people across the world believe in some kind of divine being or 'god'. They believe for various reasons — for some people, it's based on personal religious experience, but for others it's more indirect.
For many people, the fact that they're brought up in a religious environment leads to or supports belief in a god.

## Religious Belief can Start with your Upbringing

1) Children generally believe what their parents tell them, and tend to copy their parents' behaviour.
2) So, if a child is brought up by religious parents, with an upbringing that's based on religious teaching, it's more likely that they'll believe in a god.
3) For example, most Christian parents will have their children baptised soon after they're born, take them to pray in church, send them to Sunday school to learn about the Christian faith and encourage them to be confirmed as Christians when they're old enough. They'll also take part in religious festivals, e.g. performing in a nativity play at Christmas. At home, church and Sunday school, there are trusted adults who set an example of belief in God, and can help a child to develop their own faith.
4) The same would apply if you grew up in a religious community or went to a religious school (e.g. a Roman Catholic school, a Jewish Cheder or a Muslim Madrasah) where life is based on faith in one particular religion.

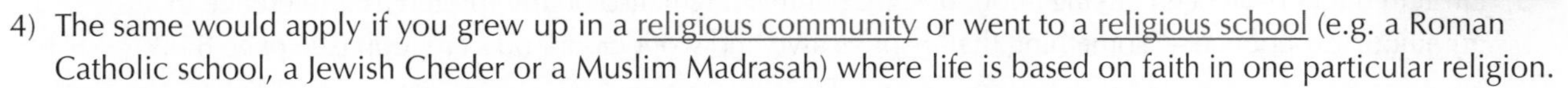

5) Different religions have different attitudes towards raising children in their faith:

**Christianity**

1) According to the New Testament, you cannot be 'born a Christian'.
2) It's said that God has no grandchildren. In other words, you can't rely on your parents' faith — you have to find your own. And your parents can't force you to accept Christianity — it's your decision.

*Evangelical Christians (see p.43-44) in particular stress this.*

**Judaism**

1) Jews believe that if your mother is Jewish, you're Jewish — whether you like it or not.
2) However, practising Jews recognise the importance of encouraging their children to 'keep the faith'.

**Islam**

1) Muslims believe that everyone is born in submission to Allah.
2) They may walk away from Allah as a result of their upbringing, but this is not the way things were meant to be.
3) If someone embraces Islam later in life, he or she is said to be 'returning'.

6) Conversion refers to the first time a person becomes a follower of a god (although it can also be used when someone changes their faith). They might say they've been 'saved' or 'born again'.

## Religious Experiences may Lead to Belief in a God

There are loads of ways that people claim to experience God.

1) Religious Scripture — some people believe that holy books (e.g. the Bible) can reveal the nature of God.
2) Prayer — this is an attempt to contact God directly and can be thought of as a conversation with God.
3) Miracles — these are amazing events that can't be explained by the laws of nature or science.
4) Numinous Experiences — these are feelings of awe, in which a person can 'sense' the presence of God.

*There's more about revelations on page 84.*

### But there are Plenty of Sceptics around...

A key concern for nonbelievers is whether miracles and other religious experiences are real.
Sceptics argue that they're just illusions brought on by religious hysteria or a desire to believe in something. Or that events that seem miraculous can actually be explained by science.

## Your upbringing can have a powerful influence on your beliefs...

What causes someone to believe in a god is different for everyone. Someone's upbringing often influences their belief, but people may convert because of religious experiences like miracles or feelings of awe.

General

# Design and Causation

There are two main philosophical arguments for the existence of a god.
These are usually referred to as the argument from design and the argument from causation.

## Design: "Someone must have designed the Universe"

1) Many people are convinced of the existence of a god by 'design' arguments.
2) The idea here is that the intricate workings of the Universe (or of life) can't have come about by random chance. There must have been some kind of designer — and this designer was God.
3) Isaac Newton's thumb theory (because every thumbprint is intricate and unique, there must be a God) and William Paley's watchmaker theory (you wouldn't think an intricate watch you found was made by chance — so why believe the world was) are both design arguments.
4) Even Albert Einstein, one of the most prominent scientists of the twentieth century (and an agnostic — see below), said: "When I see all the glories of the cosmos, I can't help but believe that there is a divine hand behind it all."

Einstein

5) Einstein might have been talking about design, but this might also be interpreted as a reference to a numinous experience — something that inspires awe and wonder at God's creation (see page 84).

## Causation: "There must have been a First Cause"

1) The Universe as we know it works on the principle of 'cause and effect' — that is, everything that happens is caused by something else.
2) So an event happening now was caused by an earlier event, which in turn was caused by an even earlier event, and so on back through time.
3) If you trace this chain of cause and effect back in time, you find two possibilities:
   a) The chain goes back forever — i.e. the Universe has always existed, it's eternal.
   b) You eventually reach a starting point — an uncaused cause or 'First Cause'.
4) Some people argue that this 'First Cause' must have been God.

## But Not Everyone is Convinced by these Arguments

1) These philosophical arguments convince many people of the existence of God.

Darwin

2) However, non-religious ideas about the origin of the world might lead a person to become an agnostic (someone who doesn't know whether or not there's a god — strictly, someone who believes it's impossible to know whether there's a god or not) or an atheist (someone who rejects completely the idea of a divine being).
3) These ideas include the theory of evolution (often called Darwinism) and the Big Bang theory (cosmology) (more about those on the next page).
4) Cosmologists argue that the Big Bang theory offers an alternative 'First Cause'. According to the theory, both space and time started with the Big Bang. If this is true, then to ask what came 'before' the Big Bang or what 'caused' the Big Bang is meaningless.

## Christians, Muslims and Jews have Similar Beliefs about God

Since Christianity and Islam both developed from Judaism, the basic concept of God (the Christian God, the Muslim Allah or the Jewish Almighty) is something that all three faiths share. God is believed to be:

OMNIPOTENT: all-powerful — nothing is impossible for God.

OMNISCIENT: all-knowing — knowing everything that we do, think or feel, now, in the past and in the future.

OMNI-BENEVOLENT: all-loving and all-compassionate — he wants only what's best for us.

## Looks like the jury's still out on this one...

Philosophers have been arguing backwards and forwards about this sort of thing for thousands of years.

# The Origins of the World

GENERAL

No one saw exactly how the Earth came to be like it is... but science and religion both have their theories.

## *Scientific Arguments — There are **Two** Main Types*

*COSMOLOGICAL THEORIES* — How the Universe came into being

Chief amongst these is the Big Bang theory. It says that the Universe began in an explosion of matter and energy. Matter from this explosion eventually formed stars, planets and everything else. The Universe still seems to be expanding today — important evidence for this theory.

*EVOLUTIONARY THEORIES* — How living things came to be like they are today

In 1859, Charles Darwin published 'On the Origin of the Species'. In this book he argued that all life on the planet originated from simple cells. Life evolved (gradually changed) over millions of years into a huge variety of forms. According to this theory, we evolved from apes — not from Adam and Eve.

These theories are at odds with many religious arguments. However, if you don't take everything in the Bible or Torah literally, scientific and religious ideas can exist in harmony. Science tells us how, religion tells us why.

## *Religions have their **Own Ideas** about all this...*

### Christian Ideas

*"In the beginning God created the heavens and the earth."* **Genesis 1:1**

1) Traditional Christian and Jewish teachings about Creation come from the same scriptures, and so are identical.
2) According to Genesis Chapter 1, God created everything. If the Bible is taken literally, the process took six days, and humankind didn't evolve from apes, but is descended from Adam and Eve.
3) However, some Christians view Genesis as a parable, or as a symbolic description of a more gradual evolution. So it's possible to believe in the Bible and science.
4) In 1996 the Roman Catholic Church accepted the Big Bang theory — definitely a significant acceptance of science.

#### *The Creation in Genesis Chapter 1*

Genesis says things were created in the following order: on the first day light and darkness; on the second day the sky; on the third day oceans, land and plants on the land; on the fourth day the sun, moon and stars; on the fifth day creatures of the water and sky (e.g. fish and birds); and then on the sixth day, land animals and people. On the seventh day, God rested.

If you ignore the fourth day, this is pretty much the same order as scientists think things appeared. So the timescale is different (millions of years rather than six days), but the general idea is the same.

### Jewish Ideas

1) Orthodox Jews, who see the Torah as the word of God and so literally true, would find it difficult to accept scientific arguments about creation.
2) Reform Jews might argue that Creation as described in the Torah is more a way for us to understand, not an explanation of, how it happened.

### Islamic Ideas

1) The Muslim creation story is very similar to that in Genesis. Muslims believe that Allah created the world and everything in it.
2) But descriptions of creation in the Qur'an aren't entirely at odds with science. In fact, scientific theories are supported by passages like this.
3) Islam differs from science when it comes to the creation of humans, though. The Qur'an states that Allah formed Adam from clay and breathed life and a soul into him — and that all humans descend from Adam.

*"Have those who disbelieved not considered that the heavens and the earth were a joined entity, and We separated them and made from water every living thing? Then will they not believe?"* **Qur'an 21:30**

## *This is a key question in the science vs. religion debate...*

Whether the Universe came to be this way through chance or design is a big question.

GENERAL & CHRISTIANITY

# Evil and Suffering

Loads of bad things happen in the world. People suffer from terrible illnesses and die in pain. Some people commit horrible crimes and other people suffer as a result. These issues often cause people to ask why. For religious people, the bigger question is: *"Why is God letting this happen?"*

## *Evil can be either **Human-made** or **Natural***

Evil and suffering can be divided into two types:

**MORAL (HUMAN-MADE) EVIL**

1) This is when suffering is brought about by the cruel actions of people.
2) This includes things like murder, war, rape and torture.
3) The person causing the evil is able to make a choice about what is morally right or wrong.

**NATURAL EVIL**

1) This kind of evil, and the suffering that comes with it, is caused by the world in which we live, and is no-one's 'fault'.
2) This includes things like disease, floods, earthquakes and hurricanes.
3) However, many recent natural disasters may have been caused by human interference in the natural world, raising the question of whether that makes those events human-made.

## ***Evil** can Lead People to **Question** their **Faith***

1) Evil and suffering may lead some people to question their belief in God — or even to reject their faith.
2) This might be because they can't believe that a God who is good would allow such things to happen, or because they feel that their prayers are not being answered (i.e. they think God could help, but doesn't).

*There's more about prayer on pages 97 and 98.*

**ANSWERED AND UNANSWERED PRAYERS**

Roman Catholics and Orthodox Christians often pray for a saint to intercede with God on behalf of someone who's suffering. These are called 'intercessory prayers'. In other Christian traditions, prayers of intercession for others are addressed directly to God, as are prayers for help in Judaism and Islam (called du'a in Islam).
Christianity, Judaism and Islam teach that no sincere prayer goes unheard or unanswered — if a prayer seems to be unanswered, it's just that we can't understand God's reply.
Since no human can ever know God's plan, it's impossible to say what's really best for us.
Praying for and helping those who suffer is seen as a key part of various faiths.

3) Other people might argue that God can't be very powerful if he is unable to prevent suffering (i.e. God can't help, even if he wanted to).

## *The **Christian** View — **Adam & Eve**, a **Test of Faith**...*

1) Christianity and Judaism teach that evil entered the world as a result of Adam and Eve giving in to temptation in the Garden of Eden — this switch from a perfect world to one containing evil is known as 'The Fall'.
2) After the Fall, every human being was born with a flawed nature, capable of causing suffering — this is the idea of original sin.
3) Christians believe God created humans with free will — it's up to us to choose whether we perform evil deeds or not, just as it was up to Adam and Eve whether to give in to temptation or not.
4) Suffering is often seen as a test of faith — God has his reasons (even if we don't know what they are). Christians believe that they should try to help people who are suffering — both practically and by praying.
5) Some (but not all) Christians believe in an evil, spiritual force known as the Devil or Satan who is working against God, bringing evil and suffering to humanity.

*Christianity and Judaism differ in that Christians believe Jesus was put on Earth to pay for the sins of all humankind.*

## *Not the cheeriest page in the book, for sure...*

So we're into evil and suffering already. Many people have tried to work out exactly what evil is.
Some argue that human-made evil is a psychological disorder that some people are more prone to than others.

# Evil and Suffering

JUDAISM & ISLAM

The problem of evil, why people suffer, and how to deal with it. It's the sort of thing religion was invented for.

## *Judaism* and *Islam* also say we have the *Choice...*

1) Both Judaism and Islam teach that humankind was created with free will.
2) Therefore, people can choose to follow God, or choose to do wrong.
3) Judaism and Islam also have similar perspectives on how to deal with suffering and evil.

## *Judaism* says *Suffering* can have *Positive Results*

1) The Book of Job in the Hebrew Bible contains a key Jewish idea on evil and suffering. Job endures terrible suffering of all kinds and he questions God. In the end Job comes to the conclusion that God is all-powerful and knows what he is doing — and that suffering must be accepted because we can't really understand the world or God's plan.
2) Judaism teaches that we have free will and are able to choose what we do (like Adam and Eve — see p.4). But we are prone to making mistakes, which could lead to suffering.
3) Like many Christians, Jews may also respond to suffering and evil through prayer.
4) The Jewish approach to suffering often stresses the idea that good can come out of terrible suffering. Suffering can bring people closer to each other and closer to God. It also allows people to make sacrifices for other people and draw on their inner strength.
5) The following passage is taken from the Midrash (a collection of Rabbinical commentaries on the Tenakh, or Jewish Bible): *"Not to have known suffering is not to be truly human."* It suggests that suffering is simply a part of the human experience and, therefore, must be accepted.

## The *Qur'an* says *"We Will Surely Test You"*

1) Muslims believe that evil is a test of humanity's free will. We have free will so can choose whether to give in to temptation or not. It's a test of faith.
2) Islam teaches that if we choose to act against the will of Allah we will have to answer for that wrongdoing on the Day of Judgement.
3) The following passage is taken from the **Qur'an 2:155-156**:

*This is remarkably similar to the moral of the Book of Job, when you think about it.*

> *"And We will surely test you with something of fear and hunger and a loss of wealth and lives and fruits, but give good tidings to the patient, who, when disaster strikes them, say, 'Indeed we belong to Allah, and indeed to Him we will return.'"*

4) The idea here is that suffering should be accepted. Muslims believe that, despite suffering in this life, there will be joy in the next as Allah is compassionate.
5) Prayer is one way of coping with evil and suffering. If people pray for forgiveness when they have done wrong they will be forgiven. One of the ninety-nine revealed names of Allah is Al-Ghaffar — The Forgiver.
6) Muslims believe that those who are suffering should be treated compassionately by others. Many Muslims work to help those who are suffering.
7) However, there is a belief in a devil (called Iblis or Shaytan) who was cast out by Allah and tries to lead people away from him. Some Muslims would argue that Allah allows Shaytan to use this power to test and tempt us — we have the free will to resist.

*Remember — there are differences in belief and tradition within Judaism and Islam, as there are within all religions.*

## *Judaism and Islam both say suffering is a test...*

Christianity, Judaism and Islam all have pretty similar ideas about this stuff: 1) Suffering is often seen as a test of faith. 2) You should always try to help others who are suffering. 3) Evil is wrong, but if you pray for forgiveness after doing something wrong, God/Allah will be merciful and will forgive you.

GENERAL & JUDAISM

# The Problem of Evil

What believers mean by the 'problem' of evil is why there is evil in the world and how we should respond to it.

## There are *Different Ideas* about the *Problem of Evil*

**CHRISTIANITY**

1) Some Christians would argue that most evil comes about because of how we humans act. After the Fall (p.4) we have the choice to do evil — and it is our responsibility not to.
2) Some Christians think that evil is necessary for there to be free will — without the choice of doing wrong, what freedom is there? They believe that there has to be evil in the world for it to be possible for us to do good — really doing good things requires that we could have acted differently. If we could only do good, how virtuous would we really be?
3) Many Christians believe that all the suffering in the world will in the end come to good — that God has a plan in which we must have faith.

**JUDAISM**

Most Jewish thought doesn't seek to explain the presence of evil, or try to explain away the problem of evil. Many Jews believe that evil requires a human response rather than a philosophical explanation — i.e. being available to help those people who are the victims.

**ISLAM**

1) Islam teaches that everything that happens is part of Allah's plan. Allah has good reasons for allowing evil, including natural evil, to occur — even if they aren't immediately apparent to us.
2) Evil also gives people the chance to do good. It's up to us to be good and help those in need. If we ourselves are afflicted by evil, Muslims believe we must meet it with patience and faith.

## The *Holocaust* Caused Jews to ask *"Where was God?"*

1) Towards the end of the 18th century, persecution of Jews living in Europe, known as anti-Semitism, spread through many countries — especially France, Germany, Austria and Russia.
2) Later, during the 1920s, Germany faced huge economic problems. The National Socialist (Nazi) Party seemed to offer solutions. It pinned the blame for the country's problems on 'non-Aryan' people (i.e. those who weren't considered 'pure Germans') living in Germany — especially the Jews.
3) In 1933 its leader Adolf Hitler became Chancellor of Germany, and laws began to be passed that gradually deprived the Jews of their citizenship rights. Eventually Hitler introduced the Final Solution — the plan to wipe out the Jews completely. Six million Jews died in the Holocaust.

The Holocaust posed very serious spiritual problems for Jews — they had to find answers to questions like:

If God exists, and he is good, and all-powerful, how could he have allowed such terrible suffering?
If we are the 'chosen people', how could God have let six million of us be wiped out?

Jews have come up with many responses to this type of question:

1) Some Jews have concluded that there is no God.
2) Some have concluded that if God does exist, he either doesn't care, or is powerless to intervene.
3) Some Jews say that the Holocaust, and all suffering, is a test of faith — if good people always got the best things in life, everyone would be good for the wrong reasons.
4) Some Jews say that God could intervene to stamp out evil if he chose to. However, he gave all human beings free will and refuses to override this even when it is abused. Also, it would be impossible for God to 'destroy all evil people' because no-one is completely evil or completely good.
5) Some Jews regard all those who died in the Holocaust as martyrs for the faith, and see their martyrdom as 'sanctifying the name of God'.
6) Some say the most important thing is to keep practising Judaism, or else Hitler will have won.

## *It'll be a problem for you too if you don't learn it...*

Some really terrible things happen. It's no wonder that this stuff is a problem for religious believers.
But most faiths try to tackle evil constructively and to help the victims of natural and moral evil.

# The Media: Belief

GENERAL

The media, e.g. TV programmes, radio programmes and films, can have a big impact on people's beliefs.

## A Christian Example: "Songs of Praise"

Dedicated religious programmes might affect people's attitudes to belief in God. One of the best-known is 'Songs of Praise', which features Christian hymns and focuses on a different community or theme each week.

**SONGS OF PRAISE — SUNDAY EVENINGS, BBC 1**

Positive effects on faith:

1) Viewers share other people's experiences of God and faith. This can help show the relevance of Christianity to people's lives, and make them feel part of a larger community.
2) The themes covered in the programme can lead to a deeper understanding of the Christian religion.
3) The programme is interactive — with hymn and prayer text on screen. This lets viewers take part in communal worship without having to go to church.

Negative effects on faith:

1) It's hard to feel personally involved in a service when you're watching it on TV.
2) The programme might be seen to trivialise the act of worship.
3) Some people find the traditional hymns boring and uninspiring.

*Christian leaders such as the Pope and the Archbishop of Canterbury often appear in the media giving their opinions on all sorts of issues. Their messages are sometimes presented out of context, though, making them sound more controversial. This makes for exciting headlines, but can give a very bad impression of Christianity.*

BBC Radio 4 broadcasts religious programmes, including 'Sunday Worship' on a Sunday morning. There's also a Christian digital TV channel — GOD TV.

## Judaism is Sometimes Stereotyped by the Media

1) You don't tend to get regular, specifically Jewish programmes on national TV or radio, and this is a cause for some concern and frustration among the Jewish community in the UK.
2) Many feel that Jewish issues are not always dealt with fairly and that Jews are shown in a stereotypical way (e.g. passive victims in Holocaust films like 'Schindler's List', neurotic intellectuals in Woody Allen films like 'Annie Hall' or pushy, overprotective mothers in US sitcoms like 'Will and Grace').

In June 2008, BBC 4 broadcast an in-depth series of programmes called 'Jews' that looked at the history, religious practices and beliefs of different groups of Jews in Britain today. Programmes like this may help Jews to reconnect with their faith, as well as educating the non-Jewish community.

3) The UK's Chief Rabbi, Lord Jonathan Sacks is a regular contributor to BBC Radio 4's 'Thought for the Day'. He also writes occasional articles for national newspapers — usually The Times.

## Islam has Been in the Spotlight Since 9/11

Since the rise of Islamic fundamentalism, Islam and its perceived link with terrorism have been all over the news.

Programmes like Channel 4's 'Qur'an' (first shown in July 2008) have tried to show a more balanced view of Islam. 'Qur'an' looked at how different groups of people interpret the sacred text differently.

Some Other Muslim Programming:

- "Devotional Sounds: Islam" on the BBC's Asian Network radio station broadcasts religious music every Saturday and Sunday morning.
- Muslim clerics regularly contribute to Radio 4's "Thought for the Day".

## An Atheist Viewpoint: "The Root of All Evil?"

1) Atheist programmes and literature might lead people to question the existence of God.
2) In January 2006, Channel 4 showed a two-part series by atheist Professor Richard Dawkins called 'The Root of All Evil?', related to his book 'The God Delusion'.
3) In these programmes, he argued that what he called 'a process of non-thinking called faith' has led to intolerance, violence and destruction whilst preaching peace and brotherhood.

# Warm-Up and Worked Exam Question

## Warm-up Questions

1) List two types of religious experience that may lead to a belief in God.
2) What is meant by a belief that God is "omnipotent"?
3) Briefly describe the most widely accepted cosmological theory.
4) Which of the following religions teach that humans have free will? Christianity, Judaism, Islam.
5) Why does the existence of evil sometimes cause people to question their faith?
6) Name one religious TV or radio programme.
   Suggest two positive and two negative effects of this programme on people's faith.

## Worked Exam Question

Read through this worked example, then have a go at the practice exam questions on the next page. Always read the instructions carefully — and don't forget to give reasons to support all the points of view you mention.

1 "Evil is a test of our free will."
Discuss this statement. You should include different, supported points of view and a personal viewpoint. You must refer to Christianity in your answer.

*Many Christians would agree with this statement. They believe that God gave humans free will, so we choose whether to perform evil deeds or not. Christians believe that our souls move on to Heaven or Hell after death. Which we go to depends on whether we chose to do good or evil with our lives, and whether we were faithful to God. If we could only choose to do good things, then doing them would not mean we were truly virtuous.*

*For top marks, include specific teachings from religious texts.*

*Other Christians believe that evil exists because Adam and Eve gave in to temptation in the Garden of Eden. This was 'The Fall', after which every human was born with a flawed nature and capable of causing evil. This does not explain natural evil, such as earthquakes, though. Some Christians would explain this by saying that God has a plan that we can never know.*

*You're told to include different points of view — so think about all the ways people might look at an issue.*

*My personal viewpoint is that evil is not a test of our free will because there is no 'grand plan', and no life after death. Evil exists purely because some people are very selfish and put themselves first without caring whether they hurt other people. Also, it would be cruel for a good God to choose to allow suffering just to test us.*

*It doesn't matter what your personal viewpoint is, as long as you give reasons for it.* *(12 marks)*

# Exam Questions

2 a) What is a "numinous experience".

*(2 marks)*

b) Do you think that religious programmes on the TV make people more likely to believe in God? Give two reasons for your point of view.

*(4 marks)*

3 a) Explain how Christians/Jews/Muslims respond to the problem of unanswered prayers.

*(6 marks)*

Answer this question for whichever religion you've studied.

b) "It is not possible to prove that God/Allah exists".

Discuss this statement. You should include different, supported points of view and a personal viewpoint. You must refer to a religion in your answer.

*(12 marks)*

4 a) What is meant by moral evil?

*(1 mark)*

b) Explain the different ways in which Jews might respond to the Holocaust.

*(6 marks)*

c) Explain from two different religious traditions the teachings about evil.

*(6 marks)*

5 a) What is meant by a 'design argument' for the existence of a god?

*(2 marks)*

b) "God created the Universe and everything in it in six days."
Refer to at least one religion in your answer.

i) Do you agree? Give reasons for your opinion.

*(3 marks)*

ii) Give reasons why some people might disagree with you.

*(3 marks)*

General

# Life After Death

Every religion in the world has something to say about death — and what comes after it.

## Life After Death — Some People Believe, Others Don't

1) Some people believe that when you die, that's it — your body decays and you cease to exist.
2) Others believe that, although your body may die and decay, your soul can live on — in other words, you move on to a different kind of existence. This is the basic idea of life after death.

## Many Religions Teach that the Soul is Immortal

1) Most religions have a concept of soul — that part of a human being that isn't a part of the physical world.
2) Most religions teach that something happens to this soul after death:
   - Some religions teach that the soul is rewarded or punished for the actions of the person on Earth.
   - Others teach that the soul is placed into another body for another life (reincarnation).
3) Even some non-religious people believe in souls. The big differences between those things that are alive (like us) and those that aren't (like rocks) suggests to some people that there might be something special inside us that isn't just more 'stuff'.
4) The fact that people are conscious (aware) of themselves in a way that even other animals aren't is taken by many to suggest that this awareness must be separate from everyday matter.

## Near-Death Experiences and the Paranormal

There are many reasons why people believe (or don't believe) in life after death.
Most religions teach that we all move on to an afterlife of some kind. For some people, this will be enough to make them believe in life after death — they have faith in what their religion teaches.
But even non-religious people can be convinced by things like near-death experiences, the paranormal and evidence of reincarnation:

NEAR-DEATH EXPERIENCES
A near-death experience usually involves an out-of-body experience when someone is close to death. While apparently physically dead, they glimpse what they believe to be an afterlife, or speak to long-dead family members.

Not everyone believes that these visions are real though. They argue that hallucinations could be a result of chemical activity in the brain when it's short of oxygen.

THE PARANORMAL
The paranormal (things science can't explain, which are thought to have a spiritual cause, e.g. ghosts) is sometimes used as evidence of life after death. Some people (mediums) claim they can talk to the dead.

Other people reckon these events have a scientific explanation — maybe we don't know what the explanation is yet, but there will be one. And some people don't believe these events happen in the first place.

EVIDENCE OF REINCARNATION
Some people claim to have evidence of reincarnation (having lived a previous life, died, and been reborn in a new body). Lots of research has been carried out with young children who claim to remember past lives, and the evidence has some people convinced. But sceptics suggest that the memories aren't real — that they must have been suggested to the children in some way.

## *Paranormal events can't be explained by science...*

The idea of life after death is pretty central to most religions — they each have their own teachings on this stuff, and you need to get your head round what they believe. Have a look at the next few pages for their beliefs.

# Life After Death: Christianity

CHRISTIANITY

What people believe will happen to them after death can influence the way they live their lives.

## Christians Believe in **Heaven** and **Hell**

1) Christianity teaches that the soul lives on after death (immortality of the soul), and that the body will be resurrected (brought back to life) for Judgement Day, just as Jesus was resurrected after his crucifixion.
2) Christians believe that God will judge you, and you'll go either to Heaven, or to Hell:

- Heaven is often portrayed as a place of great beauty and serenity, a paradise where you'll spend eternity with God — as long as you believe in Jesus, have followed his teachings and have lived a good life, that is. Those in Heaven are said to belong to the Communion of Saints.
- Hell, on the other hand, is often portrayed as a place of torment and pain — the final destination of nonbelievers and those who have led bad lives.

3) However, not all Christians believe that Heaven and Hell are real places — many Christians see Heaven and Hell as states of mind. In Heaven you'll be happy, and know God — in Hell you'll be unable to know God's love.
4) A few believe that those who God finds unacceptable will be annihilated. They had no interest in spiritual things when they were alive, therefore their spirits were never awakened and cannot survive death.
5) Roman Catholics also believe in a place, or state of existence, called Purgatory. Here sins are punished before the soul is able to move on to Heaven. This concept isn't in the Bible, so Protestants reject it.

## "Whoever lives and believes in me will **never die**"

This is how the Christian Church sees death and resurrection:

1) Human beings sin, meaning that they don't live up to God's perfect standard. Because of this, they're not fit to be accepted into Heaven.
2) But Jesus redeemed his followers by sacrificing himself to pay for our sins. He broke the power of sin and death — his power and goodness were so great that after he was crucified, death couldn't keep hold of him.
3) Jesus promised that, just as he had been saved from death, anyone who followed him would find salvation.
4) Many Christians believe that even those who have led sinful lives may find salvation thanks to Jesus's sacrifice and God's saving power.

*"I am the resurrection and the life. He who believes in me will live, even though he dies; and whoever lives and believes in me will never die."*
**John 11:25-26**

## The Idea of Heaven is **Comforting** to Believers

1) Pretty much everyone knows they're going to die one day — and for many it's a hard concept to grasp, and death is a scary thought. Many people get a lot of comfort from a belief in the afterlife.
2) Also, when someone you love dies, it's a lot nicer to think that they still exist in some form.
3) Belief in life after death is also important from a justice point of view. Lots of good people suffer greatly, and some, sadly, die young. At the same time, some evil people live out long lives and seem quite happy. It can make people feel a lot better if they believe that everything will be evened up after death.
4) So belief in Heaven and Hell might encourage some people to follow Christian teachings or do good deeds — they want to make sure they're well qualified for a good afterlife.

## Get ready to do some soul searching...

It's easy to see how belief in an immortal soul can affect how people live their lives. If you knew your life would be judged on how you'd used it, chances are you'd think twice before doing something dodgy.

Judaism

# Life After Death: Judaism

It should come as no surprise at all to learn that Judaism has something to say about death as well.

## *Sheol — the Shadowy Destination of the Dead*

1) Jewish teachings are largely concerned with the earthly life, and a person's duties to God and other people. According to the Torah, rewards for obeying God and punishments for 'breaking the covenant' are sent in this world (Leviticus 26:3-17). But Jews still have a firm belief in the immortality of the soul.
2) When the earliest Jewish scriptures were written, it was believed that after death all souls went to a place called Sheol — where the dead lived as shadows. Sheol was believed to be dark and cold, and your soul would stay there for eternity. This wasn't as a punishment — it's just what was believed to happen.
3) However, over time the Jews came to believe in the resurrection of the dead...

## *In the Messianic Age the Dead Will be Resurrected*

1) Jews believe that the Messiah, a great future leader, will bring an era of perfect peace and prosperity called the World to Come (or messianic age). (Jews don't believe Jesus was the Messiah.)
2) It's believed that the righteous dead (both Jews and non-Jews) will be resurrected to share in the messianic peace. But the wicked dead won't be resurrected — they gave up their share in the World to Come by living sinful lives.

*"Multitudes who sleep in the dust of the earth will awake: some to everlasting life, others to shame and everlasting contempt."* **Daniel 12:2.**

3) Orthodox Jews believe that the physical body will be resurrected, intact, in the messianic age. Because of this, the body shouldn't be cut after death (autopsies are frowned upon) and cremation is forbidden. A Jewish cemetery is called the 'House of Life' (Bet ha-Chaim), which reaffirms the view that the body will be resurrected.
4) Reform Jews believe that the body is simply a vessel for the soul, and reject the idea of physical resurrection. So Reform Jews accept cremation and organ donation.

## *Modern Judaism Teaches of Gan Eden and Gehinnom*

1) Modern Jews believe in an afterlife spent in places called Gan Eden ("Garden of Eden" or Paradise) and Gehinnom (a bit like Purgatory), but they don't tend to have firm beliefs on the specifics of the afterlife.
2) Some see Gan Eden as a physical place of lavish banquets and warm sunshine. But others have a more spiritual view of it — as a closeness to God. Similarly, there are different views of Gehinnom — a place of fire and physical torment, or a chance to see missed opportunities and the harm a person caused in life.
3) Only if you've lived a blameless life will you be sent straight to Gan Eden when you die.
4) Most souls are sent to Gehinnom for a period of punishment and purification first, which lasts no longer than 12 months, before ascending to Gan Eden. Only the truly wicked never reach Paradise, but there are various ideas about what happens to them, e.g. they're annihilated, or they stay in Gehinnom forever.

## *Your Behaviour During Your Life is Judged*

1) Many Jews believe that your behaviour here will determine what kind of afterlife you receive. This means that there's a strong emphasis on moral behaviour in this life — doing what is right even if it isn't easy or profitable for you.
2) However, some Jews would argue that being virtuous is its own reward — you should do good things simply because they are good.

### *Will there be exams in the next life...*

Of the three religions in this book, Judaism has the least clear ideas about the afterlife. In some ways that makes it harder to learn — you have to know more points of view. But it gives you plenty to write about.

# Life After Death: Islam

ISLAM

Islam has very definite teachings when it comes to life after death.

## The *Soul* is the *Real Person*

1) Muslims believe that human beings are Allah's greatest physical creation. They also believe that humans are different from other animals, because we know we will die.
2) Islam teaches that every soul (ruh) is unique and has free will.
3) It is the soul that will be judged after death, as it is the soul that is our consciousness. Our body is thought of as a kind of 'vehicle for the soul'.
4) Muslims call life after death akhirah — it's one of the key Islamic beliefs. Not to have a belief in life after death would make this life meaningless for a Muslim.
5) Islam teaches that nothing that happens to us during our earthly lives is accidental — Muslims believe we are being tested, and that the way we act in life will determine what happens to us after we die.
6) A key teaching of Islam is that we remain in the grave after death in a state called barzakh (the 'cold sleep') until the Day of Judgement. On this day, Allah will judge everyone — not just Muslims.

*It's free will that makes human beings different from angels — angels obey Allah perfectly.*

*Muslims believe in predestination — Al-Qadr. Although we have free will, Islam teaches we cannot do everything we want — God is still in control. In recognition of this, Muslims will often say "insh'Allah" (if God is willing).*

## The Soul Goes to *al'Jannah* (Paradise) or *Jahannam* (Hell)

1) Although the earthly life is short compared with the eternal, Muslims believe it's still very important. It's in this life that Allah tests us. On Judgement Day, it's too late to beg forgiveness for any wrongdoing.
2) Islam teaches that we are judged on:
   i) our character, ii) our reactions to good and bad events in our lives, iii) our way of life.
3) Muslims believe everything is the will of Allah — so there's no point moaning about your circumstances. We cannot know why things happen, or what Allah wishes us to learn from it. The important thing is that we react to it in the right way.
4) The reward for those who have followed Allah will be entry into al'Jannah (Paradise) — this is a place of peace, happiness and beauty. In fact, the Qur'an refers to al'Jannah as 'gardens of delight', filled with flowers and birdsong.
5) For those who don't believe in Allah, or have committed bad deeds, the reward is Jahannam (or Hell). The Qur'an describes Jahannam as a place of scorching fire, hot winds and black smoke. Here, those who have ignored Allah's teaching and failed to act righteously will be punished for eternity.
6) But Allah is also merciful, so many of those who have lived sinful lives may not be sent to Jahannam.

*Allah is merciful and compassionate, but at the same time, he's a tough judge. Basically, if you're a good Muslim, you'll go to Paradise. But if you're a bad Muslim or a non-Muslim, you deserve Hell, but you might get lucky and be sent by Allah to Paradise if he's feeling merciful.*

## Being *Obedient to Allah* is Vital for a Muslim

'Islam' literally means 'submission' or 'obedience' to Allah. And there are certain day-to-day rules that Allah expects you to follow if you want to show that you're being obedient. The key to getting to Paradise for a Muslim is obedience. The reasoning is as follows...

1) Allah expects obedience, and obedience is a Muslim's duty.
2) If a Muslim does his or her duty, that person will please Allah.
3) If a person pleases Allah enough, they will be sent to Paradise after they die.
4) And if Allah is not pleased with someone, they will be punished after they die.

So this is vital stuff. How a Muslim lives in this life will determine where he or she ends up in the afterlife.

## *Muslims believe in free will...*

Islam has very clear teachings on life after death — including descriptions of Paradise and Hell.

GENERAL & CHRISTIANITY

# Abortion

Abortion is a subject that many people have strong views about.

## Abortion — Terminating a Pregnancy

1) Abortion is when a foetus is removed prematurely from the womb, before it is able to survive.
2) Abortion has been legal in England, Scotland and Wales since 1967. It can take place until the 24th week of pregnancy, as long as two doctors agree that it's required. They must consider the quality of life of the woman, the unborn child, and any children the mother may already have.

*There are complicated arguments for and against abortion...*

i) The 'pro-choice' argument says that a woman has the right to choose what happens to her body (and since the foetus isn't independent of the woman, this argument says it must be considered part of the woman).
ii) But is it right to consider the foetus part of the mother when it's genetically different?
iii) Although many people are generally against abortion (seeing it as the taking of a life) they will agree that in certain circumstances, abortion should be permitted, e.g. if the mother's or child's health is at risk, if a woman has become pregnant through rape, or if a mother is too young to cope with a child.
iv) The question of when life actually begins is important here, too. Is it at conception (as the Roman Catholic Church says)? Or at birth? And is a foetus an actual person, or just a potential person?

## The 'Sanctity of Life' Argument

Probably the most important biblical passage regarding the Sanctity of Life argument is the sixth of the Ten Commandments, *"You shall not murder."* **Exodus 20:13**

1) Christianity, Islam and Judaism teach that all life is created by God. As God's creation, all life belongs to God and is therefore holy. This is the 'sanctity of life' argument.
2) Based on this, many religious people believe that we don't have the right to interfere with when life ends, or to prevent the beginning of a new life.

## Many Christians see Abortion as Undesirable

1) Abortion is a very complicated and emotional issue, but generally speaking, Christianity teaches that abortion is undesirable. However, the Roman Catholic Church goes so far as to say that abortion is murder.
2) Not all Christian churches see it in such 'black-and-white' terms, however. The Church of England believes that abortion is permissible in certain circumstances, while the Religious Society of Friends (the Quakers) argues that the life of the unborn child cannot be valued above that of the woman.

*"Abortion has been considered to be murder since the first centuries of the Church, and nothing permits it to be considered otherwise."* **Pope Paul VI** (Leader of Roman Catholic Church, 1970)

3) Indeed, many Christians argue that allowing a woman to choose is a way of showing Christian compassion — whether they agree with the choice made or not.
4) Although the Bible doesn't actually mention abortion, other Christian writings (e.g. the Didache, a 2nd century manual of Christian teaching) are quite specifically against it.

## It's tricky, emotional stuff..

There are no easy answers. So learn the stuff on this page, and be ready to give both sides of the argument.

# Euthanasia and Suicide

General & Christianity

Another couple of very complicated subjects...

## Euthanasia is often called Mercy Killing

Euthanasia means killing someone painlessly to relieve suffering, especially from an incurable illness. It's often called mercy killing.

1) There are two forms of euthanasia — voluntary euthanasia and non-voluntary euthanasia.
2) Voluntary euthanasia is when an ill person actively requests assistance to die, or refuses treatment which is keeping them alive, i.e. the person decides that they want to die and seeks help to achieve this.
3) Non-voluntary euthanasia is when the patient is unable to make such a request, and the decision is made by someone else — usually doctors and family members.
4) Suicide is when someone takes their own life — usually because of depression or illness. Attempted suicide used to be a crime in the UK, but it's now seen as a sign that someone needs help.
5) Assisted suicide is when a doctor provides someone with the means to end their own life, usually by prescribing a lethal dose of medication.

## Euthanasia is Illegal in the UK

1) Euthanasia and assisted suicide are illegal in the UK, but euthanasia is allowed in certain circumstances in Albania, Belgium, Luxembourg, and the Netherlands, and assisted suicide is legal in Switzerland.
2) The charity 'Dignity in Dying' believes that many people would be grateful for 'the mercy of a painless death', and many people want assisted suicide legalised in the UK. In the 2005 British Social Attitudes Survey, 80% of people said that they were in favour of letting terminally ill patients die with a doctor's help.
3) Legalisation would mean that scarce medical resources could be saved for people who could be cured.
4) A few doctors have even admitted to helping patients to die, sometimes by giving a patient an excess of painkillers, which can ease suffering but can also lead to eventual death — this is known as 'double effect', which is legal so long as the intention was to relieve pain.
5) However, there is a concern that if euthanasia were legalised, some elderly people may feel under pressure to end their life, even if they don't want to.

## "Your Body is a Temple of the Holy Spirit"

1) The passage in the subheading (from 1 Corinthians) suggests that God lives within each of us. Life is considered a sacred gift, and so both euthanasia and suicide are seen as wrong by many Christians (see page 14 — the 'Sanctity of Life' argument). However, some argue that Jesus's resurrection proves that death is not the end, and that earthly life isn't always the most important thing.
2) Roman Catholics are the most strongly opposed to euthanasia. They believe that anything that intentionally causes death is 'a grave violation of the law of God'. So even those who are unlikely to recover consciousness should be kept alive.
3) To Roman Catholics, suicide is considered so grave a sin that suicides aren't given a Christian burial. However, some Christians point out passages in the Bible that describe suicide (e.g. King Saul's death in 1 Samuel 31:4-5) without calling it a sin.
4) Many Christians suggest that the easing of suffering in euthanasia is a way of demonstrating Christian compassion, and that the use of 'extraordinary treatment' (e.g. life-support machines) to keep a person alive is not always the best approach.
5) Most Anglican denominations agree that terrible distress should not be suffered at all costs, and that death may be considered a blessing. They argue that a person's quality of life must also be considered.
6) Local churches often have links with hospices. A hospice is a place where terminally ill people can be cared for, and can discuss any fears that they may have about death.

JUDAISM & ISLAM

# Abortion, Euthanasia and Suicide

## Abortion, Euthanasia and Suicide — The Jewish View

1) As a general rule, Judaism is opposed to abortion, euthanasia and suicide — the passage on the right is often used to support this view.

> *"There is no god besides me. I put to death and I bring to life"* **Deuteronomy 32:39**

2) However, Judaism does not teach that the life of an unborn child is more valuable than that of the mother. Many Jews accept that, in certain cases, abortion should be allowed. Most rabbis allow abortion if pregnancy becomes physically or mentally dangerous for the woman concerned, or if the child is likely to be severely disabled and unable to lead a full life. But it cannot be carried out simply for convenience.
3) Reform rabbis are more likely to allow abortion than Orthodox ones.

### Only God can Decide when we Die

1) Jewish teaching is opposed to the practice of euthanasia — life is seen as a gift from God and is therefore sacred. We do not have the right to decide when a life should end.
2) The same thing applies to suicide — most Jews see it as such a great sin that those who take their own lives are not buried in the same part of the cemetery as other Jews.
3) However, most Jews who are suspected of having committed suicide are given standard funeral rites, as they are often judged to have been disturbed beyond being responsible for their actions.
4) The relief of pain and suffering is a key part of Jewish teaching. So although euthanasia is seen as wrong if it involves actively doing something to cause someone's death, it may be possible to withhold treatment, if this treatment would cause further distress.
5) The words of Rabbi Moses Isserles are sometimes used to argue that it may be reasonable to switch off a life-support machine that's keeping someone alive.

> "If there is anything which causes a hindrance to the departure of the soul... then it is permissible to remove it."

## Abortion, Euthanasia and Suicide — The Islamic View

Muslims believe that Allah created the world and everything in it. Our lives are sacred (see the 'Sanctity of Life' argument on p.14). This means that abortion and euthanasia are generally seen as wrong.

1) The passage on the right sums up Islamic teaching on abortion. But there are circumstances in which it is permissible.

> *"And do not kill your children... We provide for them and for you. Indeed, their killing is ever a great sin."* **Qur'an 17:31**

2) When the mother's life is in danger, abortion is lawful. The potential life in the womb is not as important as the actual life of the mother.
3) Within the first 120 days, abortion can also be allowed if the baby would be born with a serious defect (though not all Muslims agree with this). After 120 days, abortion is only allowed to save the life of the mother.
4) Some Muslim women argue that they should be free to choose what happens to their bodies. Those that disagree claim that in the Qur'an it says that unborn children will want to know why they were killed.

### Allah knows Why we Suffer...

1) Euthanasia and suicide are seen as wrong by most Muslims, because our lives are Allah's.
2) Muslims believe that Allah has a plan for every living person — he has decided how long each of us will live on this Earth, and we do not have the right to interfere with that plan.
3) Islam teaches that life on Earth is a test. Allah knows why we suffer, and we do not have good reason to end our own lives, no matter how bad that suffering is.
4) Instead, those who are suffering should turn to Allah, pray and 'patiently persevere' — Allah is merciful, and all will be revealed on the Day of Judgement.
5) However, in cases where a patient has a terminal illness, with no hope of improvement, Islam allows doctors to stop 'unnecessary' treatment.

# Warm-Up and Worked Exam Question

## Warm-up Questions

1) What is a "near-death experience"?
2) What is Purgatory? Which Christian denomination believes in it?
3) Describe a Christian view of Heaven and Hell.
4) What do Jews mean by the 'messianic age'?
5) What do Muslims call life after death?
6) What is suicide? Is attempted suicide legal in the UK?

## Worked Exam Question

This is a really interesting section — and you probably have your own views on some of the issues in it. But there's no getting away from the fact that you need to know the full range of religious viewpoints and the teachings behind them. Study this worked example, and then try the practice exam questions on the next page.

1 a) What is abortion?

*Abortion is when a foetus is removed from the womb before it is able to survive.*

*Make sure you learn the terminology. You need to include all the important bits in your definition.*

*(2 marks)*

b) Abortion is always wrong. It should be outlawed.

Give two reasons why a religious believer might agree or disagree with this statement.

*You're not given a specific religion — so you can draw your reasons from any of them.*

(i) *A religious believer may agree because they consider all life as belonging to God and therefore holy. Only God can choose when it starts or ends. This is the 'Sanctity of Life' argument.*

(ii) *They may disagree because allowing a woman to choose whether or not to have an abortion is a way of showing compassion. This is especially true if the mother was raped, is very young, or if the child will have serious health problems.*

*(4 marks)*

*You're asked for two reasons, but there are four marks. This means you should develop or explain each viewpoint.*

# Exam Questions

2 a) Describe Jewish beliefs about cremation.

*(3 marks)*

b) "Only religious people will obtain eternal life."
Refer to at least one religion in your answer.

i) Do you agree? Give reasons for your opinion.

*(3 marks)*

ii) Give reasons why some people might disagree with you.

*(3 marks)*

3 a) Explain what religious believers mean by the 'soul'.

*(2 marks)*

b) Explain the teachings of two different religious traditions about life after death.
(You must state the religious traditions you are referring to.)

*(6 marks)*

4 a) Do you agree with abortion?
Give two reasons for your point of view.

*(4 marks)*

b) Explain different Muslim attitudes to abortion.

*(6 marks)*

5 Look at the newspaper headlines below.

**Allow euthanasia for disabled babies?**

a) What is meant by 'euthanasia'?

*(2 marks)*

b) "Euthanasia is murder. Anyone who does it should be punished severely."

Do you agree? Give reasons for your answer, showing that you have thought about more than one point of view. Refer to religious arguments in your answer.

*(6 marks)*

# Wealth, Poverty and Disease

GENERAL

Wealth is basically money and possessions. Wealth is a big issue for religious people, because it's not very evenly distributed in society — some people are rolling in it, while other people are left struggling in poverty.

## Being **Wealthy** isn't a **Bad Thing** in Itself

*"...there came a rich man from Arimathea, named Joseph, who had himself become a disciple of Jesus."* **Matthew 27:57**

1) None of the three major religions teach that wealth is bad.
2) There are people in the Bible who are both wealthy and faithful to God, e.g. Joseph of Arimathea was a rich council member who retrieved the body of Jesus from the Roman authorities and arranged his burial.
3) And there are plenty of examples from the Jewish books of the Kings, e.g. King Solomon was one of the great kings of Israel, who rebuilt the Temple in Jerusalem: *"King Solomon was greater in riches and wisdom than all the other kings of the earth."* (**1 Kings 10:23**)
4) Muslims believe that all wealth belongs to Allah, and that personal wealth is a gift from Allah.
5) So in all three religions, it's not wealth, but a love of wealth that's a problem:

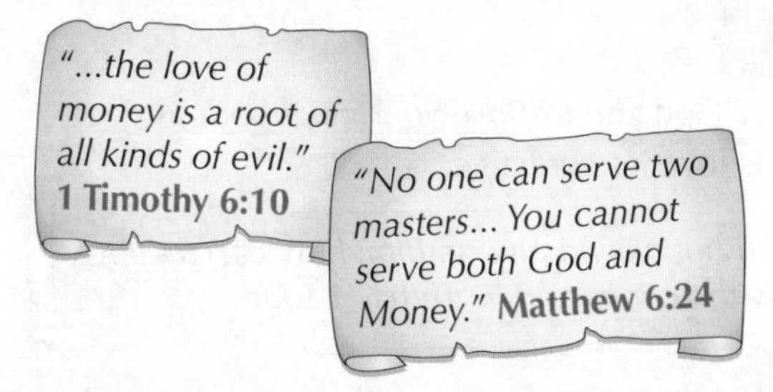


*"...those who hoard gold and silver and spend it not in the way of Allah — give them tidings of a painful punishment."* **Qur'an 9:34**

*"Whoever loves money never has money enough..."* **Ecclesiastes 5:10**

## There are Many **Causes** of **Poverty** and **Hunger**

Poverty leads to great suffering. So its causes and effects are of great concern for religious people.

1) The Brandt Report in 1980 identified an imbalance between the developed and the developing worlds. The developed world contains around 25% of the world's population but around 80% of the wealth. Little has changed since 1980. Some religious people believe that the greed of people in developed countries leads to poverty in developing countries.
2) Direct causes of poverty in the developing world include rapid population growth, war, and the sale of raw materials at low prices. This poverty often leads to hunger, because people can't afford to buy food.
3) Famine, an overall lack of food in an area, is often caused by war or climate. War stops people from working on farms, because they're either involved in the fighting or sheltering from the violence. Droughts, floods and other extreme weather conditions can destroy crops and ruin the fertility of the soil.
4) Hundreds of thousands of people die of starvation every year.
5) In the UK, causes of poverty range from unemployment to gambling and alcoholism. The poorest people become homeless and are dependent on charity for food and shelter.

## Poverty and **Disease** Often Go Together

1) Poverty and disease are very closely related. The effects of poverty, e.g. malnutrition, poor sanitation, lack of proper healthcare, etc. leave people more susceptible to disease — particularly children. The World Health Organisation estimates that around a third of all deaths worldwide are poverty related.
2) At the same time, disease weakens people, making it harder for them to work their way out of poverty.
3) Education also has an effect on patterns of disease. For example, sexually transmitted diseases like HIV and syphilis can be controlled by educating people about safe sex and avoiding promiscuity.
4) Religious organisations like Christian Aid, Muslim Aid and the Jewish charity Tzedek, aim to provide immediate help for the sick and starving, as well as long-term projects to help whole communities get themselves out of poverty. (More about that on the next three pages.)

CHRISTIANITY

# Money and Charity: Christianity

Basically, Christianity teaches that you shouldn't be selfish with your money.

## It's **What You Do** With Your **Money** that **Counts**

1) Christians believe you should only earn money in moral ways.
2) Occupations that many Christians consider immoral are those that exploit or harm other people (e.g. weapons trading or working with oppressive regimes), are damaging to the environment, or are sexual in nature.
3) Also, you mustn't use your money in ways that might harm you or others.
4) This means that many Christians (especially Methodists) disapprove of gambling (playing games of chance for money). Gambling can be addictive, and profits are made at the expense of others.
5) Christians also disapprove of the practice of usury — charging high rates of interest on loans. This is seen as profiting from someone else's poverty.

*The Roman Catholic Church and, to a lesser extent, the Church of England are very rich institutions — this is a worry for some believers.*

## Christians have a **Duty** to be **Charitable**

1) Jesus taught that the most important commandments were to love God and to *"love your neighbour as yourself"* (**Mark 12:31**). For Christians, charity means putting this love into practice:

*"If anyone has material possessions and sees his brother in need but has no pity on him, how can the love of God be in him? ...let us not love with words or tongue but with actions and in truth."* **1 John 3:17-18**

2) Christians believe they have a duty to care for other people, and use many sources of authority to stress this. The Bible contains many passages encouraging charity.

*"The man with two tunics should share with him who has none, and the one who has food should do the same."* **Luke 3:11**

*"Go, sell everything you have and give to the poor, and you will have treasure in heaven."* **Mark 10:21**

*"I was hungry and you gave me something to eat, I was thirsty and you gave me something to drink... whatever you did for one of the least of these brothers of mine, you did for me."* **Matthew 25:35-40**

3) In practice, 'charity' is any sort of help that's freely given. This could be a donation of time (e.g. visiting the sick or elderly), effort (e.g. working on a building project) or material things (e.g. giving money). A number of Christian charities exist — working both in the UK and globally, e.g. Christian Aid:

**CHRISTIAN AID**

Christian Aid was set up after World War II to help refugees. It now has over 40 member organisations in the UK and Ireland, and works globally to relieve poverty. It raises money through donations, events and collections. Most of Christian Aid's work is in development — they believe the best way to help people is by *'helping them to help themselves'*. They set up projects in the developing world, drawing on the skills of local people. Development projects set up by Christian Aid aim to help with problems such as poor sanitation, education and healthcare, as well as encouraging the use of birth control. The organisation also aims to change government policy to help reduce the suffering of the world's poor, e.g. through debt relief, and fair trade products.

4) Some religious orders (communities of monks or nuns) are dedicated to relieving suffering amongst the starving, poor and sick. One example is the Order of the Missionaries of Charity:

**MOTHER TERESA**

Mother Teresa was an Albanian Roman Catholic nun who devoted herself to the destitute and dying in Calcutta, India. She founded the Order of the Missionaries of Charity, whose nuns now work amongst the poor all over the world. She said that it isn't what you do for God that counts, but how much love you pour into it. She won the Nobel Peace Prize in 1979, and died in 1997 at the age of 87.

## Jesus encouraged people to give out of love...

Christians don't have any strict rules about how much of their income they should give to the poor (although many use 10% as a guideline). Donations are left to the conscience of each individual.

# Money and Charity: Judaism

JUDAISM

Judaism teaches that it's our duty to look after those less fortunate than ourselves.

## Jews must Deal **Fairly** and **Honestly**

1) Although Judaism doesn't teach that everyone should try to be wealthy, it does suggest that extreme poverty will make others responsible for you — so all Jews should aim to work and earn a living.
2) But the love of wealth may turn you from God — so you should neither seek nor shun wealth.
3) Unfairness and dishonesty in business are condemned — you're answerable to God for any wrongdoing.

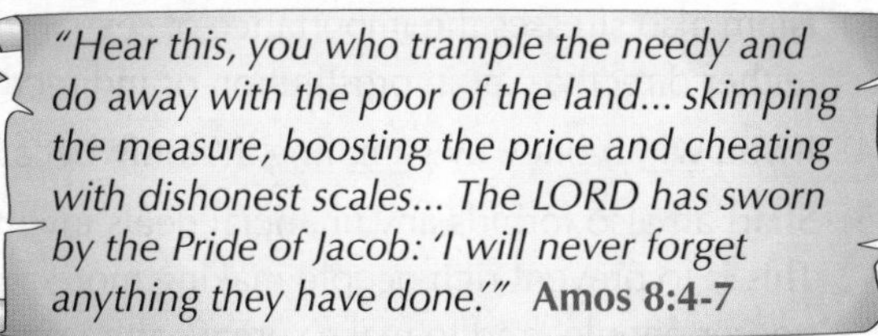


4) All money must be morally earned, so any occupation that's harmful in any way is forbidden. Jews particularly frown on work that is damaging to God's creation (e.g. unsustainable tree felling or bullfighting).
5) It's also strictly forbidden for one Jew to charge interest on a loan to another Jew (Leviticus 25:37) — a practice called 'usury'. This rule doesn't apply to loans made to non-Jews, however: *"You may charge a foreigner interest, but not a brother Israelite..."* (**Deuteronomy 23:20**).
6) Although gambling is generally frowned on, occasional lighthearted games for small stakes are allowed. For example, it's traditional to play a gambling game called kvitlech (similar to blackjack) at Hanukkah.
7) Jews try to avoid talking about or handling money on the Sabbath — the day of rest.

## **Judaism** says, "Do not be **hardhearted** or **tightfisted**..."

1) This passage from Deuteronomy sums up Jewish teaching on charity:

> *"If there is a poor man among your brothers in any of the towns of the land... do not be hardhearted or tightfisted toward your poor brother."* **Deuteronomy 15:7**

2) Also, Maimonides said that the best way to give was *"to help a person help themselves so that they may become self-supporting"*.

*Maimonides was an important Jewish Rabbi and philosopher.*

3) There are two main ways of giving to charity — Tzedakah and Gemilut Hasadim:

> *TZEDAKAH*: Tzedakah is financial aid — even the poorest in society are expected to contribute 10% of their wealth. All wealth belongs to God, and not giving to the poor deprives them of what they're owed.
>
> *GEMILUT HASADIM*: This means, literally, the 'giving of loving-kindness' and refers to any kind and compassionate actions towards others.

4) Many Jewish homes have collection boxes (called pushkes) in which money for charity can be placed. Children are encouraged to use these boxes — maybe donating some of their pocket money each week.
5) Donating clothing to people who need it, feeding the hungry, visiting someone who's sick and burying the dead are all considered Gemilut Hasadim. The most important thing is, that whatever you're giving, you don't expect anything in return.
6) There are Jewish charities that have been set up to help the poor:

**TZEDEK (Jewish Action for a just world)**

> Tzedek is a Jewish charity set up in the UK that works with poor people of all races and religions, *'providing direct support to small scale sustainable self-help development projects for the relief and elimination of poverty'*.
> Their focus is on helping local projects, e.g. health and agriculture training schemes, that improve a community's ability to get itself out of poverty and achieve a better standard of living.

### Sounds like good advice to me...

Judaism teaches that God has provided the world with everything we need, so that there should never be any poverty or hunger. Jews believe that the poverty that does exist is caused by the greed of others.

ISLAM

# Money and Charity: Islam

In Islam, the principle is much the same as Christianity and Judaism — greed and waste are frowned upon.

## *Gambling* and *Charging Interest* are *Absolute No-Nos*

1) Islam forbids using money in ways that might damage yourself or others — it's a basic principle of Shari'ah (Islamic law) that a Muslim should not harm others.
2) Islam forbids alcohol, so Muslims consider it immoral to make money from alcoholic drinks.
3) Islam also stresses the importance of sexual modesty, so making money from sex is forbidden (either directly, e.g. in prostitution or indirectly, e.g. through sexually-suggestive advertising).
4) If you win money by gambling, it's only because someone else has lost it.
5) Shari'ah also forbids any financial deals involving the charging of interest. This is to prevent rich people making more money at the expense of poorer people, and to make sure wealth is spread more fairly.

*Charging interest (particularly a high rate of interest) is called 'usury'. The Arabic word for it is riba.*

6) This means Muslims can't use most Western bank accounts. Also, Muslim businesses must be run differently from others, because the Western economic system depends on lending money and charging interest. Some Islamic banks exist to get around this.

## *Charity* is One of the *Five Pillars* of Islam

1) Muslims believe that possessions ultimately belong to Allah.
2) Islam teaches that you should act responsibly and help those in need.
3) As in Judaism, there are two main ways to help the disadvantaged — Zakah and Sadaqah:

> ZAKAH: This is one of the Five Pillars of Islam — 2.5% of your yearly savings should be given to the needy, no matter how rich or poor you are.
> SADAQAH: This is additional aid — maybe financial donations or an act of compassion and love.

4) Zakah is the Third Pillar of Islam. The Five Pillars are a guide to living a good Muslim life — they're practical ways of showing obedience to Allah. Zakah is also a way of redistributing wealth.
   - The money donated is collected by a local mosque. It's then redistributed to needy Muslims, or used for religious purposes, like running Muslim schools.
   - It's a sign of concern for others and encourages unselfishness.
5) This Hadith (saying of the Prophet Muhammad) sums up the importance of Zakah pretty clearly:

> *"Whoever is made wealthy by Allah and does not pay the Zakah of his wealth, then on the Day of Resurrection his wealth will be made like a bald-headed poisonous male snake with two black spots over the eyes. The snake will encircle his neck and bite his cheeks and say, 'I am your wealth, I am your treasure.'"* **Prophet Muhammad (Sahih Bukhari)**

6) There are Islamic charities, that help the poor globally and in the UK — e.g. Muslim Aid and Islamic Aid.

**MUSLIM AID**

Muslim Aid provides disaster relief and development aid around the world.
They aim to provide not only initial emergency aid after a war or natural disaster, but ongoing help to get people back on their feet. This help includes building new permanent housing, sanitation and schools, and offering small interest-free loans to help start-up businesses.

**ISLAMIC AID**

Islamic Aid is an international organisation dedicated to reducing poverty and deprivation.
In the UK, they work to improve the lives of Muslim immigrants, e.g. by raising awareness of 'ghettos'.

# The Media: Life and Death

General

There are a lot of sensitive issues in this section, and many people feel very strongly about them.

## The Media Sometimes **Criticises Religious Views**

1) Life and death issues are important to everyone, so they tend to crop up a lot in the media — from in-depth documentaries to soap operas.
2) But the media is often accused of insensitivity to religious views — so the big question is this: "Should the media be free to criticise what religions say about matters of life and death?"

### Arguments For

- Freedom of speech. This is the most fundamental one. In the UK, we have the right to freedom of opinion and expression — as long as anything said about a person is true.
- Education. By covering all views on topics like euthanasia and abortion, the media can help to educate people about their options, and the implications of their choices.
- Constructive questioning can help deepen a person's faith.

### Arguments Against

- Insensitive coverage of these issues can be seen as causing unnecessary offence.
- Unbalanced coverage, e.g. the media is sometimes accused of having a pro-choice bias when it comes to abortion coverage.
- Exaggerated or untrue representations of beliefs can damage a person's faith or give religion a 'bad name'.

3) TV programmes, newspaper articles and films are sometimes censored (bits of material are cut out).
4) This can happen if they contain material that's thought to be obscene or excessively violent, or if they cover subjects that society considers unacceptable.
5) Religious groups might also try to suppress material that they feel puts a 'wrong' or 'dangerous' message across, e.g. glamorising abortion or suicide.

## Example: **"Million Dollar Baby"**

1) Some religious people question whether life and death issues are treated fairly by the media.
2) A good example is the 2004 film "Million Dollar Baby", which tackles the issue of euthanasia.

What it's about: A boxing coach (a Catholic) takes on a female boxer ("Million Dollar Baby") and guides her up through the ranks. An illegal move by an opponent leaves her paralysed from the neck down with no hope of recovery. She asks her coach to help her to die, which he does in the end. (Oh yes — it's a cheery film...)

The issue: Does the coach show love by helping his student to die at her request and with dignity, or is it murder and a mortal sin?

How the film tackles it:

1) The coach spends a long time talking to his confessor and wrestling with his conscience.
2) In the end, by helping "Boxing Baby" to die, the trainer goes against his religion.
3) The film deals with beliefs, relationships and people very sensitively.
4) It gives no clear-cut answers — the viewer is left to decide whether the coach should be condemned by God.

How the film was received: The film was critically acclaimed and won four Academy Awards. But anti-euthanasia campaigners, including the bioethicist Wesley J. Smith, criticised the film for encouraging the euthanasia of disabled people.

## There's nothing like a nice cheery end to a section...

For some religious people, their religion is such a big part of their identity that they see any criticism of it as a personal insult. But does protecting them hinder other people's right to free speech? It's a complex issue...

# Warm-Up and Worked Exam Question

## Warm-up Questions

1) Describe some causes of famine in the developing world.
2) List three common causes of poverty in the UK.
3) What is charity? Give some examples of the different forms that charity can take.
4) Describe the work of one Christian organisation to relieve poverty.
5) What is Tzedakah? (*Judaism*)
6) What is Sadaqah? (*Islam*)

## Worked Exam Question

This section contains lots of specialist words that are easy to muddle up — such as Zakah and Tzedakah. It's worth learning them though, because you can't get full marks in lots of questions without using them. Read through this worked example — then try the exam questions opposite.

1 Choose one religion and explain how its followers respond to poverty.

*Judaism teaches that it is our duty to help others less fortunate than ourselves. Deuteronomy 15:7 sums up this teaching: "...do not be hardhearted or tightfisted towards your poor brother".*

*Think about what you are going to write — you need to organise your answer for this type of question.*

*All Jews are expected to give 10% of their wealth to charity. This is called Tzedakah. As all wealth belongs to God, not giving to the poor deprives them of what they are owed. Many Jewish homes also have collection boxes for collecting extra money for charity. Jews can also make charitable donations through Gemilut Hasadim. This means any kind, compassionate actions, such as donating clothes to the poor.*

*Maimonides was an important Jewish philosopher and Rabbi. He said that the best way to give was to help people to help themselves so that they become self-supporting. The Jewish charity Tzedek tries to do this through supporting sustainable, self-help development projects to help improve the ability of communities to get themselves out of poverty.*

*(8 marks)*

*Don't just write down the basic facts — you'll get more marks if you develop at least some of your points.*

# Exam Questions

2 a) What is usury?

*(1 mark)*

b) Give two reasons why many religious people are against gambling.

*(2 marks)*

c) Explain how having a religious faith might influence someone who is looking for a new job.

*(6 marks)*

d) "Religious people shouldn't be wealthy."

Do you agree? Give reasons for your answer, showing that you have thought about more than one point of view. Refer to religious arguments in your answer.

*(6 marks)*

3 a) Explain two causes of poverty in the developing world.

*(4 marks)*

b) Do you think it matters how people spend their money? Give two reasons for your point of view.

*(4 marks)*

c) Explain what Christians believe about wealth.

*(6 marks)*

4 a) Explain how having a religious faith may influence someone to campaign to have a film banned or censored.

*(4 marks)*

b) The media should be allowed to say whatever they like about religious views on matters of life and death.

Give two reasons why a believer might agree or disagree with this statement.

*(4 marks)*

GENERAL

# Attitudes to the Family

Times change, and the old 'married with two kids' kind of family isn't as common as it used to be.

## Marriage in the UK — Times are Changing

1) The number of marriages taking place in the UK each year has been decreasing for at least thirty years.
2) At the same time, it's become more popular (and acceptable) for couples to cohabit (i.e. live together) — either instead of getting married, or as a 'trial marriage' before doing it for real. (However, government statistics seem to show that a marriage is more likely to break down if the couple lived together first.)
3) In most cases, cohabitation still involves commitment. When you commit to a relationship, you promise to stay together and be faithful to each other — so you're no longer free to do whatever you please.

## Family Life in the UK is also Changing

1) There used to be two basic types of family that 'society' and the Christian Church considered 'ideal' — the nuclear family, and the extended family.
2) A nuclear family consists of parents and children. An extended family is where three or more generations live together or as close neighbours.
3) In reality, families can have very different structures — e.g. single-parent families and re-constituted families (where divorcees with children re-marry, or find new partners).
4) Family life is changing in the UK — and one of the most important changes in the past 30 years has been the growth of single-parent (or 'lone-parent') families. This is partly due to more children being born outside marriage, but it's also because more than 1 in 3 marriages now end in divorce.

## Family is Important to Christians, Jews and Muslims

### The Importance of the Family to Christians

1) Family life is seen as very important by most Christians — it's believed to be better for a child to have a father and a mother present (ideally the child's biological parents), so that he or she grows up with one role model of each sex.
2) Ideally, a stable family can give a child a sense of identity and a feeling of security, teaching him or her how to behave in different social situations, and how to give and receive love.
3) Many Christian churches offer help in raising children through Sunday schools. These schools aim to teach Christian morals and ideals through the study of Bible stories.

### The Importance of the Family to Jews

1) Family life is also very important to Jews, as it's through the family that the Jewish religion and customs are passed on. Children take part in Shabbat rituals (the special meals and prayers of the day of rest) at home from an early age.
2) At a Jewish school called a Cheder, children learn Hebrew, and study the Torah and Talmud (see p.88).

### The Importance of the Family to Muslims

1) Muslims believe that a stable family life teaches people to be kind, considerate and affectionate towards others, and that it's the duty of the father to raise his children as Muslims.
2) Local Mosques often have schools (Madrasahs) to help teach children the ways of Islam. There they learn Arabic so that they can read and understand the Qur'an, and are taught from the Hadith and the Sunnah (see p.89).

## All of the religions value a stable family life...

So family life is changing, but it's still really important. And even though marriage might not be such a big deal these days, still about 50% of women and 40% of men in the UK marry before they're 30.

# Marriage in Christianity

Christianity

Marriage — a pretty big thing in anyone's life. Including yours if you get a question about it in the exam.

## Courting is a Bit Like Dating

1) The Bible doesn't say anything about how to find someone to marry, because in biblical times marriages were arranged. However, modern Christians believe that everyone has the right to choose who they marry.
2) Many Christians find a partner by courting (dating). Couples don't usually have sex during the courtship period because sex before marriage is forbidden by God.

## A Christian Wedding has Legal, Social and Religious Features

Most Christian weddings take place in church. The details will vary according to tradition and denomination, but all combine legal, social and religious features:

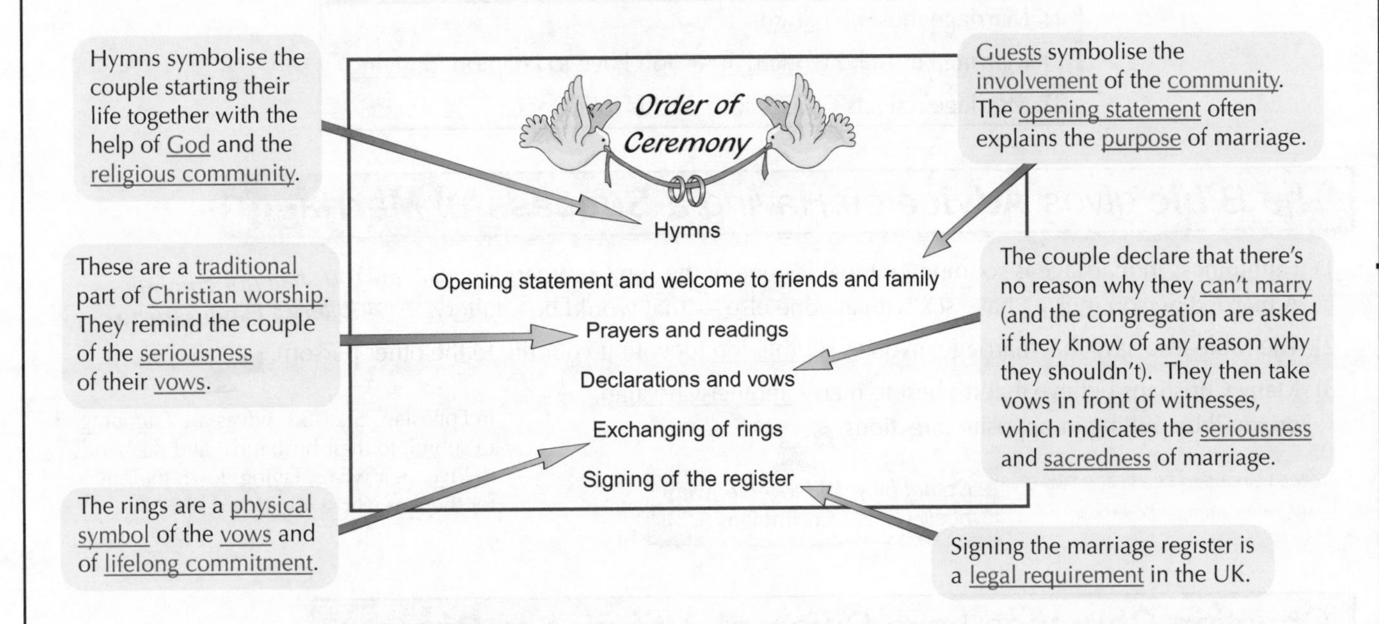


A Roman Catholic wedding may also include nuptial mass (Holy Communion).
In an Orthodox wedding, crowns are placed on the heads of the bride and groom.

## Church Weddings are Less Popular than they Used to Be

1) In the past, most people married in church. However, now only around 1 in 3 weddings is in a church.
2) The number of weddings being held in non-religious venues, like hotels or castles, is increasing. Many people also choose to get married abroad, often somewhere hot and sunny.

*You can't get married absolutely anywhere — the place has to have a special licence.*

3) The ceremony will be a civil ceremony — it'll have absolutely no reference to religion.
4) Many Christians choose to marry in church so the wedding takes place 'in front of God'.
5) The Church of England used to have strict rules about which church you could marry in — you had to have lived in the parish or worshipped there regularly. These rules were relaxed in 2008 to make it easier for couples to choose the church where they wanted to get married.

### Marriage is about commitment...

The number of marriages in the UK is falling, but that doesn't make it a less popular topic with the examiners. Make sure you learn what happens during a Christian marriage ceremony, and what each bit symbolises. When that's done, try to think of some reasons for and against getting married in a church.

CHRISTIANITY

# Marriage and Divorce: Christianity

All Christians see marriage as a lifelong commitment, but they don't all agree on what to do if it breaks down.

## Christians say Marriage Should be Forever

1) The Christian faith values marriage very highly — the joining of husband and wife in holy matrimony reflects the union of Jesus with his followers.
2) Jesus taught that marriage should be a lifelong union — marriage is seen as a covenant or contract between two people, involving commitment and responsibility. Christianity teaches that the purpose of marriage is for two people to offer love and mutual support and for procreation (to have children).
3) The Church recognises that not everyone is called to marriage (e.g. Roman Catholic priests) and from these people it demands celibacy.

*"...a man will leave his father and mother and be united to his wife, and the two will become one flesh."* **Mark 10:7-8**

| Central Biblical teachings on Marriage |
|---|
| 1) Marriage must be faithful. |
| 2) Marriage must be worked at — you have to keep on forgiving. |
| 3) Marriage reflects Christ's love for his followers. |

## The Bible gives Advice on Having a Successful Marriage

1) Faithfulness in marriage is so important that it's one of the Ten Commandments. A married person mustn't have sex with anyone else — that would be adultery.
2) The Bible also says that marriage involves submission (devoting your life to the other person).
3) Many Christians believe that it's best to marry another Christian, or you'll be pulling in opposite directions.

*"You shall not commit adultery."* **Exodus 20:14**

In Ephesians 5:21-33, wives are encouraged to submit to their husbands, and husbands to love their wives, laying down their lives for them as Christ laid down his.

*"Do not be yoked together with unbelievers."* **2 Corinthians 6:14**

*Yokes were used to attach two working animals together.*

## Christian Churches have Different Attitudes to Divorce

1) The breakdown of a marriage is seen by all Christians as a tragedy. However not all Christians agree about whether divorce is permissible, or even possible.

The Roman Catholic Church states that it is actually impossible to divorce. Marriage is a sacrament — God has made the couple into one flesh, and this cannot be undone. However, a marriage can be annulled — annulment means that it was never a true marriage in the first place. This can happen if:
- i) either partner did not consent to the marriage or didn't understand what marriage is about,
- ii) the couple didn't or couldn't have sex, or one partner refused to have children.

The Church of England states that divorce is possible and accepts that some marriages fail. Divorced people can only re-marry in church if they can find a minister willing to marry them, but this doesn't satisfy every member of the Church.

Nonconformist Churches (e.g. Baptists and Methodists) will generally re-marry divorcees, but an individual minister can refuse to do so if this goes against his or her own conscience.

2) Jesus himself was anti-divorce, but pro-forgiveness.

In **Mark 10:2-12** Jesus says that Moses allowed divorce because of people's 'hardness of heart'. But he says that marriages were meant to last for life, and if a divorcee re-marries it's the same as committing adultery.

In **John 8:1-11**, Jesus freely forgives a woman caught in the act of adultery. But he tells her, 'Go now and leave your life of sin'.

**Matthew 19:8-9** says that divorce and re-marriage are only permitted to someone whose partner has been unfaithful.

3) But some Christians view an unhappy marriage as a waste of two lives, and so see divorce as preferable. It's also argued that parents fighting can harm the emotional wellbeing of children more than a divorce.

# Marriage and Divorce: Judaism

Judaism

Traditionally all Jews have been expected to marry and have at least two children — ideally a boy and a girl.

## Marriage Matters in Judaism

1) To Jews, marriage is an emotional, intellectual and spiritual union. It is seen as the proper context for sex (seen as natural and God-given) and having children (procreation), but is also for companionship.
2) It's the Jewish custom for parents to arrange for their children to meet suitable partners. To help in this it was common to use a 'shadchan', or matchmaker (and it still is among the ultra-Orthodox).
3) Although 40% of UK Jews 'marry out' (i.e. marry non-Jews), those who take their religion seriously find this worrying — children of 'mixed marriages' are less likely to be brought up as observant Jews. Some Jews see this as a threat to Judaism's survival, and even a 'posthumous victory to Hitler'.

*Nowadays there are shadchan services available via the Internet.*

## Kiddushin is the First Part of the Marriage Ceremony

'Kiddushin' is the first part of the Jewish marriage ceremony, and is usually translated as 'betrothal'. The word comes from a root meaning sanctified, which reflects the holiness of marriage. Different Jewish communities celebrate marriage in different ways, but there are some common features.

1) The ceremony takes place beneath a chuppah, a wedding canopy — this is a piece of cloth supported by four poles. It is thought the cloth represents privacy, and the open sides hospitality.
2) Usually, the bride will circle the groom seven times.
3) The groom gives the bride a ring and makes the betrothal declaration: *'Behold you are consecrated to me with this ring according to the laws of Moses and Israel.'* This completes the kiddushin.
4) Then the ketubah (marriage contract) is read out. The traditional ketubah sets out the woman's right to be cared for by her husband and her entitlements in the event of divorce (a bit like a modern prenuptial agreement). Reform Jews have rewritten the ketubah to be a mutual statement of love and commitment, more like Christian marriage vows.
5) The sheva brachot or seven blessings are said — normally by a rabbi, who usually conducts the service.
6) The groom breaks a glass with his foot in memory of the destruction of the Temple in Jerusalem by the Romans in 70 CE. It's said that there can never be complete joy for the Jewish people until the Temple is restored — this is why it's remembered.
7) After the service there will be a festive meal and dancing, and shouts of 'mazel tov!' (good luck, best wishes). Among some Orthodox Jews, the men and women dance separately.

## Divorce is a Last Resort

1) Judaism accepts that some marriages don't work out, and that it's better for a couple to divorce than to stay together in bitterness. But divorce is a very last resort after all attempts at reconciliation have failed.
2) Traditionally, a woman cannot initiate divorce, but a divorce does require the wife's consent.
3) In Reform synagogues, if the husband will not grant his wife a certificate of divorce, a 'Get', the Bet Din (Jewish court) can do so, freeing her to re-marry.
4) In Orthodox synagogues, women who want a divorce but whose husbands will not grant one (or who aren't around to grant one) are known as 'agunot' — chained women.

## Marriage is a union of mind and body...

Christian, Jewish and Muslim teachings about marriage and morality have a lot in common. This isn't so surprising — all three religions share the same Near Eastern background.

Islam

# Marriage and Divorce: Islam

Marriage is very important in Islam. Muslims are advised to marry, and Muhammad himself was married.

## Marriage is Recommended for Three Reasons

1) Marriage provides companionship.
2) Marriage provides a secure environment for having children (procreation) and bringing them up as practising Muslims.
3) The sexual instinct is very strong and needs to be carefully channelled.

*"...He created for you from yourselves mates that you may find tranquillity in them; and He placed between you affection and mercy..."* **Qur'an 30:21**

*"Whoever among you can marry, should marry, because it helps him lower his gaze and guard his modesty."* **Prophet Muhammad (Sahih Bukhari)**

See page 31 for more about marriage in Islam.

## Choosing a Partner is often your Parents' Responsibility

Practising Muslims generally want their children to marry other Muslims. Islam affects a Muslim's whole life, and being married to a non-Muslim could create tension, especially with bringing up children.

1) Most Muslims believe it's unwise for young men and women to mix freely, and 'dating' is discouraged or even forbidden.
2) In most Muslim communities, parents search for suitable partners for their children — i.e. Muslims often have 'arranged marriages'.
3) However, as marriage is a contract, both partners must consent to it.
4) Parents also have a responsibility to help if the marriage begins to go wrong.

## The Marriage Ceremony — Customs Vary

The marriage ceremony is different in different Islamic cultures, but there's always a religious ceremony (witnessed by Allah) and a public one (witnessed by the community). They usually go like this...

1) A nikah (contract) is drawn up in advance by the families of the bride and groom, and a mahr (dowry) paid by the groom to the bride.
2) An imam (leader of prayers) is often present (though this isn't compulsory).
3) Vows are exchanged, and a marriage declaration is made by each partner. A Hadith (prophetic saying) or a khutbah (speech) may also be said.
4) There will be a big feast afterwards, though the men and women may enjoy this separately.

## Divorce is the Last Resort

*"Of all the lawful acts the most detestable to Allah is divorce."* **Prophet Muhammad (Sunan Abu Dawud)**

1) Divorce is permitted, but only as a very last resort. If things aren't going well, an arbiter from each family should be appointed to try to sort things out.
2) Muslims see reconciliation as particularly important when the couple have children.
3) But, in Islam, marriage is a contract and like any other contract it can be ended.
4) When the man says 'I divorce you' three times, the marriage is said to be over. However, there's often a period of three months after the first of these declarations. This allows time for reflection, and also to ensure that the woman is not pregnant.
5) A woman can divorce a man in this way (divorce 'by talaq') if it was written into her marriage contract. Otherwise she has to apply to a Shari'ah court for a divorce 'by khul'.
6) After divorce, both men and women are free to re-marry.

This kind of divorce isn't legal in the UK, as Islamic law isn't part of the British legal system.

## Marriage is an important part of Islamic life...

There are quite a lot of Arabic words in these Islam sections — and they're in the syllabus too, so you need to know 'em. The same goes for the sections on Judaism — they contain quite a bit of Hebrew.

# Religious Attitudes to Sex

GENERAL

Christianity, Islam and Judaism have all formulated laws concerned with sex. But this doesn't mean that religious people think there is anything wrong or dirty about having sex — quite the opposite.

## *Christianity, Islam and Judaism have a Lot in Common...*

The three faiths have a lot in common when it comes to sex.

1) Traditionally all three religions teach that the only right context for sexual activity is within marriage.
2) But nowadays you'll find liberal Christians, Jews and Muslims who'll tell you that this belief is outdated.
3) 'Orthodox' members of all three faiths say that certain moral principles never change, however.

They might argue that when the scriptures were written, contraception was unreliable and the danger of unwanted pregnancy very great. But modern methods mean this isn't the case any more. Also, allowing sex before marriage gives young people a chance to explore their sexuality and channel their sexual urges. It's argued that sexual frustration is a bad reason to get married.

4) All three religions teach that couples should wait until they are married, rather then having pre-marital sex. In fact, it's very important to most Muslims that people, especially girls, remain virgins until marriage.
5) The Christian Church teaches that the total giving of self in sex shouldn't be treated casually — self-control and sexual restraint are considered important. Christians are urged to keep sex within marriage for positive reasons more than negative ones — marriage is believed to give sex a special status.
6) Promiscuity (having many sexual partners) is seen as wrong in all three religions — in Christianity it's seen as dishonouring yourself.

### *...but they're Not Identical*

1) Judaism and Christianity are monogamous — adultery is forbidden by one of the Ten Commandments.
2) Islam permits, but doesn't encourage, polygamy. A man may have up to four wives, but only if he can support them and treat them equally.

*Muhammad actually had eleven wives during his lifetime — although not all at the same time.*

## *Homosexuality — Scriptures say it's Wrong*

Homosexuality means being attracted to members of the same sex.

1) Homosexuality is seen in other species, and many non-religious people see it as a natural alternative to heterosexuality.
2) But the scriptures of all three religions seem to say that homosexual sex is wrong — although the relevant passages are interpreted differently by some people.
3) Some (including some priests) argue that the scriptures were written against a very different cultural background from ours, so we can't apply their standards today.
4) Christianity and Judaism no longer condemn homosexuality, but it isn't seen as the ideal and many still view homosexual sex as a sin. So many religious gays opt for celibacy (they don't have sexual relationships).
5) Civil partnerships became legal in the UK in December 2005. They give homosexual couples the same rights as married couples concerning things like custody of children.
6) The Church of England doesn't allow same-sex partnerships to be blessed in a church. However, there have been some cases where vicars have gone against this rule and blessed the unions of homosexual couples anyway.
7) Reform Jews don't usually condemn homosexuality, and even allow commitment ceremonies for homosexuals — these can take place in a synagogue. They also allow homosexuals to become rabbis.
8) Homosexuality is strictly forbidden by Islamic Shari'ah law (see p.73), so in many Muslim countries it's still illegal. In some countries, e.g. Iran and Saudi Arabia, homosexual acts between men carry the death penalty.
9) As with other religions though, some moderate Muslims believe that the traditional teachings on homosexuality cannot be applied to modern society.

*"Because of this, God gave them over to shameful lusts... Men committed indecent acts with other men, and received in themselves the due penalty for their perversion."* **Romans 1:26-27**

## *Oranges are not the only fruit, but that's all you're allowed to eat, apparently...*

Oooh, here we go again... courting controversy. Whatever you think about this stuff yourself, you need to know what the religions teach. Then you can agree or disagree with them all you like — it's up to you...

GENERAL

# Contraception

Hmmm... another tricky topic...

## *Contraception — Preventing a Pregnancy*

1) Contraception (or birth control) is anything that aims to prevent a woman becoming pregnant (conceiving).
2) Contraception can be temporary (e.g. the contraceptive pill, condoms) or permanent (sterilisation).
3) The Roman Catholic Church believes that preventing conception is against 'natural law' and that the use of any artificial contraception is a grave sin. Indeed, it teaches that humans have an obligation to 'be fruitful and increase in number'. Many individual Roman Catholics disagree with this, especially because of recent concerns about AIDS. The Church does allow natural family planning though — by only having sex at the times during a woman's cycle when she's less fertile.
4) Other Christian Churches have different views on the matter. The Anglican, Methodist and Presbyterian Churches are in favour of contraception, suggesting that it lets parents plan their family in a responsible way.
5) Many Christians believe that contraception should be a question of individual conscience.

## *Jews Generally see Contraception as Bad*

1) Judaism traditionally teaches that a child is a gift from God, and contraception interferes with God's plans to bless couples with children.
2) Most Orthodox Jews only accept contraception if pregnancy could be physically or psychologically harmful to the mother or an existing child.
3) Reform Jews are happier with the idea of contraception for family planning — leaving the decision of whether or not to use it to individual conscience. (Having said that, not wanting to have children isn't a good enough reason to use contraception for many Jews.)
4) Sex should be as natural as possible, though, so hormonal contraceptives like the contraceptive pill are generally preferred to barrier methods like condoms. But their use may be encouraged by some as a means of preventing the spread of HIV and other STIs (sexually transmitted infections).

## *Islam Teaches that Life is a Sacred Gift from Allah*

1) The Qur'an encourages procreation, and Muslims believe that conception is the will of Allah. So although contraception isn't specifically mentioned in the Qur'an, it's often seen as unwelcome.

*"...He gives to whom He wills female [children], and He gives to whom He wills males ...and He renders whom He wills barren..."* **Qur'an 42:49-50**

2) Most Muslims feel that it's the right of both husband and wife to try for children, so both partners must agree to any contraception.
3) Different Muslims have different views on contraception, e.g. in Iran, contraception for family planning is actively encouraged. But more conservative scholars and clerics have campaigned against contraception.

**In most Muslim countries, contraception is permitted if:**

i) there's a threat to the mother's health,
ii) it could help a woman who already has children,
iii) there is a greater than average chance of the child being born with disabilities,
iv) the family is too poor to raise a child.

4) Only 'reversible' methods are allowed, though — permanent sterilisation and vasectomies are frowned on.

## *Nothing's ever simple is it...*

People interpret their religion's teachings in different ways, so it's difficult to give a clear-cut overview of what a religion teaches. But, all these different opinions about various issues makes for plenty to say in the exam.

# The Media: Marriage and the Family

GENERAL

Here comes another media page...

## *Soaps* Tackle some *Difficult Issues*

1) In recent years, soap operas like 'Eastenders' and 'Hollyoaks' have covered (amongst other things) homosexuality, rape, prostitution, celibacy, incest, marriage and infidelity (although rarely in the same episode).
2) Even though soaps are often seen as a form of escapism, they let us see how a variety of characters deal with issues and emotions that we could all face at some point in our lives.
3) However, characters are sometimes criticised for being stereotypes. They can easily cause offence to people.

## Films are *Classified* and there's a *Watershed*

1) Films are classified — some are only deemed suitable for people over a certain age. They may be censored too (see p.23), e.g. if they're too sexually explicit.
2) In the UK there's a television 'watershed' at 9 p.m. After this time, programmes are aimed at adults, and it's up to parents to decide whether children watch or not.
3) Many people, both religious and non-religious, object to sex and adultery being explicitly portrayed — they feel that this might promote promiscuous behaviour as 'the norm'.

**Reflection or Cause...**
Some people think that the sex and 'immorality' that we see on TV just reflects what already happens in society. But others say that showing these things has a direct influence on society.

## An Example from *Film: "Four Weddings and a Funeral"*

'Four Weddings' is a great example for marriage and the family in the media. It covers lots of different issues.

What it's about: It's a romantic comedy, but it asks lots of important questions about love, relationships and commitment. The plot centres around Charles, a single thirty-something, and his on-off relationship with Carrie, an American woman he meets at the film's first wedding. (If you haven't seen it, this is the perfect excuse.)

The issues: Promiscuity, marriage and divorce, homosexuality, committed cohabitation.

**Promiscuity:**

The central characters are "serial monogamists" — they've had a string of different sexual partners. Carrie admits to having had 33 different sexual partners. Some Christians might see this as sexually irresponsible and emotionally empty. But the film doesn't encourage this behaviour — Charles is shocked.

*"Flee from sexual immorality... he who sins sexually sins against his own body. Do you not know that your body is a temple of the Holy Spirit..."* **1 Corinthians 6:18-19**

**Marriage and Divorce:**

During the film, Carrie marries 'the wrong man' (a rich politician), which very soon ends in divorce. And Charles nearly marries 'the wrong woman' in a Church wedding. His brother stops him, because he knows Charles doesn't love her. This illustrates the importance of marrying for love.

**Homosexuality:**

For most of the film, the happiest, most committed relationship we see is that between Charles's two gay friends Gareth and Matthew. Their relationship is shown as a 'marriage', which ends suddenly when Gareth dies of a heart attack. The film challenges the idea that homosexual relationships are less committed or loving than heterosexual ones.

**Committed Cohabitation:**

At the end of the film, Charles and Carrie decide to stay together and have children, but not get married. Religious liberals accept cohabitation in a stable and loving relationship, but hope that it will be a 'prelude' to marriage. Roman Catholics and many other religious conservatives believe that when you decide to commit to someone it should be inside marriage, and both partners should be open to having and raising children.

## *TV soaps — real life stuff or total pap?*

Sex, marriage and divorce are part of a lot of people's lives, so it's no wonder they're in the media a lot.

# Warm-Up and Worked Exam Question

## Warm-up Questions

1) What is meant by "cohabitation"?
2) How has family life in the UK changed over the past 30 years?
3) Which of the following religions are strictly monogamous? Christianity, Judaism, Islam.
4) What is a civil partnership?
5) What is the attitude of the Roman Catholic Church towards contraception?
6) Name three issues that crop up in soap operas that are relevant to Religious Studies.

## Worked Exam Question

Christianity, Judaism and Islam all teach that marriage involves commitment and faithfulness. And that it's something that has to be worked at. In that respect, marriage is just like an exam paper. Before you read the answer to the worked exam question below, think about how you'd go about answering it. Then read the answer and the comments and check if you were on the right track.

1 "Contraception should be made as widely available as possible."
In your answer, you should refer to at least one religion.

(i) Do you agree? Give reasons for your opinions.

*Don't forget to state clearly whether you agree or not — it's important.*

*Yes, I agree with this statement. People are always going to have sex, both inside and outside of marriage. Contraception is vital to prevent unwanted children being conceived, who may not be loved or properly cared for. Contraception is also necessary so that people can plan their families. Most people can support a small number of children better than a large number. Also, some types of contraception prevent the spread of sexually transmitted diseases, which can cause pain and suffering to entire families.*

*(3 marks)*

(ii) Give reasons why some people may disagree with you.

*If you didn't refer to a religion in part a) then you must in part b).*

*Orthodox Jews would disagree. Judaism traditionally teaches that a child is a gift from God, and contraception interferes with God's plan. They think contraception should only be used if pregnancy could be harmful to the mother or an existing child.*

*Roman Catholics would also disagree. The Roman Catholic Church teaches that humans have an obligation to 'be fruitful and increase in number', and that using contraception is against natural law.*

*(3 marks)*

*For this question you need to refer to the beliefs of a specific religion. It's not enough to generalise about what religious people are likely to think.*

# Exam Questions

2 a) Give two reasons why many religious believers think cohabitation is wrong.
*(2 marks)*

b) Describe Christian beliefs about the significance of marriage.
*(3 marks)*

3 a) Explain how having a religious belief may influence an unmarried person who is deciding whether to have sex.
*(4 marks)*

b) "Civil partnerships should never be blessed in a place of worship."
Refer to at least one religion in your answer.

(i) Do you agree? Give reasons for your opinion.
*(3 marks)*

(ii) Give reasons why some people may disagree with you.
*(3 marks)*

4 a) Do you think divorcees should be allowed to re-marry in a place of worship?
Give two reasons for your point of view.
*(4 marks)*

b) Explain how the key features of a Christian marriage ceremony reflect religious teachings.
*(6 marks)*

5 a) What is adultery?
*(2 marks)*

b) Do you think that the way relationships are portrayed in TV programmes can cause an increase in promiscuity?
Give two reasons for your point of view.
*(4 marks)*

GENERAL

# Prejudice and Equality

The world we live in is full of people from different religious, racial and cultural backgrounds. And the way each religion deals with this is important, as it can help or hinder the building of communities.

## Prejudice has Many Causes

It's worth being very clear about what a few words mean...

| | |
|---|---|
| **Justice** | the principle of fairness — both legally and more generally. |
| **Equality** | being equal, and being treated equally. |
| **Community** | the people living in a certain place, or a group of people with the same religious or cultural characteristics. |
| **Prejudice** | judging something or someone with no good reason, or without full knowledge of a situation. |
| **Discrimination** | unjust treatment, often resulting from prejudice. |

1) Prejudice has many causes, and is often the product of early influences. It tends to be the result of widely held (yet inaccurate) beliefs of a particular community or family.
2) Discrimination comes in many forms... Individuals may discriminate by being violent and abusive. Whole societies may discriminate by passing laws which prevent certain people from doing certain things.

## Racism is One Form of Prejudice

It's a sad fact that some people are prejudiced against anyone from a different cultural or religious background, or simply because of the colour of their skin.

1) There have been many instances of racial discrimination in the UK in recent years — usually as a result of ignorance, misunderstanding or segregation. At times these have culminated in rioting or murder.
2) Racism is often based on stereotypes — fixed and standardised images of groups of people, which can be used to promote negative thoughts and actions.
3) The media has an important role to play. Television and newspapers can educate — or help fuel negative stereotypes (see p.45).
4) At the present time in the UK, Asians suffer from racism and racist attacks more than any other ethnic group. This has led to further segregation and increased hostility.

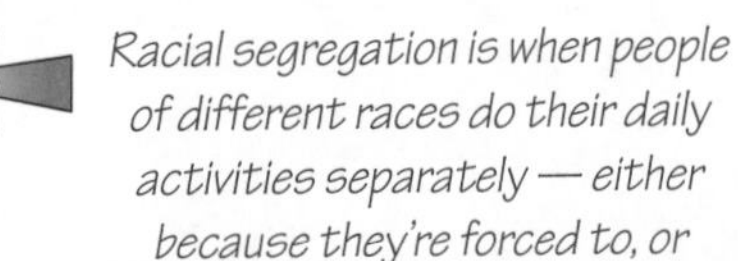

*Racial segregation is when people of different races do their daily activities separately — either because they're forced to, or because it's the social norm.*

## The Government Tries to Promote Community Cohesion

1) The UK is a multi-ethnic, multi-faith society (see p.43), so it can be hard for members of a community to feel they have much in common — they can lack 'community cohesion'.
2) This is particularly true of places where there are lots of people from ethnic minorities.
3) The Government is trying to promote the idea of 'Britishness' as something that goes beyond racial and cultural differences to help tie communities together.
4) The Race Relations Act (1976) is part of this. It makes it illegal to discriminate on the grounds of race, colour or nationality, or to publish anything likely to cause racial hatred.

## Sex Discrimination — it's also Illegal

Most societies have historically been male dominated, and have only started to change relatively recently.

1) Up until the middle of the 20th century, it was seen as a woman's role to stay at home and take care of the family. But during World War II, women had to take on traditionally male roles, e.g. factory work, while the men were away fighting. After the war, many women didn't want things to go back to the way they'd been.
2) In 1975 the Sex Discrimination Act was passed by Parliament. This made it illegal to discriminate against people on account of their gender (sexism) — especially in the fields of employment and education.

# Attitudes to Equality: Christianity

CHRISTIANITY

For Christians, the Bible has plenty to say on the subject of equality...

## The Bible has Plenty of '**Anti-Prejudice**' Stories

1) The idea of 'do to others what you would have them do to you' is a fundamental part of Christian teaching (sometimes called the 'Golden Rule').
2) Generally Christians believe that everyone was created equal by God, and so they try to avoid discrimination and promote equality. They look to the example of Jesus, who told stories about equality, and acted true to his own teaching by mixing with a variety of people himself.
3) One of the most famous stories in the New Testament is the Parable of the Good Samaritan (Luke 10:25-37) where one man comes to the aid of another simply because he is suffering.

THE PARABLE OF THE GOOD SAMARITAN

A man is beaten up and left half-dead by robbers. First a priest and then a Levite (the Levites were a Jewish priestly tribe) walking down the road see him, but carry on walking. But a Samaritan (considered an enemy by the Jews) bandages the man, puts him on his donkey, takes him to an inn and sees that he is looked after.

4) But there are plenty of other biblical verses preaching equal treatment for all — these two are from the New Testament.

*"...there is no Greek or Jew... barbarian, Scythian, slave or free, but Christ is all, and is in all."* **Colossians 3:11**

*"My brothers... don't show favouritism. Suppose a man comes into your meeting wearing a gold ring and fine clothes, and a poor man in shabby clothes also comes in. If you show special attention to the man wearing fine clothes... but say to the poor man... 'Sit on the floor by my feet,' have you not... become judges with evil thoughts?"* **James 2:1-4**

5) And Deuteronomy (a Book of Law in the Old Testament) includes these...

*"Do not take advantage of a hired man who is poor and needy..."* **Deuteronomy 24:14**

*"Do not deprive the alien or the fatherless of justice..."* **Deuteronomy 24:17**

*By the way, 'alien' means 'foreigner' here.*

## **Many People** have Fought against **Prejudice**

1) Most Christians would argue that we should avoid prejudice on the basis of race, gender, religion, age, disability, colour or class. The Bible has plenty of specific teaching on these matters.

*"...loose the chains of injustice and untie the cords of the yoke, to set the oppressed free... Then your light will break forth like the dawn..."* **Isaiah 58:6-8**

2) There are many examples of individual Christians struggling against injustice — e.g.:

   DIETRICH BONHOEFFER was a German Christian who felt the church had a duty to speak out against the Nazis' treatment of the Jews. He later became involved in an active conspiracy against the Nazi Party and was hanged in a concentration camp.

   ARCHBISHOP DESMOND TUTU and BISHOP TREVOR HUDDLESTON were active in the fight against apartheid in South Africa (see next page).

   DR MARTIN LUTHER KING was a baptist minister who dedicated his life to trying to change the way black people were treated in the USA. He organised peaceful marches, rallies and boycotts, and in 1965 blacks were given equal voting rights with whites. King was assassinated in 1968 aged only 39.

## *The Good Samaritan — what a nice bloke...*

This is a serious issue that often makes it into the news. And it's one that you might have personal experience of — and if you do, you can use that experience to help answer an exam question on it. But be careful not to just rant on about yourself — you'll need to refer to the religious teachings as well.

CHRISTIANITY

# Attitudes to Equality: Christianity

## Most Christian Churches Work to Promote **Racial Harmony**

1) Leviticus 19:33-34 contains some basic teaching on the way people from different races and cultural backgrounds should be treated.

*"When an alien lives with you in your land, do not mistreat him... Love him as yourself..."* **Leviticus 19:33-34**

This story's actually about foreigners living in Israel, but Christians argue that it also applies to the modern world.

2) There's a story about Simon Peter in Acts that's also relevant.

**Acts 10:1-35** tells a story about Simon Peter. He is told by God not to consider impure anything that God has made. So when Cornelius, a Roman soldier, sends for Peter, Peter goes willingly, even though it is against the law for Jews to associate with non-Jews. Peter says, "...*God does not show favouritism but accepts men from every nation...*"

3) The parable of the Good Samaritan (see previous page) is an example of Christian teaching on the treatment of people from other cultures. The Samaritans were a mixed race who suffered a great deal of discrimination at the time Jesus told the story.
4) More recently, Dr George Carey (the former Archbishop of Canterbury) spoke about the fundamental Christian belief that racism is wrong, that everyone is created in God's image.

*"Racism has no part in the Christian Gospel... it contradicts our Lord's command... It solves no problems and creates nothing but hatred and fear."* **Dr George Carey**

5) But although Christians generally work to improve racial harmony (people of all races living and working together peacefully), there have been occasions when this hasn't been the case...

The Dutch Reformed Church of South Africa (DRC) believed that God had divided mankind into different races and made white people superior. This idea became law in the system of apartheid.
Trevor Huddleston (an English bishop working in South Africa) argued that apartheid was against God's will. For nearly 50 years, he struggled against it using non-violent methods, until apartheid eventually ended in 1992.

## *Sex Discrimination — Not So Clear*

1) The Bible gives different messages on the subject of sex discrimination. In the New Testament, women are found among Jesus's followers and he treated them equally — remarkable for the time.
2) But this is taken from St Paul's letter to his assistant Timothy:
3) Although in Galatians 3:28 St Paul writes, "There is neither... male nor female, for you are all one in Christ Jesus."

*"I do not permit a woman to teach or to have authority over a man; she must be silent. For Adam was formed first, then Eve... it was the woman who was deceived and became a sinner. But women will be saved through childbearing..."* **1 Timothy 2:12-15**

### WOMEN IN THE CHRISTIAN CHURCH

There's evidence from the Bible that women, as well as men, taught and led congregations in the very early Christian Church, e.g. Phoebe (**Romans 16:1-2**), Priscilla (**Acts 18:26**, **1 Corinthians 16:19**, **Romans 16:3**), Mary, Tryphena and Tryphosa (**Romans 16:12**).
But for much of the Church's history, women haven't been allowed to be ordained as priests. The reasoning being that Jesus only called men to be Apostles.
Over the last 50 years, this has started to change — women can now be ordained as ministers in most Protestant denominations and as Anglican priests, but not as Roman Catholic or Orthodox priests.

## *Racism — still a big issue today, unfortunately...*

In the UK prejudice against Muslims has increased in recent years. This has led to further mistrust and calls for segregation from some, and an increased desire for tolerance and integration from others.

# Attitudes to Equality: Judaism

JUDAISM

Like Christianity and Islam, Judaism teaches that God created people equal.

## The Hebrew Bible Preaches **Tolerance**

Racism is disapproved of in Judaism. The Hebrew Bible (the Old Testament) has a lot to say on the matter.

1) The Book of Genesis suggests that all of humanity comes from the same source and is, therefore, equal before God.

   *"Adam named his wife Eve, because she would become the mother of all the living."* **Genesis 3:20**

2) Other messages of tolerance can be found in Deuteronomy 23:7, and Leviticus 19:33-34 (see p.38).

   *"Do not abhor an Edomite, for he is your brother. Do not abhor an Egyptian, because you lived as an alien in his country."* **Deuteronomy 23:7**

3) Deuteronomy 23 contains a discussion of who should be called 'the Lord's people'. This could be taken as meaning we should show tolerance for other nationalities. However, the same chapter does contain references to certain people or nations who should be excluded.
4) The Jewish people are sometimes called the 'chosen people'. This doesn't mean they think they're better than anyone else — simply that God gave them additional responsibilities.
5) The stories of Ruth and Jonah (both in the Hebrew Bible, i.e. the Old Testament) could also be used to promote social and racial harmony.

**The Story of Jonah...**

Jonah was told to preach to the people of Nineveh, who had upset God. When he preached God's message, the people of Nineveh were humble and repentant, which pleased God, and so God spared the city, upsetting Jonah. But God said he was right to spare the city, and that Jonah was wrong to be upset. The message is, *"If God can love and forgive, we should be able to live with others too."*

*Before he got to Nineveh, Jonah was swallowed by a big fish and stayed there for 3 days.*

*And Isaiah 42:6 shows that God does not want the Jews to turn their backs on non-Jews, but to be "a light for the Gentiles".*

**The Story of Ruth...**

Naomi and her husband leave Judah because of a famine — they end up in Moab. Naomi's sons marry Moabite girls — but soon after, Naomi's husband and sons die. Ruth (one of Naomi's daughters-in-law) stays very loyal to her Israelite mother-in-law, and becomes devoted to God. This bloodline eventually produces King David. The message is, *"Good things happen to those who are nice to people from other lands."*

## ***"Male and female he created them"*** — Genesis 1:27

1) The above passage is sometimes read as meaning that men and women are seen as equals before God, although different, and with different responsibilities. (God did create two different sexes after all, so he can't have wanted us all to be identical.)
2) Some people involved with the feminist movement (fighting for women's rights) argue that the expectation for women to become wives and mothers is unfair, and has hindered women's progress.
3) Judaism doesn't suggest that women should not be able to follow their chosen career. However, there is still a belief that motherhood is a privilege, and women should devote some of their life to it.
4) But there are definitely differences of opinion on this. Orthodox Jews aim to uphold many of the ancient Jewish traditions, and so would be more likely to suggest that women should remain at home as mothers and wives.
5) However, Reform Jews are willing to interpret traditional teachings so that they are, perhaps, more relevant to the modern age. For this reason they're less strict when it comes to the roles of men and women.

*There are also rules governing SYNAGOGUE WORSHIP. Usually ten men (called a minyan) are required for a service, and it is men who read from the Torah. Also, men and women in Orthodox synagogues have separate areas for prayer. Reform Jews don't accept all these rules, however — women can form a minyan, and even become rabbis.*

## *Tolerate thy neighbour...*

Jews have suffered from a great deal of racism and persecution over the years. By far the most extreme form of social injustice was the Holocaust in World War II, when discrimination became government policy. It serves as a reminder to everyone of how much suffering can arise from racial hatred..

ISLAM

# Attitudes to Equality: Islam

Islam is truly international — with followers from many countries, and many ethnic and cultural backgrounds.

## *Islam says People are Created Equal, but not Identical*

1) Islam teaches that all people were created by Allah, and were created equal (although not the same). He intended humanity to be created with differences. But this just means we're all individuals. Hurrah.

> *"And of His signs is the creation of the heavens and the earth and the diversity of your languages and your colours..."* **Qur'an 30:22**

2) Muslims all over the world are united through the ummah — the community of Islam. The ummah consists of all Muslims, regardless of colour, nationality, tradition (i.e. Sunni or Shi'ite) and so on. This can help promote racial and social harmony, as no one is excluded or discriminated against in theory.

3) Hajj (pilgrimage to Makkah) especially demonstrates equality. Those on pilgrimage all wear simple white garments, showing everyone's equal before Allah — wealth, status and colour don't matter.

4) The fact that all Muslims should pray five times a day at set times, and face Makkah whilst doing so, also demonstrates unity and equality. Men and women often pray together at home — however, they must pray in separate groups in the mosque.

Muslims are more likely to be subjected to racially motivated attacks, abuse and murder than their white neighbours in the UK.

As a result a number of peaceful pressure groups have been established — some working within Muslim communities, others working with the Government or with other faith groups.

## *The Qur'an teaches that Men and Women are Equal*

1) Men and women have an equal obligation to Allah in terms of prayer, fasting, pilgrimage and charity.

> *"Indeed, the Muslim men and Muslim women, the believing men and believing women, the obedient men and obedient women... the charitable men and charitable women, the fasting men and fasting women... and the men who remember Allah often and the women who do so — for them Allah has prepared forgiveness and a great reward."* **Qur'an 33:35**

2) All Muslims, male and female, are also obliged to seek education.

3) In the early days of Islam, there were many female religious scholars.

4) But there are also some teachings that might be interpreted as meaning men are superior, e.g.

> *"Men are in charge of women by [right of] what Allah has given one over the other and what they spend [for maintenance] from their wealth..."* **Qur'an 4:34**

Although they're usually taken to mean that men and women just have different roles within the community or family — men are responsible for providing for the family, and women are responsible for the home.

WOMEN AND THE MOSQUE

Women aren't encouraged to attend the mosque for prayer, but the Prophet Muhammad did permit it. If they do go to the mosque, they must pray in a separate group — behind (or otherwise out of sight of) the men.

Women are not permitted to lead the prayers of men, but they may lead other women. This is agreed by all traditional schools of Islam, both Sunni and Shi'ah.

Muslim feminist Asra Nomani is leading a campaign to end segregation in the mosque, and allow woman-led mixed-gender prayers. In 2005, Amina Wadud led a mixed-gender prayer in New York. Their actions have been condemned by Muslim scholars as not following the teachings of Islam.

## *We're not all the same, but everyone should be treated equally...*

In Islam, a woman's traditional role has been to create a good homelife for the family, while the man went out to work and made sure the children were good Muslims. However, not all Muslims live in this traditional way. In some Islamic cultures there is almost complete equality between men and women.

# Family Roles of Men and Women

GENERAL

Men and women have different roles in society — and different roles in family life too.

## Roles of Men and Women Have **Changed A Lot** in Society...

1) In the past, it was seen as a woman's role to take care of the home and raise children, while the man went out to work. The man was the head of the household, and his wife was expected to be obedient.
2) After World War II, these attitudes started to change in the UK (see p.36). Now it's considered perfectly normal for women to go out to work, and men to take part in housework and childcare (although women still do a lot more of this overall.)
3) Religious views on the roles of men and women have shifted over time in a similar way.

## ...And in **Christian** Families

*"Wives, submit to your husbands as to the Lord. For the husband is the head of the wife as Christ is the head of the church..."*
**Ephesians 5:22-23**

1) The Bible talks about wives submitting to their husbands (doing as they say).
2) But many Christians argue that this just reflects the ideas of society at that time, and doesn't correspond with Jesus's attitude towards women. Women are found among Jesus's followers, and he treated them equally.
3) Nowadays, most Christians believe that men and women should have equal roles in the family.

## Jewish **Women** Must Learn to Run a **Jewish Home**

1) Jewish women and men have traditional roles in the home. But these expectations are changing, especially for Reform Jews (see p.39).
2) Men and women have clear roles during the Shabbat meal — the mother lights candles and welcomes Shabbat, and the father blesses the children.

*There's lots to do to prepare for Shabbat — cleaning the house and preparing food. This is traditionally the woman's job.*

## **Mothers** are Very Important in **Muslim** Families

1) In traditional Muslim families, women are generally expected to take care of the home and the children, and men are expected to support their wives (see p.40).
2) However, it's quite acceptable for women to go out to work if their husbands agree.
3) Even though they're not head of the household, mothers have a very high status in Muslim families.
4) Modern interpretations of the teachings of the Qur'an say that husbands should consider what's normal in society when dealing with their wives, and that family decisions should be taken together.

*"Who amongst the people is most deserving of my good treatment? He said: Your mother, again your mother, again your mother, then your father..."*
**Prophet Muhammad (Sahih Muslim)**

### Men and women have different roles...

Religious texts are read within the context of society. As the roles of men and women have gradually changed in society, the different religious texts have been interpreted differently.

GENERAL

# Religious Help for Immigrants

Over 100,000 people move to the UK every year — either looking for work or to find refuge from persecution (asylum seekers). And there are plenty of religious organisations out there to help them...

## *Immigrants Often Face **Difficulties***

1) Many immigrants arrive with either no, or very poor, English — so they need interpreters while they learn the language.
2) They're often unfamiliar with British customs and laws, so can find themselves in trouble without understanding why.
3) Many asylum seekers have suffered physical, mental, emotional or sexual abuses in their countries, which can leave them seriously traumatised.
4) Without good English and an understanding of the system, it can be very difficult to get good-quality legal advice, register for healthcare or find accommodation.
5) Immigrants are frequently exploited as unofficial, cheap labour, paid well below the minimum wage.
6) Some people accuse immigrants of taking homes and jobs from local people. This attitude can lead to discrimination and abuse (ranging from playground name-calling to physical attacks).

## *Religious Organisations Offer **Practical Help***

Christianity, Islam and Judaism agree that all human beings should be treated fairly and humanely. So there are organisations from all three faiths working to improve the lot of immigrants to this country. You need to know some examples of these religious organisations and the work they do:

**The Boaz Trust**

A Christian organisation based in Greater Manchester, set up to help failed asylum seekers. These are people whose asylum applications have been turned down but are too scared to go home. They aren't allowed to work in the UK and get no help from the Government, so they're entirely dependent on charity for food, accommodation and any legal help they might need for an appeal.

**The Jesuit Refugee Service**

An international Roman Catholic organisation, with bases in over 50 countries worldwide. JRS offers pastoral services (taking care of people's spiritual well-being), counselling, English-language teaching and help with healthcare and legal representation. They also campaign across Europe against the detention of asylum seekers. (Detention means holding asylum seekers in a centre while deciding if they should be allowed into the community or sent back to where they came from.)

**The Jewish Council for Racial Equality (JCORE)**

A Jewish organisation, based in the UK. They campaign for the rights of asylum seekers, raise awareness of the problems faced by immigrants and offer all sorts of practical help. For example, they have a 'refugee doctors project' that gives information and practical help to trained immigrant doctors, to help them re-train to practise in the UK.

**Islamic Aid**

An international Muslim organisation dedicated to reducing poverty and deprivation. Their work in the UK centres on improving the lives of Muslim immigrants, e.g. by raising awareness of the problem of 'ghettos' and tackling unemployment among UK Muslims.

## *Bienvenue, Willkommen, Witajcie, Swaagatam, Huan yin...*

There are tens of thousands of failed asylum seekers in the UK, living off the charity of organisations like Boaz and JCORE. They have no home, no legal way of making money, no access to medicine or education for their children — it's a terrible way to live. But as far as the law's concerned, they have no right to be here at all...

# The UK as a Multi-Faith Society

GENERAL

All through history, people from different cultures have come to settle in Britain, bringing with them their own beliefs and customs. It makes our society rich and diverse, but can sometimes cause problems.

## The UK is a *Diverse, Multi-Faith Society*

1) Your identity is what makes you you. It's how you see yourself and how others see you. It's made up of basic stuff like your name, age, appearance, as well as 'deeper' stuff such as your beliefs and attitudes.
2) The United Kingdom is a very diverse, multi-faith society — there are a wide range of Christian denominations, and about 6% of the population practises a non-Christian religion.
3) In most major towns and cities you'll find a variety of places of worship — including different churches, synagogues and mosques.
4) Children in UK schools are taught about all major world faiths in an attempt to increase understanding and tolerance.

*Although some Roman Catholic and other church schools limit the amount of time spent looking at other religions.*

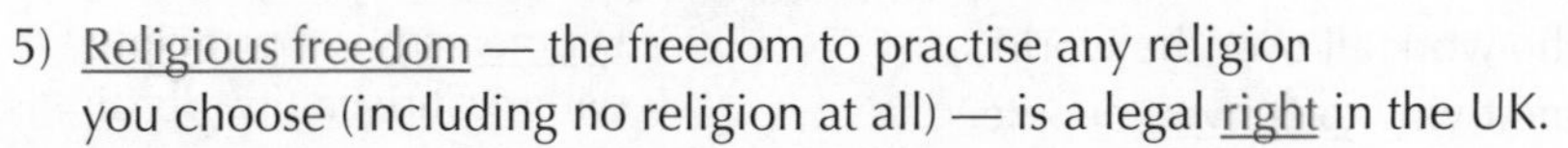

5) Religious freedom — the freedom to practise any religion you choose (including no religion at all) — is a legal right in the UK.
6) The religious diversity of the UK provides a great opportunity for increasing understanding, and for finding common ground between the different faiths.
7) But that isn't the only advantage of a multi-faith society. Along with their faiths, these different cultural groups bring their customs, dress, art, music, food, architecture...
8) All this helps to make the UK a really vibrant and interesting place to live.

## *Conversion and Interfaith Marriages are Issues in the UK*

But along with religious diversity and freedom come the issues of conversion and interfaith marriages.

*CONVERSION*

In the past, Christians often believed they had the right to make people take up their faith. In general, Christians are much more tolerant now, but evangelical Christians still consider it a priority to 'win people for Christ'. This is because they don't believe that a person can get to Heaven any other way (see next page).

Muslims are happy to accept converts, but they don't usually go out trying to convert people. However, rejecting Islam to take another faith (apostasy) is a sin that's still punishable by death.

While the early Jews accepted converts to the faith, modern Orthodox Jews aren't very keen to at all. Reform Jews will accept converts after a period of study (usually about 18 months) but they don't encourage conversion either. In the Middle Ages, many Jews were forced to reject Judaism, but encouraging other Jews to do the same carried the death penalty.

*INTERFAITH MARRIAGES*

As a rule, interfaith marriages are disapproved of — unless either the husband or the wife intends to convert at some point.

Children of a mixed marriage are much less likely to be brought up as observant members of either religion (although the child of a Muslim is considered a Muslim, and the child of a Jewish mother is considered Jewish — whatever the faith of the other parent).

And it can be difficult for any member of the family to really stay a part of their own faith community. There are groups like the 'Inter-Faith Marriage Network' that offer advice and support for mixed-faith couples.

## *Pluralists say there's Room for Everyone*

1) Most religious believers are happy to live alongside other faiths in the UK. Organisations representing every major faith in the UK belong to the 'Inter Faith Network for the UK'.
2) The aim of this network is to promote mutual understanding, combat prejudice and help build community cohesion.
3) This is an example of religious pluralism — the idea that every faith has as much right to exist as any other, and that there's room for everyone.

*The Inter Faith Network for the UK describes itself as based "...on the principle that dialogue and cooperation can only prosper if they are rooted in respectful relationships which do not blur or undermine the distinctiveness of different religious traditions".*

GENERAL

# Attitudes to Other Religions

Christianity, Judaism and Islam have a great deal in common, and their approach to other religions is generally one of tolerance and mutual understanding. Over the years, though, there have been times of misunderstanding, ignorance and intolerance, which have led to discrimination and war (e.g. the Crusades).

## Christianity Teaches that Jesus is the **Only Path** to **God**

*"I am the way and the truth and the life. No one comes to the Father except through me."* **John 14:6**

1) Christians generally believe that people have the right to practise any faith, although they might argue that only Christianity has the truth about God. This passage stresses the Christian belief that it's only through following the teachings of Jesus Christ that people can reach God.
2) In the Decree "Ad Gentes", the Roman Catholic Church makes it clear that "*...the Church still has the obligation and also the sacred right to evangelise all men*". 'Evangelise' means spread the Christian message with the aim of converting people (see previous page).
3) There are also Christian missionaries who work all over the world spreading the message of Christianity and trying to convert people.
4) This approach could be described as exclusive — it doesn't really welcome other faiths, and may even reject them because Christianity is seen as the only way.
5) But not all Christians accept this. Christian inclusivists believe that there's at least some truth in what other religions say about God.

Ecumenism is a principle within Christianity. Its aim is to create unity amongst the different Christian traditions, e.g. Roman Catholics, Anglicans, Methodists, etc.

## Jews believe Judaism is the **Only True Faith** (for Jews)

1) Judaism teaches that it is the only true faith for Jews to follow, but is tolerant of other faiths.
2) Most faiths have similar moral and spiritual laws and so are tolerated by Judaism. Because of this, there's no real desire to convert people.
3) People of any religion are generally deemed to be righteous if they follow the Noahide Code — moral laws given to Noah after the flood that prohibit idolatry, murder, theft, sexual immorality and blasphemy.
4) Islam and Judaism have very similar beliefs in one all-powerful God. However, some Jews have difficulties with the Christian belief that Jesus Christ was the incarnation of God. And with the use of statues and icons in Roman Catholic and Orthodox Christianity, which they see as idolatry.
5) But there's still a great deal of mutual respect, and Jewish participation in interfaith groups (see previous page) is common. One example of an interfaith group in the UK is '*The Council for Christians and Jews*'.

## Muslims believe Islam is the **Only True Faith**

1) Muslims believe that Islam is the only true faith — although there is an acceptance that all righteous people will be favoured by Allah, as he knows all we do.
2) Muslims believe that men like Adam, Ibrahim (Abraham), Musa (Moses) and Isa (Jesus) were all Prophets of Allah. So the Torah and the Bible are also holy scriptures revealed by Allah (albeit edited from their original form). This suggests that Islam is an inclusive faith.

*"Indeed, those who believed and those who were Jews or Christians... those [among them] who believed in Allah and the Last Day and did righteousness — will have their reward with their Lord..."* **Qur'an 2:62**

3) But some Muslims interpret the scriptures to argue that Islam should be exclusive, and shouldn't have anything to do with other faiths. And like Christians, some Muslims feel they have a mission to lead non-Muslims to Allah.
4) However, many Muslims in the UK live side by side with other religious believers, and some take part in interfaith groups.

*E.g. The Centre for the Study of Islam and Christian-Muslim Relations.*

## Exclusive, inclusive or pluralist...

Exclusivists believe that their religion is the only way to salvation. Inclusivists believe that other religions have some truth in them. And pluralists believe that many different religious viewpoints are valid.

# The Media: Religion and Society

General

Community cohesion isn't much of a story until it goes wrong. But when it does, it gets everyone's attention.

## The Media Raises *Sensitive Issues*

With community cohesion issues, the media has to strike a balance — drawing attention to problems that may be of public concern, but without encouraging racism or xenophobia (fear or hatred of people from other countries).

### *Immigration* is Regularly in the *News*

The mainstream British press would deny that it ever carries a racist or discriminatory message, but some people argue that it encourages prejudice.

1) Elements of the British media have described immigration as a big problem and have called for stricter controls on who's allowed to settle in the country.
2) They point to the strain placed on social services, the competition for jobs and the fact that immigrants often send a large proportion of the money they earn back to their country of origin.
3) Some think this media attention has made life harder for migrants, by turning people against them, and ignores the positive impact they have — creating economic activity often in deprived areas.

## *Islamophobia* is a *Serious Problem*

1) Islam is often portrayed by the media as a violent religion, which threatens the security of the nation. This attitude was reinforced by the London bombings in 2005, conducted by four Muslims.
2) Many people feel that the influence of the media has contributed to Islamophobia — hatred and fear of Islam.

The Forum Against Islamophobia and Racism (FAIR) was set up in 2001 to monitor media coverage of Islam, and to work with media organisations to combat misrepresentation.

### Rioting in *2001* Highlighted *Tensions*

1) In 2001, activity by the far-right group, the National Front, sparked off rioting in Oldham and Burnley. This unrest spread to Bradford, a city that had seen decades of high immigration, which had developed a number of ethnically segregated neighbourhoods.
2) Much of the violence was focused in Manningham, a mainly Pakistani area of the city, where it was reported that around one thousand Asian youths confronted riot police.
3) News reports featured local religious leaders — including the Archbishop of Bradford and members of local Muslim organisations — expressing their distress and appealing for calm.
4) In the aftermath, the leaders of Bradford's different religious groups met up with the Home Secretary to try to end the mistrust between their communities.
5) While some in the media applauded the role played by religious organisations, others complained that focusing on religion took attention away from the problem of racism, and the real social and economic difficulties faced by the people of Bradford.

In 2006 Channel 4 made *Bradford Riots*, a drama which tells the story of Karim, a Muslim student from Bradford, who gets caught up in the rioting and ends up being given a harsh prison sentence.

- Religion plays an important, but background role in the film. The Imam in the mosque offers spiritual guidance rather than practical advice.
- Religion is seen as an inescapable part of the characters' identities — but one that they are sometimes reduced to. At the end, Karim's cellmate calls him simply 'Muslim-boy'.
- The film reflects on the uncertainty and vulnerability felt by Britain's Muslim communities in the wake of the 9/11 terrorist attacks.

## *The media can influence your view of religions...*

The nature of the media means that when religion is covered, it's more likely to be a story about a riot, or an extreme weird cult, than about people practising their faiths quietly, as they have done for years.

# Warm-Up and Worked Exam Question

## Warm-up Questions

1) What is racial harmony?
2) How are the roles of women different from those of men in a traditional synagogue? (*Judaism*)
3) List three problems faced by immigrants to the UK.
   Describe the work of one religious organisation which tries to help them.
4) How is conversion viewed by a) Christians, b) Jews, c) Muslims?
5) What do missionaries do? (*Christianity*)
6) What is Islamophobia? (*Islam*)

## Worked Exam Question

This section has been about the issues faced by our twenty-first century society — prejudice, discrimination, intolerance... A question about them is likely to crop up in the exam, so make sure you practise the exam questions on the next page. To get you off to a flying start, here's a worked example.

1 Explain why many Christians are against discrimination.

*Christianity teaches that everyone was created equal by God, and so discrimination is wrong. Many Bible passages are anti-discrimination and promote the idea of equality, e.g. "…there is no Greek or Jew… barbarian, Scythian, slave or free, but Christ is all, and is in all." Jesus's attitude to discrimination is illustrated by the Parable of the Good Samaritan. In this parable, one man came to the aid of another who was suffering, even though the men were from enemy tribes.*

*Remember — the question is about Christianity, so include specific Biblical teachings.*

*Also, the 'Golden Rule' of Christianity is to "do to others what you would have them do to you". So if a Christian wouldn't want to be discriminated against, he or she shouldn't discriminate against others.*

*But there may be other reasons that aren't directly related to what it says in the Bible...*

*Christians may also be guided by influential Christians who have fought against discrimination. E.g. Archbishop Desmond Tutu was active in the fight against Apartheid in South Africa.*

*(8 marks)*

*You have to think of this type of question as a 'mini essay' if you want top marks. Organise what you want to say and use clear English. And make sure your spelling is correct.*

## Exam Questions

2 a) Explain what religious believers mean by 'community'.

*(2 marks)*

b) Do you think the media encourages community cohesion?
Give two reasons for your point of view.

*(4 marks)*

3 a) What is prejudice?

*(2 marks)*

b) Choose one religion other than Christianity and explain why followers of that religion might strive for racial harmony.

*(8 marks)*

4 a) Do you think religious people should marry someone of the same faith?
Give two reasons for your point of view.

*(4 marks)*

b) "Men and women should have different roles in the home."
Do you agree? Give reasons for your answer, showing that you have thought about more than one point of view. Refer to religious arguments in your answer.

*(6 marks)*

5 a) Explain from two different religious traditions the attitudes of their followers towards other religions. You must state the religious traditions you are referring to.

*(6 marks)*

b) "No more immigrants should be allowed into this country."

Refer to at least one religion in your answer.

(i) Do you agree? Give reasons for your opinion.

*(3 marks)*

(ii) Give reasons why some people may disagree with you.

*(3 marks)*

GENERAL & CHRISTIANITY

# Moral Guidance

A moral code is a list of what someone believes to be right and wrong. Different people use different sources of moral guidance. For most religious people, the first place to start is sacred texts.

## People Look for **Moral Guidance** in Different Places

Religious people look in various places to find the 'truth' about what's right, and what God wants.

**SACRED TEXTS**

Believers most commonly look to sacred texts (e.g. the Bible, the Qur'an or the Torah and Talmud) for moral guidance. Some people claim that the religious texts were written for a society with different values, and should be interpreted to suit the times. Others argue that they're the Word of God and so must be obeyed to the letter. (There's loads more about sacred texts on pages 87-89.)

**THE EXAMPLE OF TEACHERS/PROPHETS**

Religious people may also look at the lives and actions of teachers like Jesus and Muhammad to guide them along the right path (more about that later).

**CONSCIENCE**

Your conscience is that little voice in your head telling you what's right or wrong. Some believers argue that this is the voice of God, so we should listen to it very carefully and always trust what it's telling us. Others say that it's just the result of your upbringing — e.g. your parents' opinions, things you've read or heard, religious teachings... If this is true, then your conscience is only as trustworthy as the things it's based on. Some people believe that your conscience has to be schooled in the teachings of your faith, or it might lead you astray.

*"My conscience is clear, but that does not make me innocent. It is the Lord who judges me."* **1 Corinthians 4:4**

## Jesus Set an **Example** for Christians Today

### Jesus **Challenged** Laws and Traditions in the name of **Love**

1) Jesus's Jewish opponents often accused him of breaking religious laws — for example, he healed people on the Sabbath when Jews were not supposed to do any work.
2) Jesus thought the Jewish authorities had missed the point of God's law, and that the 'spirit' of the law was more important than the 'letter'. He also criticised the Pharisees for allowing ritual and tradition to become too important, e.g. in **Mark 7:1-22** he challenges 'ritual washing' and 'unclean' things.
3) In fact, he taught that your motivation was even more important than your actions — being angry with someone could be as bad as killing them (**Matthew 5:21-22**).
4) Above all else, Jesus wanted his followers to love. When asked which was the most important commandment, he gave a pretty neat answer that summed up his beliefs...

*"Love the Lord your God with all your heart and with all your soul and with all your mind and with all your strength... love your neighbour as yourself."* **Mark 12:30-31**

### Jesus set an Example of **Self-Sacrifice**

1) Christians believe that in his willingness to suffer and die on their behalf, Jesus set an example which they themselves should be prepared to follow. In **Mark 8:34** Jesus says, *"If anyone would come after me, he must deny himself and take up his cross and follow me."*
2) In dying on the cross, Christians believe Jesus paid for all the sin of mankind. The Bible teaches that God is merciful, but he is also just, so our sins have to be paid for.
3) Christians believe that everyone who has died will be judged. Most Christians believe that only those that have followed Jesus's teachings, and have behaved morally (or have repented and sought forgiveness for any immorality) will enter Heaven as a result of his sacrifice.

# Moral Guidance: Christianity



The main source of moral guidance for most Christians is the Bible (see page 87).

## The Ten Commandments are about Showing Respect

The most famous moral laws in the Bible are the Decalogue (i.e. the Ten Commandments):

From **Exodus 20**:
You shall have no other gods before me.
You shall not bow down before idols.
You shall not misuse the name of the Lord.
Observe the Sabbath and keep it holy.
Honour your father and mother.
You shall not murder.
You shall not commit adultery.
You shall not steal.
You shall not give false testimony (lie).
You shall not covet (want to possess) someone else's things or wife/husband.

Basically the Ten Commandments are about showing respect — to God, and to other people.

## Churches have a Powerful Influence on their Followers

1) Some Christians look to religious leaders (e.g. the Pope or the Archbishop of Canterbury) and religious traditions to find moral truth.
2) Church leaders are respected and trusted, so the teachings of Churches (particularly the Roman Catholic Church) exert a strong influence on issues like medical ethics, war and justice.

**THE MAGISTERIUM** — this is the teaching authority of the Pope and bishops of the Roman Catholic Church.

1) To Roman Catholics, the authority of the Church rivals that of the Bible itself.
2) The Pope is believed to be infallible on questions of faith and morals (i.e. he can't make a mistake).
3) Dogmas are firm beliefs of the Catholic church — some come from the Bible, but some are Church traditions (e.g. the belief that the Virgin Mary was born without sin). Most of them are set out in a series of statements called the Catechism, to help its members understand what they should believe.

But religious leaders are human, and humans have failings — so can Christians trust that they speak for God? The same goes for the traditions of the Church. All religious institutions were founded by humans.

## Situation Ethics is all about Showing the Greatest Love

1) Situation Ethics is a Christian principle based on the idea that the only intrinsically good thing is Christian love — that is an unselfish, absolute and unconditional love for all people.
2) The principle states that all decisions should be made to achieve the greatest amount of love. So any Biblical or Church law can be broken, if breaking it results in more love.
3) This is quite a hard thing to get your head around, because the sort of love we're talking about isn't cuddly or sentimental. These decisions are usually about causing the least harm overall.
4) Here are a few real examples of where Situation Ethics could come into play:
    - A homeless man steals a loaf of bread to feed himself.
    - A widow marries someone she doesn't love, but who will care for her children.
    - A dictator is murdered to end a harsh regime.
    - Tens of thousands of civilians die, to end a war that had killed millions *(Hiroshima)*.
5) In each case, from the perspective of 'greatest love', it could be argued that the end justifies the means.

## The most loving thing isn't always the nicest...

In practice, most Christians will base their moral judgements on a combination of lots of different sources. But respect and love are the basic principles of Christianity, and they're always a good place to start...

Judaism & Islam

# Moral Guidance: Judaism and Islam

Observant Jews believe they should live in a way that's pleasing to God — this means obeying the 613 mitzvot.

## **Morality** Matters in Judaism

The most famous mitzvot (commandments) are the Ten Commandments (see previous page) — but they're not the only ones. There are 613 mitzvot in total, which can be divided up in different ways...

248 of the mitzvot are positive, telling Jews what they should do. 365 are negative, telling them what they shouldn't be doing.

Ritual mitzvot are about Jews' relationship with God. Moral (ethical) mitzvot are about Jews' dealings with other people.

The first four of the Ten Commandments are ritual mitzvot, and the last six are moral mitzvot.

The singular of mitzvot is mitzvah.

1) Observant Jews think it's vital to live by a moral code, and will generally regard a moral individual as someone who combines religious observance with concern for other people.
2) In deciding how to behave, Jews look first to the Torah, then to the Talmud (there's more about these on p.88), then to the wider body of traditional Jewish teaching. But an individual Jew can always ask someone who knows more about these things than they do.

The word 'mitzvah' is sometimes translated as a 'good deed'.

3) Jews realise that no one can live by all 613 mitzvot all of the time. But they believe that God is merciful and will always forgive someone who is truly sorry for his sins. Yom Kippur (see page 70) reminds Jews of this every year.
4) For Reform Jews, the buck stops with the individual conscience. They're expected to use all the traditional sources of authority on moral behaviour, but in the end they must decide for themselves what's right.
5) Orthodox Jews tend to believe that the correct moral judgements are to be found by sticking as close as possible to traditional Jewish teaching — from the Torah, the Talmud or from other respected sources.

## Muslims Follow the **Qur'an** and **Muhammad's Example**

1) According to the Qur'an (p.89), the prophets bring Allah's message so that people know how to behave.
2) Allah's mercy and compassion mean he can't just leave us to mess up our lives. So Allah gives messages to angels, who then pass on his words to prophets (or rasuls).
3) Allah sent many prophets as messengers, maybe because we seem to forget the plot quite quickly. But Muhammad was the last prophet (the 'seal of the prophets'), and Allah revealed the Qur'an to him.
4) As Allah's last prophet, Muslims regard Muhammad as a very moral, trustworthy man, that they should try to be like. Collections of his sayings (Hadiths) are a source of moral and spiritual guidance for many Muslims — particularly Sunni Muslims.
5) The Sunnah is a record of Muhammad's life and actions. It's seen as the model for a correct Muslim life.

## **Khalifah** — Taking **Responsibility** in Allah's Name

1) Muslims believe that they have a duty to obey Allah.
2) Allah has laid down rules for living a moral life in the Qur'an (e.g. rules on dress, money and food), so any Muslim who doesn't obey those rules is disobeying Allah.
3) Muslims believe that they will pay for any disobedience on Judgement Day, when Allah will judge us on the basis of our actions.
4) Muslims also believe they have been appointed khalifah (vice-regents or trustees) of the Earth. This is the idea that while we're on Earth we should take responsibility for the world in Allah's name, and make it the sort of place he wants it to be. This sometimes means applying the teachings of the Qur'an to new situations, and relying on our conscience to tell us what's right and wrong.

# Human Rights

GENERAL

Human rights are the moral, legal and political rights that ought to apply to every human being on Earth.

## The United Nations Defined Human Rights in 1948

1) In 1948, the United Nations (UN) published the Universal Declaration of Human Rights. The aim was to lay down minimum rights for every person, in every country in the world.
2) It states that all human beings are born free and equal in dignity and rights. It also contains 'articles' that lay down specific rights, e.g. the right to life, freedom from slavery, freedom from imprisonment or exile without good reason, freedom of opinion and expression, the right to seek work and to receive an education.
3) The Universal Declaration of Human Rights is a statement of how things ought to be, but means nothing in a court of law. So in 1953, the Council of Europe brought into effect its European Convention on Human Rights. This is a similar list of rights that's enforceable by the European Court of Human Rights in Strasbourg.
4) These rights became part of the UK's domestic law in 1998, with the Human Rights Act.

- This act protects the human rights of UK Citizens under UK law.
- Most of the rights in the Human Rights Act are limited. That means a person's rights can be restricted to prevent a crime or protect the rights of others.
- The rights of the wider community are put before the rights of one individual.

## Most Christians Strongly Support Human Rights

Whatever their denomination (Roman Catholic, Anglican, Methodist, etc.) most Christians agree that:

1) All human beings deserve to be treated fairly and with respect, simply because they're human. This is based on a belief in human dignity — the idea that all human life is valuable, because people are created in the image of God.

*"So God created man in his own image, in the image of God he created him; male and female he created them."* **Genesis 1:27**

*"You, my brothers, were called to be free. But do not use your freedom to indulge the sinful nature; rather, serve one another in love."* **Galatians 5:13**

2) Everyone is free — to think and to choose how to behave (although Christians hope people will choose to live in love).

Protestant ministers were heavily involved in the drafting of the Universal Declaration of Human Rights.

## The Government and Charities Protect People's Rights

1) The Government provides all UK citizens with free healthcare, free education up to the age of 18 and support to help find a home or job (the welfare system). Charities like Barnardo's and Shelter are also there to help people stay alive and healthy if they fall through the gaps in the system.
2) The Government also works to reduce social injustice. This is where groups of people are unfairly disadvantaged (i.e. discriminated against), or there's an uneven distribution of wealth in society.
3) But other rights, such as freedom of opinion, freedom of expression and freedom from imprisonment, aren't universal. The Government will limit these rights if they think it's for the good of the community, e.g. you're not allowed to say anything that might encourage racial or religious hatred, and terrorism suspects can be held for up to 28 days without charge.
4) Human rights charities, like Amnesty International and Liberty, constantly challenge these decisions to limit people's rights. They argue that any limitations on freedom of speech are dangerous, since they can restrict debate on important issues.

## Freedom and equality — human rights in a nutshell...

Some governments don't agree with the idea of human rights. They argue that the UN declaration was written by Western countries, reflecting Western values — so it isn't always appropriate for non-Western countries.

GENERAL

# Democracy

Whether you're interested in politics or not, you can't get away from how important it is and how much it affects everyone's lives — yours included. In fact, it's so important that they've put it on the Religious Studies syllabus... well, obviously... the connection's quite clear... ahem...

## Democracy is 'Rule by the People'

1) The UK is a democratic society — the people select representatives (e.g. MPs) to run the country.
2) We elect MPs to form a government every five years or so. If a government makes lots of unpopular decisions, they can be kicked out at the next general election. This helps keep their power in check.
3) But democracy is about more than voting — in a democratic society, people can speak out, or take part in peaceful protest if they want something changed.

## Democratic Processes are Important

A democratic process is any way in which citizens can take part in the running of a country:

- **VOTING** — This is the most obvious way to affect government. UK citizens can be asked to vote for a representative (e.g. in local council, general or European elections) or on a particular issue in a referendum. A referendum is a "yes" or "no" vote on a question that's considered too important to be decided by representatives, e.g. the UK joining the Euro.
- **PROTESTING** for or against a government decision — This can take many forms, e.g. writing to your representative, signing a written petition or taking part in a protest march.
- Joining a **PRESSURE GROUP** — These organisations try to influence government decisions on particular issues, e.g. Greenpeace or the Stop the War Coalition.
- Joining a **POLITICAL PARTY** — Political parties are groups of (usually) like-minded people who try to get elected based on policies. There are three main parties in the UK — Labour, the Conservatives and the Liberal Democrats. Party members can stand as candidates for election, campaign on behalf of a candidate or just donate money to help pay for election campaigns.

It's really important to take part in these processes, because they give you a say in how the country's run. Decisions that affect your lives are being made every day by the people in power. Democratic processes let you make your opinions known, to help you influence those decisions.

Democracy can bring about real social change — changes in the structure, behaviour and attitudes of society (for better or for worse). Many religious people believe they have a duty to try to make society fairer and more loving, so they ought to take part in democratic processes.

## Electoral Processes — Organising the Voting System

1) In the UK, every citizen over 18 has the right to vote (unless they're in prison).
2) Voting happens at a polling station — somewhere local with easy access, such as a village hall. Voting is secret so it's fair — you're not bullied into voting for one particular candidate.
3) There are two electoral systems used in the UK:

**First-past-the-post:** This is the system used in most UK elections. The country is divided into voting areas called constituencies (for general elections) and wards (for local elections). The candidate with the most votes in each constituency or ward is elected to represent that area.

**Proportional representation:** This is only used in European elections, and in elections to the Northern Irish, Scottish and Welsh assemblies. Each person votes for a political party. The number of representatives elected from that party is proportional to the total number of votes they got.

## Democracy — power to the people...

Yeah, yeah, politics — how dull, yawn. But free and fair elections and the right to peaceful protest are vital parts of our society, and they should never be taken for granted. Once you get the vote — use it wisely.

# Christian Teachings on Responsibility

CHRISTIANITY

Christians believe that they have a responsibility to care for other people.

## The **Golden Rule** — a Moral Rule of Thumb

Christian moral teachings on duty and responsibility come down to this one basic rule:

> *"So in everything, do to others what you would have them do to you, for this sums up the Law and the Prophets."* **Matthew 7:12**

1) That means Christians should always think about others, not just themselves.
2) It's the same sort of vibe as *"love your neighbour as yourself"* (**Leviticus 19:18**). But Christians have a responsibility to put this love into practice, e.g. by offering support, shelter, food or clothing to someone in need.
3) Many Christians also believe that they have a duty to be socially responsible. Social responsibility is the idea that we should consider the impact our actions have on the rest of society, not just the impact they have on our own lives — it's basically about not being selfish.

*Most Christian denominations remind people to "Go out to love and serve the Lord" at the end of a service.*

## The **Sheep** and the **Goats** is a Parable of **Judgement Day**

1) In the Gospel of Matthew (**Matthew 25:31-46**), Jesus tells a story about the end of the world and how everyone will be judged and separated into the good (the sheep) and the bad (the goats).

> *"He will put the sheep on his right and the goats on his left. Then the King will say to those on his right, 'Come, you who are blessed by my Father... For I was hungry and you gave me something to eat, I was thirsty and you gave me something to drink, I was a stranger and you invited me in, I needed clothes and you clothed me, I was sick and you looked after me, I was in prison and you came to visit me.'"* **Matthew 25:33-36**

2) But the people won't remember helping Jesus (and let's face it — it's not the sort of thing you'd forget)...

> *"The King will reply, 'I tell you the truth, whatever you did for one of the least of these brothers of mine, you did for me.' Then he will say to those on his left, 'Depart from me, you who are cursed, into the eternal fire... ...whatever you did not do for one of the least of these, you did not do for me.'"* **Matthew 25:40-41 & 45**

3) Jesus is saying that helping any other person is just as good as helping him. And that if you don't help a starving person, it's as bad as leaving Jesus hungry.

## **Genesis 4:1-10** — "Am I my Brother's Keeper?"

1) **Genesis 4:1-10** is the story of the brothers Cain and Abel.
2) Cain commits three sins: i) he's jealous of his brother Abel; ii) he acts on his jealousy by killing Abel; iii) then he lies to God about it.
3) When God asks Cain where Abel is, he replies: *"I don't know... Am I my brother's keeper?"*
4) The story of Cain is referred to later, in the New Testament, where Cain represents those without love for others. This quote is from the first letter of John.
5) John is saying that it's not enough to go around talking about love and charity and claiming to be Christian. A true Christian acts to help people who need it.

> *"...We should love one another. Do not be like Cain, who belonged to the evil one and murdered his brother... We know that we have passed from death to life, because we love our brothers... This is how we know what love is: Jesus Christ laid down his life for us. And we ought to lay down our lives for our brothers. If anyone has material possessions and sees his brother in need but has no pity on him, how can the love of God be in him? Dear children, let us not love with words or tongue but with actions and in truth."* **1 John 3: 11-18**

## Faith by itself isn't enough...

For Christians, it's not enough just to feel sorry for people — they have a duty to actively help them.

# Warm-Up and Worked Exam Question

## Warm-up Questions

1) List three possible sources of moral guidance for a religious person.
2) What is your conscience?
3) List the Ten Commandments.
4) Explain what is meant by the words: a) mitzvot *(Judaism)*, b) khalifah *(Islam)*.
5) Give a Christian argument in favour of human rights.
6) Name four ways that people can take part in democratic processes.
7) Briefly describe Christian teachings on love and responsibility to others.

## Worked Exam Question

Read through this worked example carefully, then have a go at the practice exam questions on the next page. Even though part b) is an "opinion" question, you need to give good reasons for your point of view — just saying "yes" or "no" won't get you the marks.

1 a) What is Situation Ethics?

*An ethical principle based on the idea that Christian love is more important than strict rules. So any commandment in the Bible can be broken if it means doing something that's more loving.*

*(2 marks)*

b) Do you think people should always trust their conscience?
Give two reasons for your point of view.

*No, I don't think people should always trust their conscience.*

*State your opinion clearly.*

*Your conscience is just the result of things of you've learned during your upbringing, e.g. from the TV, books or other people's opinions, so it's only as trustworthy as those sources.*

*In his first letter to the Corinthians, St Paul said "My conscience is clear, but that does not make me innocent. It is the Lord who judges me." Paul didn't just rely on his conscience — he believed that Jesus was the only one who truly knew what was right or wrong.*

*Examiners love it if you stick a bit of scripture into your answers — as long as it's relevant.*

*(4 marks)*

# Exam Questions

2 a) What is meant by a 'moral code'?

*(1 mark)*

b) Explain how Christians can follow the example of Jesus when making decisions on moral behaviour.

*(6 marks)*

c) "Moral judgements should be based only on sacred texts."

Discuss this statement. You should include different, supported points of view and a personal viewpoint. You must refer to a religion in your answer.

*(12 marks)*

3 Do you think that all people should have the same human rights? Give two reasons for your point of view.

*(4 marks)*

4 a) Explain how pressure groups and political parties can help to bring about social change.

*(8 marks)*

b) "It is important for religious people to take part in democratic processes." Refer to at least one religion in your answer.

(i) Do you agree? Give reasons for your opinion.

*(3 marks)*

(ii) Give reasons why some people may disagree with you.

*(3 marks)*

5 a) What is the 'Golden Rule'?

*(2 marks)*

b) Explain how the Parable of the Sheep and the Goats illustrates Christian teachings on responsibility.

*(8 marks)*

GENERAL

# Environmental Issues

Humans have come up with all sorts of different ways damaging the environment...

*Our surroundings, that we depend on for survival.*

## ***Global Warming*** *could be* ***Very Serious***

1) Gases in the atmosphere, called 'greenhouse gases', help keep the Earth warm.
2) Over the past century, the amount of greenhouse gas (e.g. carbon dioxide) in the atmosphere has increased, and measurements show that the Earth has got hotter. This effect is called global warming.
3) There's now a consensus among climate scientists that the increasing levels of greenhouse gases have caused most of the increase in temperature. There are still a few scientists who don't agree with the consensus view. They argue that the warming either isn't significant, or can be explained by natural effects.
4) Nobody knows for sure what'll happen if the Earth keeps getting hotter. But if climate scientists are right, there are plenty of reasons to be worried about global warming:
   - As the sea warms up it will expand, making sea levels rise, which could flood low-lying places (e.g. the Maldives, the Netherlands, etc.).
   - Higher temperatures make ice melt. Water that's currently 'trapped' on land (as ice) could run into the sea, causing sea levels to rise even more.
   - Weather patterns might be affected (climate change), leading to more hurricanes, droughts and floods.
5) Governments hope to reduce greenhouse gas emissions and prevent climate change. But it's almost impossible to set worldwide targets.
6) Some governments look to short-term benefits, rather than long-term care for the planet. They may say they're trying to do the best for their people, and that people should be our first priority.
7) Competition means that businesses often feel forced to put profit before the welfare of the planet — if they don't, they may not survive.
8) And developed countries are the worst, but not the only polluters. Developing nations often claim that they're only doing now what richer countries did in the past, and that it's hypocritical to tell them not to.

## *We Produce* ***Lots of Different Pollutants***

**In Water:** Sewage, agricultural chemicals and toxic chemicals from industry can pollute lakes, rivers and seas. These pollutants harm the plants and animals living in and around the water, including humans.

**On Land:** We use toxic chemicals for farming (e.g. pesticides and herbicides). We also bury nuclear waste underground, and we dump a lot of household and industrial waste in landfill sites. These toxic chemicals can kill plants and animals, and cause cancer in humans.

**In the Air:** Smoke and gases from vehicles and industry can pollute the air, e.g. sulfur dioxide and nitrogen oxides can cause acid rain, fine dust called 'particulates' can cause health problems in humans and CFCs damage the ozone layer.

## *And We're* ***Running Out*** *of* ***Natural Resources***

1) The Earth's population is increasing — it has more than doubled in the last 50 years. At the same time, our standard of living is improving — particularly in developing nations.
2) We use more raw materials and more energy for manufacturing processes every year. If we carry on as we are, these natural resources will eventually run out.
3) Fertile land for growing crops is also in danger of running out. Each year, overgrazing and irresponsible farming methods turn more fertile land into desert.

*A natural resource is just anything found naturally that's useful to humans.*

## *If you've ever fancied seeing the Maldives — do it soon...*

You might be wondering what any of this has to do with Religious Studies. All will be revealed on the next page...

# Stewardship

General

Most religious believers think that it's not just a good idea to care for the Earth — it's our God-given responsibility.

## There are Ways to Reduce Pollution

1) There are now tight restrictions on the types and amounts of chemicals that can be released into waterways.
2) Many farms are moving towards organic solutions, which are less damaging to land and water.
3) Most air pollutants can now be removed from waste gases before they reach the atmosphere.
4) Recycling cuts down on the amount of rubbish that goes to landfill, and helps to conserve natural resources — both by reducing the amount of raw materials (e.g. metal ores) used and the amount of energy needed.

*Conservation means protecting and preserving things, particularly natural resources.*

## Religious Ideas about the Environment — 'Stewardship'

**CHRISTIANITY**

1) Christians of all denominations believe that the Earth is God's creation. They believe that God gave us the Earth, but expects us to care for it — this idea is called 'stewardship'. We have no right to abuse God's creation, but must act responsibly.
2) There's pressure on governments and companies to sell goods and services, even at the expense of the environment. Although it can be difficult to balance taking care of the Earth with providing for humankind, this is what Christians believe we must try to do.

*"We have a responsibility to create a balanced policy between consumption and conservation."* **Pope John Paul II, 1988**

3) Christianity teaches that everything is interdependent (i.e. everything depends on everything else), so driving species of animal or plant to extinction, or harming the planet, eventually ends up harming us.
4) Christian organisations such as CAFOD, Christian Aid and Tearfund® are concerned with putting this responsibility into practice. They put pressure on governments and industry to think more about how we are abusing the planet.

*"You made him [humankind] a little lower than the heavenly beings, and crowned him with glory and honour. You made him ruler over the works of your hands; you put everything under his feet:"* **Psalm 8:5-6**

*"The earth is the Lord's, and everything in it, the world and all who live in it; for he founded it upon the seas and established it upon the waters."* **Psalm 24:1-2**

**JUDAISM**

1) Jews also believe in the concept of stewardship. Concern for the natural world is often seen as being at the heart of Jewish teaching.
2) God's creations should remain as he intended, and we have no right to abuse them. Everything is interdependent, with trees being particularly important. Since the creation of Israel in 1948, millions of trees have been planted to aid the reclamation of the desert and help rebuild the nation.
3) Jews also believe that as custodians, they're responsible for making the world better — this is called *Tikkun Olam* ('mending the world'). Tikkun Olam isn't just about the environment — it's a general ideal that includes helping the poor, and behaving morally.

*"The Lord God took the man and put him in the Garden of Eden, to work it and take care of it."* **Genesis 2:15**

**ISLAM**

1) Muslim teaching on environmental issues is very similar to that of Judaism.
2) At the Day of Judgement questions will be asked of us. We will be required to answer for any ill-treatment of the planet and its resources.
3) The Earth is seen as being a product of the love of Allah, so we should treat it with love.

**Dr Abdullah Omar Nasseef** stated at the 1996 World Wide Fund for Nature conference that, *"His [Allah's] trustees are responsible for maintaining the unity of his creation, the integrity of the Earth, its flora and fauna, its wildlife and natural environment."*

## Stewardship — being responsible for what you do to the planet...

Once again, the ideas of all three of these religions are very similar. Which is good for me, since I don't have to write as much. And good for you, since you don't have to remember as much. Applause all round then...

GENERAL

# Animal Rights

Religions usually say be nice to other people. But what about animals...

## *Christianity says Animals come Below People*

Animal rights issues are of interest to many Christians. For example...

i) Animal experimentation (e.g. to develop new medicines),
ii) Factory farming,
iii) Hunting,
iv) Zoos and circuses,
v) Vegetarianism.

1) One of the major issues for Christians is whether animals have souls or not. Many people believe that animals don't have souls, meaning that God created us as superior to them. Some people argue that animals are here for our use.

*"...Rule over the fish of the sea and the birds of the air and over every living creature that moves on the ground."* **Genesis 1:28**

2) Christianity teaches that we should treat animals with kindness, but that they can be used to benefit mankind (as long as their suffering is considered). It's also thought that excessive money shouldn't be 'wasted' on animals when human beings are suffering. So humans are very definitely 'on top'.
3) The Roman Catholic Church tolerates animal experimentation, but only if it brings benefit to mankind (e.g. if the experiments lead to the development of life-saving medicines). The Catechism of the Catholic Church (paragraph 2417) says that animal experimentation is allowable so long as it *"remains within reasonable limits and contributes to caring for or saving human lives."*
4) But some Christians think that it's always wrong to cause suffering to animals just to increase our scientific knowledge — particularly since medicines don't always have the same effect on humans as they do on animals.
5) Some Christians point out that as everything is interdependent, our treatment of animals reflects on us. Indeed, the Church of England teaches that the medical and technological use of animals should be monitored 'in the light of ethical principles'.
6) Certain denominations are generally opposed to any ill-treatment of animals. For example, the Society of Friends (Quakers) are particularly likely to frown on zoos, animal circuses, hunting and wearing fur.
7) Unlike some other religions, there are no specific food laws to be followed in Christianity. So vegetarianism (not eating meat) and veganism (not eating or using any animal products) are matters for individual Christians to decide about.

## *Judaism and Islam have Similar Views*

Deuteronomy 5:14 says that animals deserve a day off on the Sabbath, just like people.

JUDAISM

1) The Noahide Laws (see p.44) clearly forbid cruelty to animals. Animals are here to help us, and not to be abused. There are many stories in the Torah that demonstrate care for animals.
2) In Judaism, if meat is to be eaten, the animal must be slaughtered in a 'humane' fashion. This involves cutting the throat of the animal with a very sharp blade to bring about a quick death.
3) Experiments on animals may be tolerated if they result in a benefit for mankind, but only as a last resort. Cruel sports (e.g. bullfighting) are seen as an abuse of God's creatures.

ISLAM

1) Khalifah is the idea that we're responsible for the Earth — khalifah means vice-regent, or trustee (see p.50).
2) Cruelty to animals is forbidden, as is their use simply for our pleasure.
3) Muslims believe in demonstrating mercy and compassion for all living creatures, and animals used for meat must be slaughtered humanely.
4) Muslims will generally only allow animal testing if it is done to produce genuine medical advances for humans. The animals should be treated humanely, and no unnecessary pain should be inflicted on them.

*"...when you slaughter, slaughter in a good way. So every one of you should sharpen his knife, and let the slaughtered animal die comfortably."* **Prophet Muhammad (Sahih Muslim)**

## *Most religions believe we have a duty to look after animals...*

There's another Christian view of the role of animals in Genesis 2:18-20 — that they were created to help man.

# Humanity and Talents

GENERAL

If you're reading this page, then you must be a part of humanity.

## Humanity — Homo Sapiens and What Makes Them Special

1) The term humanity can be used in different ways:

- It can simply mean all the human beings on the planet — all nearly seven billion of us.
- Or it can mean human nature. In particular, all the good ways of acting and feeling that most humans have in common, such as feeling compassion, and doing altruistic (unselfish) deeds.

2) Humanity is what sets us apart from the animals.
3) Christians, Jews and Muslims all believe that humans are special because they were created by God in his image, and that humans have two parts, a physical body and a soul (see p.10).

## The Big Question — Why Are We Here?

This is a huge question — one that people have been debating for thousands of years.

**RELIGIOUS VIEWS**

1) Christians believe that we were created by God, for him. Quite simply, he enjoyed creating us, and he likes to love us and have a relationship with each of us.
2) Some verses of the Bible suggest that God created us to look after the rest of his creation (see p.57).
3) Many Christians, Jews and Muslims believe that what happens after our deaths (see p.10) depends on how we lived. So the purpose of us being here now might be a sort of test — of our morals or faith.
4) Muslims believe that Allah created humans to serve and worship him.

*"And I did not create... mankind except to worship Me."* **Qur'an 51:56**

**SCIENTIFIC VIEWS**

1) A scientific view is that we're not here for any purpose. No one designed us — we're just the products of evolution (see p.3). Like everything else, we're just 'the way things turned out'.
2) It's argued that 'special' human characteristics, e.g. altruism and compassion, are things that have evolved to help our genes survive and be passed on (e.g. if you help someone in need, they're more likely to help you in return).
3) So human beings are simply another type of animal — just a very brainy type.

## Talents — It's What We Do With Them That Counts

1) Most religious people believe that talents are given to us by God, so it's our duty to use them to serve God.
2) For example, good singers could use their talent to worship God in a church choir, good bakers could make cakes to sell to raise money for religious projects, good public speakers could preach religious messages...
3) The Parable of the Talents (**Matthew 25:14-30**) explains the Christian attitude to talents:

A man was going away, and entrusted some money to each of his three servants. To the first he gave five talents, to the second he gave two talents, and to the third he gave one talent.
The first two servants used their talents wisely, and doubled them. When their master came home, he was pleased with them both.
The third servant had buried his talent, for safe-keeping. The master was very angry with him, took the talent off him, and threw him out.

*The 'talents' in this parable are actually units of currency. But it's been interpreted as talking about any of God's gifts, such as our inborn skills. In fact, this is thought to be where our word 'talent' comes from.*

*It doesn't matter how many talents you have, it's what you do with them that counts.*

*It's when you don't even try that God gets angry.*

4) There are lots of organisations that'll help you use your talents to care for planet. They won't make you plant trees if you're the type that cries if you break a nail — they'll find something that your talents will suit.

Faiths4Change is an organisation in the North West of England that helps people from all faiths to improve their local environments. For example, they run projects that help children to grow vegetables in their school grounds.

GENERAL

# Fertility Treatment

There are many similarities in the attitudes of Christians, Muslims and Jews towards fertility treatment. All believe that a child is a gift, and therefore all allow some methods of fertility treatment.

## *Infertility* means an *Inability* to *Conceive* a Child

Nowadays, there are various kinds of fertility treatment that can be used to help.

*Artificial Insemination by the Husband (AIH)* — sperm from the husband is injected into the wife's womb.
*Artificial Insemination by Donor (AID)* — sperm from a sperm bank (i.e. an anonymous donor) is used.
*In Vitro Fertilisation (IVF)* — eggs are fertilised in a test tube and 1 or 2 are implanted in the mother's womb.
*Egg Donation* — where an egg from a different woman is used as part of IVF.
*Surrogacy* — where a different woman bears the child for the couple. This can involve IVF, using the couple's eggs and sperm, or artificially inseminating the surrogate with the husband's sperm.

## *Christianity* sees Children as a *Blessing from God*

1) Most Christian Churches believe that it's okay for science to help childless couples to conceive — as long as the process doesn't involve anyone else.
2) So AIH is permissible. The couple can be blessed with a child, and the sanctity of marriage isn't interfered with. Many Roman Catholics still aren't keen though, since the sperm comes from an 'unnatural' sex act.
3) Some Christians believe that if AIH fails, a couple should adopt instead. Though many other Christians consider IVF an appropriate treatment if the wife's egg and husband's sperm are used.
4) AID and egg donation are much less favoured methods, since a 'third party' is involved.
5) The Roman Catholic Church is opposed to IVF in all forms, as it often creates 'spare' embryos that are thrown away. Many Catholics argue that life begins at fertilisation, and that even an embryo has rights.

## *Judaism* allows most *Methods*

1) In Jewish teaching, there's an emphasis on having a family.
2) So it's left to individual married couples to decide whether or not to use scientific methods of conception.
3) A Jewish couple might seek advice on the matter from their rabbi (religious leader).
4) AIH is usually permitted, but not AID, as the use of donated sperm might be seen as a form of adultery.
5) IVF is generally approved of — as long as the egg and the sperm are from the married couple involved.
6) Egg donation is seen as okay, though the couple will often prefer the egg to come from a Jewish woman. This is because, according to Orthodox teachings, you're only a Jew if your mother is a Jew.

*"Be fruitful and increase in number; fill the earth..."*
**Genesis 1:28**

## *Muslims* allow some *Fertility Treatments*

1) Some scientific methods are permissible, as long as all natural methods of conceiving have failed.
2) Artificial insemination and IVF are both okay, as long as the egg of the wife and the sperm of the husband are used. But AID is not acceptable as the sperm is donated. Many Muslims see this as a sin comparable with adultery, as the woman has become pregnant using the sperm of a man other than her husband.
3) There are also concerns about diseases that could be inherited from an anonymous sperm donor (although most sperm banks screen donors for serious genetic disorders).
4) Shi'ite Muslims sometimes allow egg donation, so long as the donor is a Muslim woman, and there's no other way for the couple to have a child.

### *Religions welcome some fertility treatments, but not others...*

If the technology exists to help a couple have a child, but their religion is against it, what should they do? Tricky...

# Transplant Surgery

GENERAL

Transplant surgery is fairly commonplace nowadays. A lot of people carry a donor card (which says that they'd like their organs to be donated to someone else after they die).

## *Transplant Surgery can **Save Lives***

1) Transplant surgery is the replacement of a faulty organ with a healthy one.
2) Transplants can be used to replace organs that have been damaged. They can also be used to cure disorders like leukaemia (with a bone marrow transplant) and diabetes (with a pancreas transplant).
3) Some organs, e.g. kidneys (which we've got two of) and bone marrow (which we can replace) can be donated from living donors. But most organs, e.g. heart, liver, pancreas, eyes, etc. can only be transplanted shortly after the death of the donor.
4) There's a worldwide shortage of organs for transplantation, though, so about 60% of all patients waiting for a transplant die on the waiting list.

## *Most **Christians** are **in Favour** of Organ Donation*

Many Christian organisations encourage organ donation, but not all Christians feel the same way:

**ARGUMENTS FOR ORGAN DONATION**

- Christians have a duty to help and care for others.
- Donating your organs (before or after death) to save a life is an act of Christian love and charity.
- Most Christians believe God won't need bodies to be intact to resurrect them at Judgement Day, so there's no harm in donating organs after death.

**ARGUMENTS AGAINST ORGAN DONATION**

- The human body is sacred and so shouldn't be tampered with after death.
- As a living donor, you put your own life at risk.
- Family members can feel pressurised to allow a loved-one's organs to be donated.
- Transplants could encourage harvesting and sale of organs from developing countries.

The Jehovah's Witnesses used to ban their members from receiving transplants, because they saw it as cannibalism. Transplants are now allowed, so long as the organ is completely drained of blood.

## ***Saving Life** is Very Important to **Jews** and **Muslims***

**JEWISH VIEWS**

1) Jews believe that the human body is sacred, so it's usually forbidden to mutilate a body, e.g. remove organs. It is also forbidden to benefit from a corpse.
2) Most rabbis are prepared to overrule these objections to save a life.
3) For Orthodox Jews, this usually means organ donation is allowed if there's a specific person who needs the organ right then. Reform Jews will also allow organs to be taken where there isn't a known recipient yet.
4) In all cases, it has to be very clear that the donor is actually dead, beyond resuscitation (i.e. brain dead), before the organs are taken. The organs must be removed respectfully, with the minimum damage to the body.

**MUSLIM VIEWS**

1) Muslims have very similar views to Jews about the sanctity of the human body, and the respect that it should be shown. Some Muslims also believe that human organs belong to Allah, so we have no right to give them away.
2) Others argue that, according to Shari'ah (Islamic law), even some forbidden things are allowed when the alternative is death. They also argue that you should always choose the lesser of two evils.

*"...But whoever is forced [by necessity], neither desiring [it] nor transgressing [its limit], there is no sin upon him. Indeed, Allah is Forgiving and Merciful."*
**Qur'an 2:173**

### *Save a life — carry a donor card...*

In the future, xenotransplantation (using genetically modified animal organs) or growing organs in the lab could get rid of the need to take organs from other humans. But they have medical and ethical issues of their own...

GENERAL

# Genetic Engineering

Scientific advances mean we can now alter the genes of any living thing to try to get the features we want. But just because we can, that doesn't necessarily mean we should...

## You Need to Know about **Genetic Engineering** and **Cloning**

There are ethical issues involved with lots of different biotechnologies.
The two that you need to know about are:

**GENETIC ENGINEERING:** Manipulating genes, e.g. moving genes from one organism to another to make an organism with more useful features. Bacteria can be engineered to produce human insulin for people with diabetes, and crop plants can be made more nutritious or more resistant to disease.

**CLONING:** Producing offspring that are genetically identical to the parent.

1) These technologies have the potential to solve many problems (e.g. helping treat diseases or making food production more efficient).
2) Genetic engineering could be used to create an organism (e.g. a crop plant) with all the right characteristics, then that organism could be cloned to produce as many copies of it as we need.
3) For example, genetically modifying crop plants to increase the nutritional value and yield could mean that we can produce more than enough food for everyone.
4) Animals can be engineered to produce medicines in their milk to treat diseases.
5) But not everyone thinks it's such a great idea...

## There are **Practical Issues** with Biotechnology...

Some people disagree with genetic engineering and cloning for practical reasons:

1) Creating very successful crop plants is likely to affect the number and variety of weeds living in and around the crops. This could reduce biodiversity.
2) Not everyone is convinced that genetically modified crops or farm animals are safe to eat.
3) There's a risk that transplanted genes could get out into the natural environment — e.g. herbicide resistance could be picked up by wild plants, creating 'superweeds'.
4) Some people feel that we don't understand genes well enough to know the full effects of tampering with them. Transplanting a gene could create unforeseen problems.
5) Cloning has the problem of reducing the gene pool. Lots of copies of the same organism mean fewer different genes in the population. That leaves the population more susceptible to disease.
6) Also, cloning animals is a difficult process — embryos formed by cloning often don't develop properly, and the adults produced tend to suffer health problems and die young.

## ...as well as **Purely Moral** Ones

1) Some people think it's wrong to change the characteristics of an organism purely for human benefit.
2) Others worry that we won't stop at engineering plants and animals — that those who can afford it might decide which characteristics they want their children to have, creating a 'genetic underclass'.
3) Therapeutic cloning means creating an embryo that's a clone of an ill person, then taking stem cells from it to grow new organs. This destroys the embryo, which some Christians feel denies the sanctity of life.
4) Other Christians worry that any clone who lived to adulthood wouldn't have a soul.
5) Many Roman Catholics and other Christians are completely opposed to genetic engineering and cloning — they see them as 'playing God'. Christianity teaches that all creation belongs to God, so by creating new organisms ourselves, some Christians believe we're trying to step into God's shoes.

## *Genetic engineering has possibilities — and problems...*

Cloning humans has the added ethical question of why someone's doing it. Some people might want to achieve immortality that way. But of course, the clone wouldn't be them — it would be like an identical twin.

# Warm-Up and Worked Exam Question

## Warm-up Questions

1) Describe three environmental issues faced by the world today.
   Suggest ways for people to reduce their environmental impact.
2) What is meant by the phrase "Tikkun Olam"? *(Judaism)*
3) According to Christians, Jews and Muslims, are animals as important as humans?
4) What does the word "humanity" mean?
5) Describe three different types of fertility treatment.
6) Give two arguments against genetic engineering.

## Worked Exam Question

And I bet you thought Religious Studies was all about God and churches and stuff. No such luck.
Read this worked example carefully and then have a go at the exam questions on the next page.

1 "Humans have the right to use animals in medical research."

Discuss this statement. You should include different, supported points of view and a personal viewpoint. You must refer to Christianity in your answer.

*Many Christians believe that animals don't have souls, and that God created us as superior to them. In Genesis, God says "rule over the fish of the sea and the birds of the air and over every living creature that moves on the ground". Some Christians argue that this means we can use animals for whatever we need, including medical research.*

*You're asked to give different points of view — so try to look at both sides of the argument.*

*However, Christianity also teaches that we should treat animals kindly and not cause them unnecessary suffering. So some Christians believe that animals should only be experimented on in order to develop life-saving medicines. Some Christians argue that animal testing shouldn't be used, because animals often respond to treatments in a different way from humans. The benefit to humans is not clear, so the suffering of animals cannot be justified. Other Christians think that animal experimentation is always wrong, because it's wrong to make animals suffer, even if their suffering will benefit humans.*

*Don't forget to give your own personal response.*

*I believe that humans should use animals for medical research, because discoveries may be made that could save thousands of lives in the future. However, the animals should not be caused pain unless it is absolutely necessary, and should be kept in suitable surroundings, e.g. not in tiny cages.*

*(12 marks)*

# Exam Questions

2 a) What is stewardship?

*(2 marks)*

b) Do you think it's important to conserve natural resources?
Give two reasons for your point of view.

*(4 marks)*

c) "Humans should use the environment for their benefit."
Give two reasons why a religious believer might agree or disagree with this statement.

*(4 marks)*

3 a) State two ways in which animals are used by humans.

*(2 marks)*

b) "Religious people are more likely to treat animals well."
Do you agree? Give reasons for your answer, showing that you have thought about more than one point of view. Refer to religious arguments in your answer.

*(6 marks)*

4 a) Explain what religious believers mean by talents.

*(2 marks)*

b) Explain how having a religious faith might lead someone to believe that humans are more important than animals.

*(4 marks)*

5 a) Do you think genetic engineering should be used to create better crops?
Give two reasons for your point of view.

*(4 marks)*

b) Choose one religion other than Christianity and explain its followers' beliefs about fertility treatment.

*(8 marks)*

c) "Religious people should carry a donor card."
Refer to at least one religion in your answer.

(i) Do you agree? Give reasons for your opinion.

*(3 marks)*

(ii) Give reasons why some people may disagree with you.

*(3 marks)*

# Peace and War

GENERAL

World peace — a pretty tall order, but there are a lot of people striving for it...

## The United Nations (UN) works for World Peace

1) The UN works to find peaceful solutions to disputes, to encourage global cooperation on law, security and economic development and to protect people's basic human rights. It has 192 members (the only fully recognised, independent state that isn't a member of the UN is Vatican City).
2) Its main function is to promote world peace — an end to all wars, all over the world.
3) If a country breaks the rules, the UN can impose economic sanctions (stop people trading with them) and send in peacekeeping troops.

UN Peacekeeping and Conflict Resolution

- A lot of the UN's work is in conflict resolution — ending wars in a way that leads to lasting peace.
- The first step, before any negotiations, is a ceasefire (everyone stops fighting while they talk).
- It's the job of UN Peacekeepers to make sure both sides stick to the ceasefire, to protect aid workers and civilians, and to help people rebuild. The UN currently has about 15 peacekeeping missions in progress, including those in Kosovo, Darfur and the Democratic Republic of the Congo.

## There are Religious Peace Organisations Too

**PAX CHRISTI — Roman Catholic**
Pax Christi is an international, non-profit organisation working for human rights, disarmament, reconciliation (see page 69) and peaceful conflict resolution. For example, they are currently calling for the protection of civilians from fighting in the Democratic Republic of the Congo.

**JEWISH PEACE FELLOWSHIP — Jewish**
The JPF is a pacifist organisation, originally founded to help conscientious objectors (see page 66) in World War II. The organisation believes that military action never solves conflicts, and that active non-violence (e.g. negotiations, promoting social justice) is the only way to settle disputes.

**MUSLIM PEACE FELLOWSHIP — Muslim**
The Muslim Peace Fellowship is dedicated to making the '*beauty of Islam*' present in the world. It promotes peace through Islam, and works to bring about changes in society to make it fair and compassionate to all people.

## Wars can have Many Causes

Most wars have causes that are a combination of loads of different factors:

- RELIGION — see 'Holy War' on the next page.
- DEFENCE — e.g. a pre-emptive strike (see p.67).
- TRIBALISM — this tends to trigger wars where a group of people fight for their own independent state.
- HONOUR — wars fought to defend the honour and dignity of a country, or to save face.
- ECONOMICS — acts of aggression (attacking without provocation) are condemned by the UN, so purely economic wars (e.g. raids and invasions to gain territory) are few and far between. Economic factors still have an impact though — poverty and economic imbalances can make wars more likely.

1) In some wars, weapons of mass destruction (WMDs) have been used.
2) WMDs are weapons that can destroy large areas of land and/or lots of people all at once, e.g. chemical, biological and nuclear weapons. They're indiscriminate — they harm soldiers and civilians alike.
3) Chemical and biological weapons are banned by international law — using them is considered a war crime.
4) Many organisations, including the Church of England, want countries to reduce the number of nuclear weapons they have. However, it recognises that unilateral disarmament (where just one country gives up its weapons) is a difficult thing for a government to do.

CHRISTIANITY

# War: Christianity

Although Christianity is generally 'anti-war', many denominations accept that a war can be 'just' (i.e. justified). Individuals may not agree with this, however. They may be against war under any circumstances.

## There are **Five Conditions** for Declaring a **Just War**

1) Christianity teaches that peace is the ultimate goal for all human beings.
2) Peace doesn't just mean a lack of war — it's more positive than that. Peace is a total freedom from distress and disturbance that Christians believe can be brought about by 'good will' and faith.
3) Although Christians recognise that war goes against the teachings of Jesus, most Christian denominations accept that there can be such a thing as a 'just war'. According to the Catechism of the Roman Catholic Church (see p.49), a just war should satisfy these conditions:

*This isn't always listed as a separate point.*

**Proper Authority** A war must be declared by a proper authority, e.g. an elected government or a president (that way, you can be pretty sure the other conditions will have been thought about).

**Just Cause** A war must be defensive, preventing damage that would be *"lasting, grave and certain"* (Catechism of the Catholic Church: para 2309). This doesn't necessarily mean self-defence — defending a friendly nation or innocent people (e.g. preventing genocide in Rwanda) is also seen as 'just'. In some versions of 'just war' theory (but not in the Catechism) there's a separate condition of right intention. Even if there is a just cause, that cause mustn't be used as an excuse to achieve an unjust goal — e.g. to punish an enemy or gain land.

**Last Resort** All other ways of resolving the conflict must have been tried first.

**Achievable Aim** A war must have a reasonable chance of success. Fighting a war you have no chance of winning is considered a waste of lives.

**Proportionality** Any harm caused by fighting the war mustn't be as bad as the harm it's trying to prevent. For example, using weapons of mass destruction (nuclear, biological and chemical weapons) would nearly always violate this condition.

As well as all that, there are conditions for fighting a war justly. These are:

Discrimination: war should discriminate between combatants and civilians — it's not seen as 'just' to deliberately target civilians.

Proportionality: the military advantage gained by an attack must outweigh any harm caused to civilians.

*This is different from the 'proportionality' used to justify the war. This is about individual attacks.*

A 'Holy War' is one where people believe that God is 'on their side' — e.g. in the 11th, 12th and 13th centuries, Christians went on crusades to 'free' the Christian holy places in Palestine.

## **Pacifists** are Opposed to **All Violence**

1) A pacifist is someone who has strongly held beliefs that war and physical violence are wrong under any circumstances. Pacifists believe that all disputes should be settled peacefully.
2) Some Christians believe that all violence goes against Jesus's teachings to love your enemy and 'turn the other cheek' (**Matthew 5:38-48**).
3) There were pacifists in Britain who refused to fight in the world wars. These 'conscientious objectors' went to prison rather than go against their beliefs — they were prisoners of conscience. They suffered humiliation in prison, and after they'd been released.

"Put your sword back in its place... for all who draw the sword will die by the sword."
**Matthew 26:52**

The Religious Society of Friends (the Quakers) is a Christian denomination that's opposed to war under all circumstances.

### *Just war, just cause — just learn it pal...*

In the age of weapons of mass destruction, Pope Benedict XVI has questioned whether a 'just war' is possible any more. With these weapons, it's impossible to discriminate between fighters and civilians.

# War: Judaism and Islam

JUDAISM & ISLAM

Despite the fact that there have been a number of wars between Muslims and Jews, there are many similarities in the way the two religions approach the subject of war.

## The Jewish View — Obligatory and Optional Wars

1) The universal greeting amongst Jews is 'shalom' (peace) — this is the ideal. War is hated, but there's a belief that war is sometimes necessary to bring about peace.
2) War is divided into two categories — milchemet mitzvah (obligatory war) and milchemet reshut (optional war).
3) An obligatory war might be:
   i) a war fought in self-defence.
   ii) a pre-emptive strike in order to avoid being attacked — the Six-Day War in 1967 for example.
   iii) a war to help neighbouring countries — so that your own country is not invaded.
   iv) a war commanded by God.
4) An optional war should only take place when all attempts to secure peace have failed.
5) No war should be fought to colonise or take revenge. This is forbidden.
6) Pacifism is considered a good choice when it's the only way to survive, or when using violence would be pointless. This is why Jews generally don't respond violently to anti-Semitism.
7) But at other times, Jewish teaching demands the use of violence. If a Jew sees someone trying to murder someone else, they must do all they can to save the person's life — even if this means killing the murderer.
8) However, using the minimal necessary force is encouraged in Judaism.

**The Six-Day War**

In June 1967, Israel launched a series of attacks against its much larger Arab neighbours, destroying the Egyptian Air Force on the ground. After six days' fighting, Israel had won a war against Egypt, Jordan and Syria.

*In the Holocaust (see p.6), the Jews were victims.*

## The Islamic View — 'Hate Your Enemy Mildly'

Muslims believe that war is sometimes necessary, although the concept of jihad is often misunderstood. These passages sum up Muslim teaching:

*"He who fights that Allah's Word should be superior, fights in Allah's Cause."* **Prophet Muhammad (Sahih Bukhari)**

*"Hate your enemy mildly; he may be your friend one day."* **Ali ibn Abi Talib**

### Jihad — There are Two Kinds

1) There are two kinds of jihad (or 'striving')...
   i) the Greater Jihad (see p.83), which is when a Muslim makes a special effort to be a 'pure' Muslim, or fights against his or her own selfish desires.
   ii) a Lesser Jihad is fought against an external enemy — war is an example of a lesser jihad, but it must be fought only as a last resort. These wars are often thought of as 'Holy Wars'.
2) Military jihad has very strict rules, and is similar to the Christian idea of a 'just war':
   i) It is justified if it will bring about freedom from tyranny, restore peace, combat oppression, or right injustice.
   ii) It must not be used to colonise, suppress or impose Islam on non-believers.
   iii) The sick, the elderly, women and children should not be harmed, the natural world must not be damaged, and indiscriminate killing should be avoided.
   iv) Jihad must be in the name of Allah, and according to his will. It must be declared by a religious leader, not any old politician.
   v) Dying in the service of Allah turns a Muslim into a martyr. True martyrs go straight to paradise as an instant reward — martyrs don't have to wait for the Day of Judgement.
3) There is no real concept of pacifism in Islam, although peace is always the goal of war.

GENERAL

# Bullying and Family Conflict

Sadly, bullying happens a lot.

## *Bullying is* ***Exploitation***

1) Exploitation means taking advantage of a weaker person or group. And that's what bullying is all about.
2) A bully intimidates, frightens and controls other people that are weaker than them.
3) Acts of bullying can be: physical (e.g. hitting), social (e.g. enforced isolation) or emotional (e.g. verbal abuse, belittling someone or neglect). Bullies often pick on differences like race, religion or disability.
4) All schools have anti-bullying policies. These include:

- Listening to and supporting the victims of bullying.
- Dealing with those responsible for the bullying. This usually emphasises counselling and reform (see page 74) rather than punishment. Punishing a bully can just make them resentful, and not change their beliefs or behaviour at all. Many bullies are insecure, and pick on other people to make themselves feel strong.
- Encouraging everyone in the school to respect other people (to be considerate of other people and their feelings) and to appreciate their differences, to help prevent bullying.

## ***All*** *Religions are* ***Against*** *Bullying*

1) Christians, Muslims and Jews believe that all people are created by God, so mistreating another person is mistreating God's creation.
2) In all three faiths, it's a sin to attack someone else without cause — physically or verbally. Judaism specifically forbids spreading nasty rumours about people.
3) All three religions teach that it's important to protect the weak and to free the oppressed.
4) People of all three faiths believe they will answer to God on Judgement Day for harming, or failing to protect, the innocent.
5) Christians also believe that they have a duty to actively care for others (see page 53).
6) St Paul summed up the Christian attitude to bullying in his letter to the Ephesians.

*"...loose the chains of injustice and untie the cords of the yoke... set the oppressed free and break every yoke..."* **Isaiah 58:6**

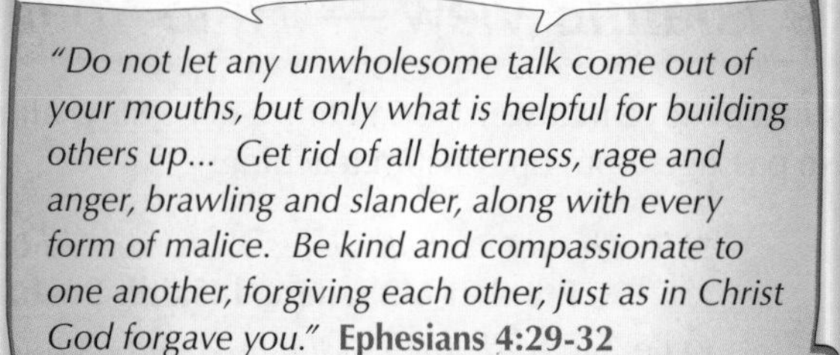


## ***Religion*** *can Cause* ***Conflict*** *within Families*

Religion can help to bring families together, but it can also cause conflict. Young people might not want to follow the traditions of their family, particularly in a multicultural, secular (non-religious) country like the UK. Some of the issues that can spark conflict are:

1) **SEX/MARRIAGE** — this could be sex before marriage, using contraception, homosexuality, marrying outside the faith, etc. Traditionally, Christianity, Judaism and Islam have had very strict teachings on this sort of thing. They say that sex should be between a man and a woman, inside marriage, and with the intention of having children. Mixed-faith marriages are rarely approved of, since children from them are unlikely to be raised as observant members of either faith.
2) **RITUALS/WORSHIP** — not keeping religious observances, e.g. community worship, food laws, Shabbat (for Jews). Religious observance is generally declining across the country, particularly amongst the young.
3) **TRADITIONS** — e.g. arranged marriages and the role of women in the family. Modern equal rights legislation means that women now have all the same opportunities as men. Some daughters of conservative families want a good education and a career — they don't want to settle down and have children.

## *Bullies like to feel strong by making you feel weak...*

Being bullied can leave you feeling ashamed. But remember, it's never your choice and it's never your fault.

# Forgiveness and Reconciliation

CHRISTIANITY

Love is all around us — it's everywhere I go. That's good news.
But Jesus said forgiveness is also important.

## In Christianity **Love** and **Forgiveness** go Together

1) Forgiveness means stopping being angry with someone who's done something wrong. Christianity teaches that forgiveness comes from love.
2) Christians believe that Jesus died on the cross to atone for the sins of all those who believed in him, so that God might forgive our sins.
3) Jesus taught that God is always ready to forgive us, but we must accept that forgiveness, and forgive others in turn.

> *"For if you forgive men when they sin against you, your heavenly Father will also forgive you. But if you do not forgive men their sins, your Father will not forgive your sins."* **Matthew 6:14-15**

4) Forgiveness is closely related to repentance. Christians believe that God's forgiveness can only come when we repent of our sins (i.e. say we are sorry, and turn our backs on them).
5) If we repent, and put our faith in God, God forgives us and we are reconciled with him. Christians believe the same sort of reconciliation (coming together and making peace) is needed between people.

**Zacchaeus (Luke 19:1-10)**

A story illustrating Jesus putting forgiveness into practice... Jesus goes as a guest to the home of the hated tax collector Zacchaeus, whose life is completely changed after he decides to repent.

## Jesus Taught His Followers to **Forgive** Their **Enemies**

1) Jesus taught that people shouldn't seek revenge — he said that they should 'turn the other cheek'.

> *"If someone strikes you on the right cheek, turn to him the other also."* **Matthew 5:39**

2) But this doesn't mean being a submissive victim — just that a Christian's response should be based on the principles of love and forgiveness.
3) For example, most Christians believe that if someone commits a crime (anything from petty theft to starting a war), we shouldn't just do nothing. Punishment can be used to reform an offender and to deter others from offending (see page 74).
4) Some people think that it's wrong to keep forgiving people — that if they reoffend they shouldn't be forgiven again — although Jesus said we should forgive...

> *"...not seven times, but seventy-seven times."* **Matthew 18:22**

There are also some evils that are very hard to forgive.
Should we forgive Adolf Hitler or Josef Stalin?

Many Christians would say 'yes' — it is better to forgive, for the sake of the forgiver, and leave judgement in the hands of God.

> *"Anyone who hates his brother is a murderer, and you know that no murderer has eternal life in him."*
> **1 John 3:15**

## *Christianity teaches that we should forgive those who do wrong...*

By preaching 'love your enemies', Christianity isn't trying to tell everyone that they need to be a submissive victim. But it does mean exercising a bit of imagination when it comes to responding to difficult situations.

Judaism & Islam

# Forgiveness and Reconciliation

Judaism and Islam's views on forgiveness are very similar...

## Jews and Muslims have Similar Ideas about Forgiveness

1) Both Jews and Muslims believe that, just as God is forgiving and merciful towards them, they should forgive other people.
2) They should also seek forgiveness and make atonement for any wrongs they've committed.
3) The Torah and the Qur'an both encourage people to be forgiving and to seek forgiveness so that they can be reconciled with each other and God.

## There are Some Specifically Jewish Beliefs About Forgiveness

1) The Medieval rabbi Maimonides wrote in the Mishneh Torah:

*"It is forbidden to be obdurate...*
*When asked by an offender for forgiveness, one should forgive with a sincere mind and a willing spirit."*

2) Jews believe that you can only be forgiven by the one you've injured — so God can only forgive a sin against God, not another person.

Each year, before Yom Kippur (the Day of Atonement), Jews seek forgiveness from anyone they feel they've hurt during the year.

Then at Yom Kippur itself, Jews seek God's forgiveness for their sins at the start of the Jewish Year.

They believe that, at the end of Yom Kippur, God 'seals' their fate for the coming year based on their behaviour and the repentance they've shown. Yom Kippur is the holiest day of the year for many observant Jews.

Jews fast on Yom Kippur. There's more about that on p100.

## And Some Specifically Muslim Beliefs About Forgiveness

1) The Qur'an allows Muslims to seek retribution for injuries, but encourages them to forgive instead:

*"And the retribution for an evil act is an evil one like it, but whoever pardons and makes reconciliation — his reward is [due] from Allah..."* **Qur'an 42:40**

2) Muslims believe that injuries should be forgiven if the offender is sorry and tries to make amends.
3) There are also many Hadith describing the Prophet Muhammad's acts of forgiveness, and other Muslims try to follow his example.
4) According to the Qur'an, the only sin Allah will not forgive is idolatry.

## If God is forgiving then so should we be...

Members of all faiths believe that there can be no true reconciliation without forgiveness on both sides.
And that means not only apologising when you've done something wrong, but not being bitter about it afterwards.
You also have to be prepared to forgive other people, and never hold grudges.

# Warm-Up and Worked Exam Question

## Warm-up Questions

1) What is the United Nations?
2) List five different possible causes of war.
3) In the context of a 'just war', what is meant by:
   a) right intention, b) proportionality, c) discrimination?
4) Give an example of a situation in which a Jew might be obliged to use violence. *(Judaism)*
5) What is exploitation?
6) Give three religious arguments against bullying.
7) How is the Jewish festival of Yom Kippur related to forgiveness? *(Judaism)*

## Worked Exam Question

You know the drill by now. Read through the worked example, make sure you can see where the answer came from, then have a go at the exam questions on page 72.

1 Explain why some Christians are pacifists and others are not.

*Christianity teaches that peace is the ultimate goal for all human beings. A pacifist believes that this goal can only be achieved if physical violence is never used — they believe violence is wrong under all circumstances.*

*In the Sermon on the Mount, Jesus taught that people should love and forgive their enemies and turn the other cheek. Christian pacifists, e.g. Quakers, take this to mean that all disputes should be settled peacefully. Also, Jesus said "all who draw the sword will die by the sword", suggesting that violence towards others only leads to more violence in return.*

*The question asks about Christian views in particular, so make sure you refer to specific Biblical teachings.*

*But there are many examples in the Old Testament of wars fought in self-defence or to right injustice. This has led other Christians to conclude that war is justified in some circumstances to bring about or to restore peace. This is known as a 'just war'.*

*(8 marks)*

# Exam Questions

2 a) In war, what is aggression?

*(2 marks)*

b) Describe how one religious organisation works for world peace.

*(3 marks)*

c) "Religion is the best way to achieve world peace."
Refer to at least one religion in your answer.

(i) Do you agree? Give reasons for your opinion.

*(3 marks)*

(ii) Give reasons why some people may disagree with you.

*(3 marks)*

3 a) Briefly describe what Jews mean by an 'obligatory war'.

*(3 marks)*

b) Briefly describe what Muslims mean by a 'lesser jihad'.

*(3 marks)*

c) Explain the Christian concept of a 'just war'.

*(8 marks)*

4 Explain how religion can lead to conflict within families.

*(8 marks)*

5 a) Do you think people should always forgive?
Give two reasons for your point of view.

*(4 marks)*

b) Choose one religion and explain its teachings on forgiveness and reconciliation.

*(8 marks)*

# The Need for Law and Justice

GENERAL

Religious beliefs about justice centre around the idea of responsibility — both in terms of answering for the things you do wrong, and of taking responsibility for the care of others.

## Law and Justice are Essential to Most Societies

1) Most nations believe that the rule of law is the best way of protecting people in society.
2) Without law there's the risk of chaos. With it, people know what they can and cannot do.
3) Laws are rules made by Parliament and enforced by the courts.
4) Christianity, Islam and Judaism all teach that God has commanded us to follow law. But some religious believers think that religious law is more important than the laws of the land.
5) Where religious law and state law disagree some believers think it's better to commit a crime if it means they avoid committing a sin (see below).
6) Justice is the idea of each person getting what they deserve, and maintaining what's right. In the context of the law, that means making sure the guilty are suitably punished, and that the innocent are protected.

## Crime or Sin — State Law versus Religious Law

1) For Christians, there's a difference between a sin and a crime. A sin is when religious law is broken, i.e. when God's teaching is disobeyed. A crime is when the state laws are broken.
2) Christians believe that justice is very important, since we are all equal in the eyes of God. Christians have a duty to look after other people, and try to guide them to do what's right and repent of their sins.
3) But Jesus taught that judgement and punishment belong to God:

*"Therefore, it is necessary to submit to the authorities, not only because of possible punishment but also because of conscience."* **Romans 13:5**

*"Do not judge, or you too will be judged. For in the same way you judge others, you will be judged, and with the measure you use, it will be measured to you."* **Matthew 7:1-2**

*Passing judgement on others is seen as hypocrisy.*

## Jewish Laws are Called Mitzvot

*"Appoint judges... and they shall judge the people fairly."* **Deuteronomy 16:18**

1) Judaism teaches that Jews should obey the laws of the land that they live in, as well as following the 613 mitzvot (religious commandments) in the Torah (p.88).
2) Rabbinical courts (Bet Din) exist in many countries to sort out Jewish disputes.
3) Justice is a huge part of Judaism — both in terms of what's due to God, and to fellow Jews. It's sometimes called a 'legalistic' religion.
4) The Torah is filled with details of laws, rewards and punishments. But, for many modern Jews, the punishments listed in the Torah are considered too extreme.

## Muslims Try to Follow Shari'ah

1) Muslims have a clear and detailed religious law (Shari'ah), and this is often the basis for state law in Islamic countries. Saudi Arabia, for example, is run according to this religious law.
2) Muslims believe strongly in justice. The Qur'an teaches that Allah is just and merciful, and that Muslims should treat all people fairly and equally.
3) Muslims consider maintaining justice to be part of their role as 'khalifah' (see p.50) — vice-regents of Allah's creation.

Muslims believe that Allah sees all. He will know if you have committed a crime and you will be made to answer for it on the Day of Judgement. A truly repentant sinner, however, will be forgiven.

## Law and Order is a really contentious issue...

For many religious people, justice doesn't have to come in this life. Christians, Muslims and Jews all believe that God is a fair judge, and that the guilty will be punished and the good rewarded in the afterlife.

GENERAL

# Theories of Punishment

Punishment can be used to 'get back' at someone for committing a crime, or to prevent crime in the future.

## The *Courts* Force Criminals to Take *Responsibility*

1) The courts pass judgement in cases of law — they decide whether or not someone is guilty of committing a crime, and what punishment they should face if they are guilty.
2) One goal of the court process is to make people take responsibility for their actions, and acknowledge that they owe a 'debt to society'.
3) This 'debt' can be paid in the form of many different punishments. The punishment given will depend on the severity of the crime, whether or not the criminal has broken the law before and whether or not they show repentance (are sorry for what they've done).

## *Punishment* can have Various *Aims*

There are several different theories of what punishment is for.

**Deterrence:** The idea that if a punishment is sufficiently bad in some way (e.g. expensive, embarrassing, restricting, painful) it will put people off committing the crime. This is the idea behind telling people in advance what the punishment for a given crime is — so they understand the consequences. Critics argue that people don't stop to think about punishment before they commit a crime, especially if they've taken drugs or alcohol, so deterrence doesn't work.

**Protection:** If a criminal is considered dangerous, this is the idea that their punishment should protect the rest of society, e.g. imprisonment. Not many people would disagree with this, but some would argue that you protect society best by reforming offenders.

**Reform:** The idea that punishment should aim to change criminals so that they won't reoffend once their punishment is over. This theory is based on the idea that nobody is inherently bad — and that with help, criminals can become useful members of society again. Programmes to help criminals reform include counselling sessions, visiting victims of similar crimes and working in the community.

*"Be merciful, just as your Father is merciful."* **Luke 6:36**

**Rehabilitation:** This is the idea that punishment should prepare the criminal for a return to a normal, useful life. It's closely related to the idea of reform, but a bit more practical. Rehabilitation usually involves the offender improving their education or learning a trade, which helps improve their self-esteem as well as giving them better job prospects. Some people think this sort of treatment is a waste of money. They argue that criminals will reoffend whatever you do to help them, and that the money would be better spent on hard-working, law-abiding people.

**Retribution:** Some people think of punishment as a way of taking revenge on a criminal, of making them 'pay' for what they've done. Critics of this way of thinking argue that revenge doesn't put right the wrong — that it's better to look for a more constructive solution.

*"If anyone injures his neighbour... eye for eye, tooth for tooth. As he has injured the other, so he is to be injured."* **Leviticus 24:19-20**

## *Punishments are used for lots of different reasons...*

Not for the first time, I'll say that this is a subject with lots of different shades of grey. Should we just lock people up and throw away the key... or is there something else we should be doing...

# Capital Punishment

GENERAL

Capital punishment is killing someone for committing a crime.

## There are Lots of Different Ways of Punishing People

1) Punishment can take a variety of forms, including: community service, a fine, probation, a prison sentence, corporal punishment (inflicting pain, e.g. flogging or beating) and capital punishment (death).
2) These different punishments have different aims. For example, fines are designed as deterrents, whereas a prison sentence is primarily to protect society, although most prisons have active reform programmes too.
3) Different countries and religions favour different types of punishment. In general, the punishments given in scripture are fines, corporal punishment or capital punishment.

## Capital Punishment Isn't Used Much Nowadays

1) Capital punishment has been used at some time by most societies, for crimes ranging from petty theft to mutiny. Capital punishment has been abolished in many places, including most of Europe and South America. Elsewhere, it only tends to be used for very serious crimes like murder, espionage and treason.
2) There are arguments for and against capital punishment:

**FOR CAPITAL PUNISHMENT**

- The risk of death might act as a better deterrent to violent criminals than a prison sentence. (Some statistical studies support this view.)
- If you execute a murderer, it's impossible for them to kill again. Imprisoned murderers have been known to order killings from inside jail, or to reoffend when released on parole.

**AGAINST CAPITAL PUNISHMENT**

- A lot of murders are committed in the heat of the moment (they're not premeditated), so many murderers won't be thinking about the consequences (not an effective deterrent).
- Execution doesn't give the offender the chance to reform.
- There have been cases where someone has been proved innocent after having been executed.

3) There tend to be more murders in countries that use the death penalty than in those that don't. This is often used as an argument against capital punishment, but it's not clear whether one causes the other.
4) Many Christians are opposed to capital punishment, as it doesn't allow for reform, or show mercy. In **Matthew 5:38-42**, Jesus said that we should set aside *'an eye for an eye'*, in the name of love and forgiveness. However, some Christians in the United States believe that it's a good thing. They say it protects the innocent.

*The 'Howard League for Penal Reform' was set up by Christians to campaign for punishments that allow offenders to reform.*

5) The position of the Torah is very clear on the issue. So Judaism will allow execution for murder if the case is absolutely certain (i.e. there are reliable witnesses). Most Jews are in favour of mercy, though.

*"If anyone takes the life of a human being, he must be put to death."* **Leviticus 24:17**

6) The Qur'an also clearly states the crimes that can be punished by death, but encourages the family of the victim to accept compensation instead.

*"...prescribed for you is legal retribution for those murdered — the free for the free, the slave for the slave, and the female for the female. But whoever overlooks from his brother anything, then there should be... payment to him with good conduct. This is an alleviation from your Lord and a mercy..."* **Qur'an 2:178**

For the death penalty to apply in Islam, there must be a confession, or witnesses to the crime.

## Capital punishment is only used for very serious crimes...

Capital punishment is a very difficult issue for modern religious people. The Bible and Qur'an both say that death is an appropriate punishment for some crimes (have a read of Leviticus chapters 20 and 24 — they're quite scary). But we tend to be a bit more squeamish about killing people these days.

GENERAL

# Drugs and Alcohol

Everyone has a view on drugs and drug abuse. But not all drugs are the same.

## Most Drugs are Illegal or Age-Restricted

### Illegal Drugs: Heroin, Cocaine, Hallucinogens, Cannabis, etc...

1) The Misuse of Drugs Act splits illegal drugs into three categories: Class A (e.g. heroin, cocaine, LSD), Class B (e.g. amphetamines (speed), cannabis) and Class C (e.g. valium, steroids). Some of these drugs can be prescribed by doctors as medicines.
2) The penalties for possessing and supplying Class A drugs are much harsher than those for Class B and Class C drugs. E.g., the police don't usually arrest people for possession of Class C drugs unless they suspect an 'intent to supply'. Supplying Class A drugs carries a maximum penalty of life imprisonment.
3) These classifications are because some drugs are more dangerous than others. In general, Class A drugs are highly addictive, cause serious psychological or physical damage and are easy to overdose on (see 'Problems' below).

### Age-Restricted Drugs: Alcohol and Tobacco

1) It's illegal to sell tobacco or alcohol to people under the age of 18.
2) That doesn't mean it's illegal for you to drink or smoke under 18 — you're just not allowed to buy them yourself. In theory, that means the decision to let you drink or smoke is made by responsible adults.
3) Campaigners argue that alcohol and tobacco are as addictive and harmful as many illegal drugs, so it's inconsistent for some to be legal and others not. Some people use this as an argument for the criminalisation of tobacco or tighter controls on alcohol. Others use it to argue that other 'social' drugs that are currently illegal (e.g. cannabis) should be legalised.

## Drugs can Cause Health and Social Problems

Most drugs are addictive — either physically or psychologically, or both. An addiction is a compulsion to keep doing something, even if you know it's harming you. A physical addiction is where your body chemistry has been changed by the drug, so you get withdrawal symptoms if you stop taking it. A psychological addiction is where you crave the feeling the drug gives you, and get anxious or depressed without it.

**Social Problems**

1) Most drugs affect people's judgement, which can make them more likely to take risks.
2) People on a 'high' sometimes feel invincible, and dangerous activities like sharing needles and unprotected sex are more likely to happen under the influence of drink or drugs.
3) Some addicts stop caring about other aspects of their life, and ignore their responsibilities.
4) At the extreme, some addicts turn to crime to help fund their habit.

**Health Problems**

1) Different drugs cause different health problems.
2) Alcohol, if drunk in excess, can cause liver disease, brain damage, and heart failure. It also doesn't mix well with other drugs. Even a small dose of some drugs mixed with alcohol can kill.
3) Smoking cannabis can cause lung diseases in a similar way to smoking tobacco. Recent studies have also suggested that it might trigger psychological disorders in vulnerable people.
4) Hallucinogens like LSD and 'magic mushrooms' can cause permanent psychological damage.
5) The biggest health risks with heroin are overdose, diseases transferred by needle sharing (e.g. HIV) and poisoning by other things it's cut (mixed) with. The drug itself doesn't cause much damage in small doses, but deaths from overdose are very common.

## There are lots of issues associated with drugs...

One of the biggest dangers in buying drugs off the street is that you never actually know what's in them. A bag of white powder sold as cocaine could be mixed with anything from local anaesthetic to rat poison. Some people argue that drugs should be legalised and controlled to stop this sort of thing from happening.

# Drugs and Alcohol

GENERAL

I suppose we'd better have the religious take on all this now — this is Religious Studies, after all.

## Christianity, Judaism and Islam all say **Drugs are Bad**

1) *"Your body is a temple of the Holy Spirit..."* — although this is a line from the New Testament (**1 Corinthians 6:19**), the message is similar for Christianity, Islam and Judaism. Drugs are seen as bad, as they damage the mind, abuse the body God has given to us, and can lead to poverty or even death.

2) Hard drugs (e.g. heroin and cocaine) and hallucinogens are completely disapproved of by Christianity, Judaism and Islam. They're seen as a way of escaping the realities of life, and existing instead in an artificial fantasy world.
3) They're also illegal, and all religions teach that you should obey the laws of the land you're living in (see page 73).
4) All three religions teach that the mind and the body are gifts from God, and that we do not have the right to abuse them. On a more practical level, drug taking is also seen as leading to irresponsible behaviour (e.g. neglecting your family or responsibilities), and possibly criminal activity.
5) Drugs taken to enhance performance in sport are also disapproved of, as they do not allow a person to properly display the skills they have been given. Again, they create a false world.
6) Islam is against cannabis for the same reasons it's against alcohol (see below). And Sheikh Ibn Taymiyyah (a famous scholar and Islamic teacher) had this to say on the subject: *"Sinful people smoke hashish (i.e. cannabis)... it disturbs the mind and temperament... excites sexual desire."*

## The Religions have **Different** Views on **Alcohol**

1) Most Christian denominations allow the consumption of alcohol — it's used in Holy Communion after all. However, drunkenness is frowned on, and some denominations are more disapproving than others.

    MODERATIONISTS (e.g. Roman Catholics, Anglicans and Lutherans) argue that alcohol is a gift from God to be enjoyed in moderation (while being aware of its dangers). Jesus and the Apostles drank wine at the last supper, and wine has always been used in Holy Communion.

    ABSTENTIONISTS (e.g. Methodists and the Salvation Army) believe that alcohol can be a bad influence, and so it's not wise to drink it. In **Proverbs 31:4-7**, the Bible says that alcohol can make you forget your responsibilities. Abstentionists don't believe alcohol is inherently evil though.

    PROHIBITIONISTS (e.g. Seventh Day Adventists) believe that drinking alcohol is a sin. They argue that all references in the Bible to Jesus and the Apostles drinking wine referred to grape juice.

2) In Judaism, alcohol is permitted, although drinking to excess is disapproved of. The Midrash (a collection of moral stories) contains the line, *"wine enters, sense goes out."*
3) Alcohol is forbidden in Islam, as it causes people to lose control — it's seen as a weapon of Shaytan (the Devil). People are more likely to do stupid things when they're drunk, and stop thinking about other people or Allah. A Muslim should have a clear mind when praying, and so there can be no place for alcohol.

### Christianity, Judaism and Islam have similar views on drugs...

This is a big social issue, so you'd expect every religion to have something to say on the matter. But as with all Religion and Society topics, come exam time, you'll need to give your own opinions too. That's what makes this subject interesting — sometimes there are no right or wrong answers, just different opinions.

# Warm-Up and Worked Exam Question

## Warm-up Questions

1) What is meant by:
   a) a sin, b) Shari'ah *(Islam)*
2) List five possible aims of punishment.
3) Give two reasons for and two against capital punishment.
4) Describe two social problems that can be caused by taking drugs.
5) Describe three health problems that can be caused by taking drugs.

## Worked Exam Question

Christians, Jews and Muslims have similar views about law and justice, but there are some differences. Read through this worked example, then have a go at the exam questions on the next page.

1 Choose one religion and explain its teachings on drugs.

*Christians strongly disapprove of drugs. They're seen as a way of escaping the realities of life and living in a fantasy world. Christians believe that drugs make people forget their responsibilities to other people and to God.*

*Clearly state which religion you're writing about.*

*Drugs like heroin and cocaine are also illegal. Christianity teaches that people should always obey the laws of the land they're living in. In his letter to the Romans, St Paul says "it is necessary to submit to the authorities, not only because of possible punishment but also because of conscience."*

*Christians believe that our bodies and minds are gifts from God, and in his first letter to the Corinthians, St Paul said "your body is a temple of the Holy Spirit". By taking drugs, Christians believe that people are damaging and abusing this gift.*

*It's not enough to just stick in some Bible quotes — you have to explain how they're relevant to the question.*

*Christians are also strongly against the use of performance-enhancing drugs, e.g. steroids, in sport. Sport should be an opportunity for people to display the gifts that God has given to them, but the use of drugs prevents them from doing this properly.*

*(8 marks)*

## Exam Questions

2 a) What is justice?

*(2 marks)*

b) "Religious people should always obey the laws of the land they live in."

Refer to at least one religion in your answer.

(i) Do you agree? Give reasons for your opinion.

*(3 marks)*

(ii) Give reasons why some people may disagree with you.

*(3 marks)*

3 a) Do you think punishment acts as a deterrent?
Give two reasons for your point of view.

*(4 marks)*

b) "The aim of punishment should always be rehabilitation."

Discuss this statement. You should include different, supported points of view and a personal viewpoint. You must refer to a religion in your answer.

*(12 marks)*

4 Explain why some Christians support the use of capital punishment but others do not.

*(6 marks)*

5 a) What is addiction?

*(2 marks)*

b) Do you agree that drugs such as cannabis and heroin should be illegal?
Give two reasons for your point of view.

*(4 marks)*

c) "Religious people shouldn't drink alcohol."

Refer to at least one religion in your answer.

(i) Do you agree? Give reasons for your opinion.

*(3 marks)*

(ii) Give reasons why some people may disagree with you.

*(3 marks)*

GENERAL

# The Nature of God and Religion

The question of what God is like has occupied religious thinkers for hundreds of years. There are three main issues:

## 1) Is God a 'Person' or a 'Force'?

1) The term 'personal god' refers to God as a 'person' — albeit an almighty and divine person. If this were the case, prayer would become part of our individual relationship — a 'conversation' with God.
2) The problem with this is that God is meant to be omnipresent (everywhere at once) — which poses the question of how a personal god can be everywhere at once.
3) The term 'impersonal god' refers to God as a concept, a force or an idea of goodness and light.
4) The obvious problem here is how you can have a relationship with a force or an idea.

## 2) Is God Within or Outside the Universe?

1) An 'immanent' God is a God who is in the world with us — a God who has taken an active role in the progress of human history and continues to do so.
2) The problem here is that an immanent God may appear small and fallible.
3) On the other hand, a 'transcendent' God is outside the world and doesn't directly act in human history.
4) This view of God makes him remote and separate from our experience on Earth. However, Christians who see God as transcendent might argue that it is they who do the work of God and that he is working through them.
5) Unfortunately, this definition is a bit too abstract for a lot of people to understand.
6) Religious believers (and Christians in particular) often try not to deal with extremes of any of these ideas, preferring instead to draw on different aspects for different occasions. Many would argue that God needs to be a blend of all of the above.

## 3) Is There Just One God or are There Many Gods?

1) Monotheism is the idea of one God. This exists in Christianity, Judaism and Islam.
2) Polytheism is the belief in more than one god, e.g. in Classical Greek and Roman civilisations, and some forms of Hinduism.

*Although Christianity is monotheistic, there is a belief that God is actually three in one (the Trinity — see next page and p.105-106).*

## Religion is Important to All Societies

1) Although religion might only seem relevant to people who practise it, it is a fundamental part of all societies. Even secular societies, where religion and government are kept completely separate.
2) People in a secular society are free to follow whichever religious faith they choose, just as they're free to have nothing to do with religion. But the Government won't take religious views into account when setting laws, or fund schools that only take children of a particular faith, etc. Some people believe that this system is fairer, as it gives no advantage to followers of any particular religious faith.

3) But even in a largely secular society, religion can play an important role. Religions continue to provide community traditions, e.g., festivals like Easter, Christmas and Hanukkah.
4) Religion also provides believers with an authority on how they should behave. It can make people more likely to live moral lives and to obey the law — resulting in a more peaceful society.
5) It can bring people together and give them a sense of community — and even non-religious people can enjoy the facilities, events and activities offered by religious groups.

## These questions have been worrying loads of people for ages...

But, tricky or not, you'll have to understand all these arguments to do well in your GCSE.

# Beliefs About God

Christianity & Judaism

There are many different ideas about what a god is. But Christian, Jewish and Muslim beliefs are quite similar.

## Christianity and Judaism say Similar Things about God...

1) As Christianity grew directly from Judaism, the basic concept of God is something the two faiths share.
2) The Judeo-Christian God is usually seen as male (referred to as He or Father) although nowadays many religious believers would argue that this is simply because when these religions were founded society was male-dominated, and that God is actually neither male nor female.
3) Both faiths share the ideas that God is omnipotent (all-powerful), omnipresent (everywhere) and omniscient (all-knowing), that God is divine, supreme, totally good and totally perfect, and that God has given us free will (see p.4).

*However, many Jews and Christians believe that our lives are predestined — we control individual actions, but not the ultimate outcome of our lives.*

### ...but There are Some Big Differences

1) The biggest difference is the Christian belief in the Trinity. Jews never believed Christ was the Son of God.
2) Another key difference between Jewish and Christian teaching is that Jews are forbidden to draw or make images of God.

## "Hear O Israel: the Lord our God, the Lord is One"

Jews don't all believe exactly the same things. They have many different opinions on many important issues. Most believe these 11 things about God. They believe God is...

| | |
|---|---|
| ...ONE | Jews believe there's only one God. The heading above comes from Deuteronomy 6:4 — it's the opening of a very important Jewish prayer called the Shema. |
| ...A PERSON | i.e. he's not just a 'force', but neither is he an old man with a beard. Human beings were made 'in his image' (but this needn't mean he looks like us). |
| ...THE CREATOR | i.e. he made the Universe and everything in it. Jews don't invent clever arguments for God's existence — they say that creation makes it obvious that he's there. |
| ...THE SUSTAINER | i.e. he didn't just create the Universe and then sit back — his energy keeps it going. |
| ...HOLY | 'Holy' means 'set apart' or 'completely pure'. God (or YHWH in Hebrew) is so holy that some Jews won't even write or say the word 'God' — they write G-d and say Hashem ('the Name') or Adonai ('the Lord', or 'the Master'). |
| ...OMNIPOTENT | i.e. all-powerful — although he still allows each person free will. |
| ...OMNISCIENT | i.e. he knows everything, even your darkest secrets and your wildest dreams. |
| ...OMNIPRESENT | i.e. present throughout the whole Universe. |
| ...THE LAWGIVER | Jewish tradition says 'God wrote himself into the Torah'. |
| ...THE TRUE JUDGE | Jews believe they shall all face him one day, for death is not 'the end'. |
| ...THE REDEEMER | Jews believe God is merciful. He will save his people from sin and suffering. |

## The Trinity — Father, Son and Holy Spirit

1) The Christian idea of the Trinity is that God exists in three 'persons' — the Father, the Son and the Holy Spirit. This is covered in detail on pages 105-106.
2) God the Father might be described as the transcendent part of God, the Son as the immanent and personal part, and the Holy Spirit as the immanent yet impersonal part (see p.80).

## Jews and Christians — similar but different...

Make sure you know the differences between Jewish and Christian beliefs — and take care not to get them mixed up. List the 11 things most Jews believe about God and learn the list. Make sure you know about the Trinity too.

ISLAM

# Beliefs About Allah

Islam shares a lot of history and beliefs with Judaism and Christianity.
But Muslims believe Islam is the "final word of god".

## The **Muslim** name for God is **Allah**

'Allah' written in Arabic

1) For Muslims, God is called Allah — and the word 'Islam' can be translated as meaning 'submission' or 'surrender' to Allah.
2) According to Islamic teaching, Allah is the creator of everything.
3) He is referred to by ninety-nine names in the Qur'an — these names tell you what Muslims believe about Allah and his power. They include:
   Ar-Khaliq — The Creator, Ar-Rahman — The Merciful, Ar-Aziz — The Almighty.
   He is also called The Provider, The Just, The Maintainer, The Hearer and The Real Truth.

## *"He is **Allah**, the **One**, Allah is **Eternal** and **Absolute**"*

1) This passage is taken from Surah 112 and describes the basic principle that Allah is one. Islam is a monotheistic religion (see page 80) and this belief in the oneness or the unity of Allah (called Tawhid) is a fundamental principle of Islam.
2) The ninety-nine names sum up much of the nature of Allah. He is loving and compassionate, he is the creator and judge of all humans, and knows everything they do.
3) Muslims believe Allah cannot be thought of in human terms — he is the Supreme Being and has no equal.
4) To Muslims, Allah is both immanent and transcendent (see page 80).
   He is transcendent in that he is the power behind the Universe and is outside, above or beyond both his creation and time itself. His immanence is demonstrated in this passage:
   *"And We have already created man and know what his soul whispers to him, and We are closer to him than [his] jugular vein."* **Qur'an 50:16**
   (In this passage 'We' refers to Allah and 'him' or 'his' refers to humankind.)
5) Human lives are predestined by Allah — but humans do have free will (see page 5).

## *There are **Five** Main Ways to **Know Allah***

1) Muslims believe that Allah has intervened in human history and that this is one way of knowing him and his power. His message was delivered by the prophets, of whom twenty-five are mentioned in the Qur'an. These include Musa (Moses) and 'Isa (Jesus). The last was the Prophet Muhammad, who brought Allah's message to the people.
2) Allah has also performed miracles (see p.85).
3) The Five Pillars of Islam also provide opportunities to know and be close to Allah.
   These are: Shahadah (a statement of belief)
   Salah (prayer) — see p.98
   Zakah (charitable duty) — see p.22
   Sawm (fasting) — see p.100
   Hajj (pilgrimage)

   Muslim prayer ritual — see page 98.

4) Muslims believe that the Qur'an is the word of Allah and allows humans to know him. Many Muslims learn it off by heart, and all try to live according to the guidelines found within it.
5) Muslims believe Allah is good and kind. However, there is a belief in a devil (called Iblis or Shaytan) who was cast out by Allah and tries to lead people away from him. Some Muslims would argue that Allah allows Shaytan to use this power to test and tempt us — we have the free will to resist (see p5).

## *Immanent AND transcendent? — tricky to get your head round...*

At the end of the day, it seems Christians, Jews and Muslims all agree on the fundamentals — that God/Allah is divine, supreme, all-powerful and all-knowing, that our lives are predestined and that we have free will.

# Vocation

General

A vocation is something God calls someone to do — it's their 'calling in life'. It can be a job, but isn't always. God will have created them with special gifts and talents for their mission.

## You can Respond to God Through a Vocation

1) You'll probably know if something's your vocation — you'll feel drawn to it, then when you're doing it, you'll feel 'at home'. But vocations are meant to be challenging rather than the easy option. Christians believe you need God's help to do them.
2) There are lots of different vocations a Christian might be called to. Here are a few examples:

- joining a religious order as a monk or a nun, to live a life of prayer and contemplation.
- a life of serving the Church, perhaps by training to be a priest.
- missionary work — trying to convert people to Christianity, maybe in a remote part of the world.
- a non-religious job such as a doctor, teacher or social worker, in order to help people.
- volunteering in the community — e.g. running a youth group.
- charity work — either religion-based (e.g. Christian Aid), or secular (e.g. Greenpeace).
- marriage and raising children.

3) Non-religious people often feel they have a 'vocation' too — they just don't believe that God called them to it.
4) You have to actually choose to follow your vocation — it doesn't just happen.

## The Covenant Gave Jewish People Their Chief Vocation

1) The covenant is the contract that God has made with the Jewish people. It commits them to serving God and to living as the Torah says they should. Many Jewish people consider this their vocation in life.
2) The Hebrew phrase 'Tikkun Olam' means 'mending the world' (see p.57). Jews are all expected to join in this task, although they can't complete it alone.
3) Jewish people may also share many of the same vocations as Christians, e.g. marriage and having children is considered very important in Judaism.
4) Jewish people can train for religious jobs — for example, as a rabbi or as a chazan. (Although in Orthodox Judaism, only men are allowed in these roles.)
5) Jewish people don't believe that they need to convert people to Judaism — so missionary work wouldn't be a Jewish vocation.

*"Be fruitful and increase in number; fill the earth..."*
**Genesis 1:28**

## The Greater Jihad is the Vocation of a Muslim

1) The Greater (or Internal) Jihad is the personal struggle of a Muslim to live their faith as best they can — it involves fighting their own desires in order to please Allah.
2) This means following all the rules making up the Five Pillars, being totally devoted to Allah, living as he commanded, and doing everything they can to help other people.
3) For a Muslim, the Greater Jihad may involve anything from learning the Qur'an by heart, to volunteering in the community, or perhaps becoming an imam (an imam is often a community leader as well as a spiritual leader).
4) Pleasing Allah is really important to a Muslim — if someone pleases Allah enough, they'll be sent to Paradise on Judgement Day.

*The Qur'an doesn't cover every detail of how Muslims should live. Extra day-to-day guidance is found in the law code called the Shari'ah (see p.73). This is based on Islamic tradition, as well as religious texts, and covers modern issues, such as drugs.*

## A vocation is your calling in life...

Make sure you know the main vocations of Christians, Jews and Muslims.

GENERAL

# Belief and Revelations

Upbringing, philosophy, comfort and personal religious experiences can all be reasons for belief.

## Different People Believe for Different Reasons

1) People brought up by religious parents or in a religious community are more likely to believe in a god (see p.1).
2) The presence of religion in the world gives some people faith, based on the good work that religion does — whether it be for individuals, communities or those who are experiencing suffering.
3) Some people are drawn to the purpose, structure and comfort it provides — or simply to the desire to have something to believe in.
4) Some people are convinced that there's a god by philosophical 'design' or 'causation' arguments (see p.2).
5) Some people's faith is strengthened by the feelings they experience during worship and the way God reveals himself to them (see below).
6) The search for meaning can also spark someone's interest in religion — people want to find answers or find out why life is as it is, and they might believe religion can help.
7) This desire to find out why we are here or why bad things happen in the world might also explain why some people move from one religion to another.

## Revelation — God Reveals His Presence

There are loads of ways people claim to experience God. He can reveal his presence in different ways...

### Revelation of Sacred Texts

Christians, Muslims and Jews believe that the truth about the world, and their rules for good behaviour were revealed to them by God. These revelations were written down in the scriptures — the Bible (p.87), the Torah (p.88) and the Qur'an (p.89).

### Revelation through Mystical and Religious Experiences

The revelation of the scriptures was something that happened a long time ago, but religious people believe that God still reveals himself today, through religious experiences.

1) PRAYER (p.97-98) — This is an attempt to contact God directly. It usually involves words and can be thought of as a conversation with God. A person might feel the presence of God in an answered prayer, e.g. if an ill person they pray for is cured, or if they are filled with a sense of inner peace or wonder.
2) MEDITATION — In meditation, a believer clears their mind of distractions and focuses on God. This could involve repetitive prayer, reading scripture or fasting. It doesn't need to be in a place of worship (you can meditate anywhere) and can result in visions or voices as the believer draws closer to God.
3) MIRACLES — Some people believe miracles occur today (e.g. healing at Lourdes, statues of the Virgin Mary crying blood), and that these miracles show God's power and presence (see p.85).
4) RELIGIOUS ECSTASY — These experiences range from singing, dancing, shaking or crying during worship to 'speaking in tongues' (unknown languages), having visions or prophesying (speaking a message from God).
5) SACRAMENTAL RITUALS — These are the rituals in which Christians believe God makes his presence felt directly. According to Roman Catholics, there are seven sacraments (see p.113) including Holy Communion. In Holy Communion, Catholics believe that bread and wine actually become Christ's body and blood (called transubstantiation) (see p.114).

### Revelation through the World

Many believers feel that God reveals himself constantly in the world through numinous experiences. This describes an experience that inspires awe and wonder, where someone can feel God's presence, e.g. a beautiful sunset, a wild sea or a butterfly's wing might convince you there must be a creator.

### A revelation is an experience of God...

Revelations, eh... Wow. I mean, just imagine. It's just mind-blowing...

# Miracles

GENERAL

Religion is a great source of stories of weird and wonderful events.

## Miracles — when Something Extraordinary Happens

1) Christianity, Islam and Judaism all teach that at some points in history the normal course of events was suspended, and something amazing happened.
2) Some believers, such as some Roman Catholics, think miracles continue to happen up to the present day (e.g. healing at Lourdes) — other Christians believe that we don't live in a time of miracles any more.
3) Others argue that the miracles in religious texts should be interpreted symbolically rather than literally.

## The New Testament Contains Many Miracles

The miracle stories are some of the best known of the Bible.

### Jesus Controls Nature — Inspiring Awe and Wonder

Jesus performs many miracles in the Gospels. He performs them basically for two reasons — to show that he has God's power, and to demonstrate the importance of faith.

*Jesus feeds the 5000* (**Mark 6:30-44**) A crowd has gathered around Jesus and the disciples, but there are only 5 loaves and 2 fish to eat. Jesus gives thanks to God, and breaks the bread. All 5000 people have enough to eat, and there's enough food left over to fill 12 baskets.

*Jesus walks on water* (**Mark 6:45-52**) Jesus catches up with his disciples' boat by walking across the water. Although they have seen him feed the 5000, they are still shocked at his powers.

### God has Intervened through Jesus and the Holy Spirit

1) Christians believe that the birth, death and resurrection of Jesus were miracles in their own right (see p.11).
2) At the feast of Pentecost (also known as Whitsun) Christians celebrate the descent of the Holy Spirit on to Jesus's early followers who were instantly able to speak many different languages and were filled with the power to speak out and do amazing things like Jesus did.
3) Many Christians believe that God continues to act in the world today through the Holy Spirit. They believe that the Holy Spirit guides them to do good in this world.

## Judaism has Plenty of Miracles of its Own

1) There are many miraculous events described in the Hebrew Bible. Examples include God parting the Red Sea for Moses during the flight from Egypt (Exodus 14) and the fall of the walls of Jericho (Joshua 6).
2) Some Liberal Jews argue that the purpose of the stories of these miracles is to impart a spiritual message, and they don't have to be believed in literally. More orthodox believers might argue that the events actually occurred as described in scripture.
3) More importantly for Jews, God intervened in the world by sending his prophets — such as Isaiah — who they believe represented God's will to the Jews. Jews consider Moses the greatest of the prophets.

## The Qur'an is a Miracle in Itself

1) Muslims believe the Qur'an is a miracle — the direct word of Allah, with a style that it's impossible to copy.
2) Some Muslims believe that the Qur'an contains 'scientific miracles' — where facts discovered centuries later are described, such as the development of the human embryo (Qur'an 23:12-14). Others argue that the Qur'an is for our spiritual and moral guidance, rather than a source for scientific theories.
3) The Prophet Muhammad didn't work miracles — but many Muslims believe that Allah took him on a journey from Makkah to Jerusalem and on a tour of the heavens in one night. Some Muslims believe it was a spiritual rather than a physical journey. Most Muslims believe that Allah's greatest miracle is creation itself.

GENERAL

# Revelation Through the Prophets

## Jesus Doesn't just Reveal God — ***He is God***

1) Most Christians believe that the Jewish prophets spoke for God (see below), but they believe that God revealed himself fully in the person of Jesus. Christians believe he was both fully God and fully human.
2) Jesus's teachings were written down during his life and passed on in the Gospels. They include the Sermon on the Mount (**Matthew 5-7**) which many believe is Christ's most important revelation.
3) In his death and resurrection, Christians believe Jesus showed his divine nature to man.

## *Jews Believe God **Spoke** to them through the **Prophets***

In Judaism, prophets are believed to speak for God among the people. A whole section of the Tenakh (p.88), called Nevi'im, is made up of the words of prophets such as Isaiah, Jeremiah and Ezekiel. According to Jewish traditions there have been many thousands of prophets, although not all have been remembered.
Here are two of the most important:

**Abraham (between 2000 and 1800 BCE)**

1) Jews call him Avraham Avinu ('our father Abraham'). He was the first of the patriarchs — the founders of Judaism.
2) Unlike his neighbours in Ur, he believed in one god. God told him to leave Ur and go to Canaan, also known as The Promised Land, The Holy Land, and later Israel. God promised this land to his descendants.
3) God made a covenant with Abraham which forms the basis of Jewish beliefs. God promised Abraham many descendants that God would never abandon. In return they had to be circumcised. The covenant was renewed at Mount Sinai with the giving of the Torah. Jews regard their history as the story of the covenant.

**Moses (around 1300 BCE)**

1) Abraham's descendants had to leave Canaan and escape to Egypt because of a famine. In Egypt they multiplied and the Egyptians made them slaves for 400 years.
2) With the help of God's direct intervention (sending the Ten Plagues on the Egyptians) Moses then led the Jews to freedom — an event called the Exodus. Their journey back to Canaan took 40 years.
3) On the way back, God revealed the Ten Commandments (Exodus 20) to Moses. Moses is regarded as the greatest of the prophets, and is traditionally believed to have been the divinely inspired author of the Torah (see p.88)

## *Muslims Believe there were **Many Prophets***

Muslims also believe that there have been many thousands of prophets in history, across all nations, revealing the nature of Allah and calling people to him. They believe that Muhammad was the final and greatest of these prophets. Muslims have special reverence for Ibrahim (Abraham), Musa (Moses) and 'Isa (Jesus) who are seen as delivering special messages from Allah to their people, but whose messages later got added to and distorted.

### *Muhammad was the **Final Prophet***

Muhammad was around 40 years old when he was called to receive Allah's final revelation.

1) While he was meditating in a cave on Mount Nur, Allah sent the angel Jibril (Gabriel) to him.
2) Although Muhammad was initially frightened, his wife Khadijah helped him realise that Allah was calling him to be a prophet.
3) Muhammad received many revelations from Allah, over 20 years. The Qur'an (p.89) records the exact wording of these revelations.

This was the message that the Prophet Muhammad had to take to the people of Makkah:

i) People were to worship one God, Allah — not many gods.

ii) People were to listen to him, because he was Allah's Prophet.

iii) People were to conduct their business honestly, and to look after the poor.

iv) If they did not do all this, they would be sent to Hell.

# Sacred Texts — The Bible

CHRISTIANITY

The Bible is a collection of books in different styles and languages written over a period of at least 1000 years. It's also the Christian Scripture — meaning that for Christians, it's sacred.

## The Bible — the Old and New Testaments

The Bible's divided into two main parts — the Old and New Testaments:

**THE OLD TESTAMENT**

The Old Testament is the Jewish Scriptures (i.e. it's considered sacred by Jews). Written in Hebrew and Aramaic, its 39 books include the Creation story, the books of the Law (Torah), the 10 Commandments, various histories of Ancient Israel, prophecy, poetry and psalms.

**THE NEW TESTAMENT**

The New Testament is the specifically Christian part of the Bible. Written in Greek in the 1st Century CE, its 27 books include the 4 Gospels, the Acts of the Apostles (describing the early years of Christianity), 13 letters by St Paul (giving advice about the Christian life), 8 letters by other early Christian leaders, and the Revelation of St John — an apocalyptic vision.

*The 4 Gospels are Matthew, Mark, Luke (called the Synoptic Gospels, as they are all very similar stories of Jesus), and John (which portrays Jesus in a very different way). The word 'Gospel' means 'good news', and the Gospels tell the good news about Jesus Christ.*

## The Bible is used as a Christian Faith Guidebook

Christians accept the Bible as authoritative in forming their beliefs and guiding their actions.

1) Christians believe the Bible offers directions for living a moral life. It presents Jesus Christ as our example for godly living, and teaches that we best love God by showing love to others.
2) Both the Old and New Testaments (but especially the New) include rituals for worship, large parts of which are still included in modern worship services (e.g. Holy Communion and baptism).
3) The faith of the Roman Catholic Church is based largely on the Scriptures, but Catholic tradition and the Magisterium (i.e. the teaching of the Pope, his cardinals and bishops) are also very important. The Protestant Churches claim their authority mainly from the Scriptures.
4) Different groups of Christians interpret the Bible in different ways:

(1) **Literalism** Many Christians believe that pretty well everything in the Bible is literally true, e.g. Jesus really did 'walk on water'.

*Some people argue that there are contradictions in the Bible, and so it's impossible for everything in it to be literally true.*

(2) **Fundamentalism** This is a form of literalism. Fundamentalists believe that it's wrong to question anything in the Bible, since it was dictated by God.

(3) **Conservative View** This view is probably the most common among Christians. They believe that the Bible was inspired by God but not dictated — the writers' own interests also come through. Readers must use their intelligence and the guidance of the Holy Spirit in order to understand the writers' intentions.

(4) **Liberal View** Liberals believe that pretty well everything in the Bible can be interpreted 'symbolically', e.g. Jesus didn't really 'walk on water' — the story has some other 'spiritual' meaning.

## The Bible has been Influential for Centuries

1) There are many different versions of the Bible in use today, and loads of translations into other languages.
2) The Gospels (which contain the teachings of Jesus) are central to Christian faith.
3) Christians often meet to study the Bible and to pray, and it's also read for guidance, or as an act of devotion towards God.

## The Bible — sells more than any revision guide...

The Bible has profoundly affected countless lives (e.g. the saints, missionaries, campaigners for social change), and arguments over its interpretation continue to be a legal matter in some countries — e.g. courts in the USA have had to legislate recently on whether schools should teach the Bible's Creation story as fact or fable.

JUDAISM

# Sacred Texts — The Torah & Talmud

The 'Jewish Bible' is the Tenakh (often just called the Torah). This is basically the same as the Christian Old Testament, except that it's in a different order. The word 'TeNaKh' even helps you remember what's in it.

## The Tenakh — its Letters tell you its Contents

### T = Torah (Instructions / Law / Teachings)

The Torah is the first five books of the Bible (Genesis to Deuteronomy). It contains 613 commandments (see p.50) which Jews are supposed to live by. Jews regard the Torah as the holiest part of the Tenakh, as it was given to Moses directly by God.

*But many people use the word 'Torah' to refer to the whole Tenakh.*

### N = Nevi'im (Prophets)

This collection of books is divided into two. The Former Prophets trace the history of the Israelites after the death of Moses. The Latter Prophets contain the words of Isaiah, Jeremiah, Ezekiel and 12 Minor Prophets. All these men encouraged the Jews to keep their part of the covenant, and their words are believed to have been inspired by God. However, the books in the Nevi'im do not have as high a status as the Torah.

### K = Ketuvim (Writings)

This is a hotch-potch of other stuff, chiefly the three 'P's: Psalms (hymns), Proverbs (wise and witty sayings), and Philosophy. This part of the Tenakh is less authoritative than the others.

## Torah means Different Things to Different People

Some Jews use the word 'Torah' to refer to the whole Tenakh. Others use it to mean the enormous body of teachings which grew up over the centuries to explain how the Torah should be applied in a changing world. Although some of these teachings were originally passed on by word of mouth (and were known as the Oral Torah), they eventually they got written down in a number of collections:

**1 The Mishnah ('Learning' or 'Repetition')**
This was a collection of Oral Torah written down by Rabbi Judah the Prince (roughly 200 CE). It ran to 63 volumes.

**2 The Gemara ('Completion')**
This is an extended commentary on the Mishnah.

**3 The Talmud (the Mishnah and Gemara combined)**
Some Jews think that God gave the entire contents of the Talmud to Moses, so it has avery high status and authority.

**4 The Codes**
The Talmud was so huge that summaries had to be made. An important example is the Mishneh Torah written by Maimonides in 1167. Another is the Shulchan Aruch from the 16th century.

**5 The Responsa**
New questions arise as technology develops, so panels of rabbis meet to give 'responses' to tricky questions, e.g. whether people should drive on the Sabbath.

## Orthodox Jews Live Strictly by the Torah

1) Orthodox means 'right belief'. Orthodox Jews think that traditional Jewish beliefs and practices are still important today. Roughly 80% of British Jews belong to Orthodox synagogues.
2) Orthodox Jews believe that the Tenakh and Talmud are of divine origin, and are to be followed to the letter.

## Progressive Jews Interpret the Torah Less Rigidly

1) Progressive Jews apply the Torah to modern life in a very different way. They believe that it's merely people's interpretation of the word of God.
2) They consider the moral commandments binding (although open to interpretation), but the ritual laws can be adapted or abandoned in response to changes in society. In Britain, there are two Progressive movements: Reform and Liberal Judaism.

# Sacred Texts — The Qur'an

ISLAM

Muslims believe the Qur'an is the most important book in the world, as it records the exact words of Allah. They call these words revelations, because they were revealed by Allah to the Prophet Muhammad.

## The *Qur'an* is Treated with *Respect*

For Muslims, the Qur'an is...

1. **A complete record of Allah's words:** The Prophet never forgot any revelations, and his followers recorded them at once, and learned them by heart.

2. **A totally accurate and unchanged record** The early Caliph (Muslim ruler) Uthman made sure there was only one version and that it was completely correct.

3. **A complete guide to Islamic life** The Qur'an says what Muslims must believe, and how they must live, in order to get to Paradise. In the Qur'an, Allah tells Muslims what they need to know, so that they can please him. Since Muslims believe the Qur'an came direct from Allah, they trust it completely. Basically, if the Qur'an says 'Do this,' then a Muslim must do it.

Allah gave the Qur'an to the Prophet Muhammad in Arabic. If you read it in another language, you might not get the proper meaning. So all Muslims must learn Arabic to be sure they are reading the real Qur'an.

Because the Qur'an is so important, Muslims treat it with great respect. Many Muslims will:

1) keep their Qur'an wrapped up to keep it clean,
2) wash their hands before touching it,
3) keep it on a higher shelf than all other books,
4) place it on a special stand when they read it.

The Qur'an is also read during private and public prayers, so Muslims get to know it really well. In the month of Ramadan, it's read from beginning to end during worship at the mosque.

## The Qur'an is Divided into *114 Surahs*

1) The Qur'an is organised into 114 Surahs (chapters).
2) The Surahs are arranged in order of length — longest first, shortest last (apart from Surah 1, the Fatihah, which is a short and punchy statement of central beliefs).
3) Each Surah is made up of Ayat (verses).
4) Most Surahs begin with the Bismillah — an Arabic phrase meaning 'In the name of Allah, the Entirely Merciful, the Especially Merciful'. This means that when Muslims start to read any Surah, they are reminded of the mercy and kindness of Allah.

## The *Hadith* and the *Sunnah* are also Important Texts

Muslims also pay a lot of attention to the guidance and example they get from the following:

— the sayings of the Prophet Muhammad that were not part of the Qur'an. These were Muhammad's words, not Allah's.

2. **THE SUNNAH** — the actions and way of life of Muhammad.

Because Muhammad was chosen by Allah to be his last Prophet, they regard him as a very remarkable man, and pay special attention to his words and actions.

### The Qur'an describes what Allah is like...

When Muslims read the Qur'an, they're learning about what Allah's like, how he relates to humans, and how to live the way Allah wants so they can get to Paradise and avoid the 'unpleasantness' of Hell.

# Warm-Up and Worked Exam Question

## Warm-up Questions

1) What is meant by a belief that God is "transcendent"?
2) Name two world religions that are monotheistic.
3) What is meant by revelation?
4) State two important religious texts used by a) Jews, b) Muslims.
5) a) What role did Jesus play in the revelation of God to the Christians? *(Christianity)*
   b) What role did Muhammad play in the revelation of Allah to the Muslims? *(Islam)*
   c) What role did Abraham play in the revelation of God to the Jews? *(Judaism)*

## Worked Exam Question

This is where you find out how much you've remembered about this section. Go through the questions and try to answer them. If you can't answer one, go back through the section to find the answer. Keep repeating this till you can answer them all without checking back. The first one is done for you.

1 a) Describe Christian beliefs about the nature of the Holy Spirit.

*Use specialist terms wherever possible — you'll get extra marks.*

*The Holy Spirit is part of the Trinity — the idea that God exists in three 'persons'. The Holy Spirit is the immanent, yet impersonal part of God — God's presence in the world which guides Christians.*

*If your exam paper has dotted lines to write on, use these as a guide for how much to write.*

*(3 marks)*

b) Explain what different Christians believe about the Bible.

*All Christians believe that the Bible is sacred. They consider it an authority on how to live a moral life and love God. Many Christians believe that reading the Bible shows devotion to God.*

*Some Christians believe that everything in the Bible is literally true because it is God's word, and some believe that it's wrong to question anything in it.*

*The question asks what <u>different</u> Christians believe. That's a huge reminder that they don't all believe the same thing — you should include these different beliefs in your answer.*

*Other Christians believe that the events described in the Bible should be interpreted symbolically, and that everything in it has a spiritual rather than a literal meaning.*

*Most Christians believe the Bible was inspired by God, but not dictated by Him. Because of this, the intentions of the humans who wrote it also come through.*

*(6 marks)*

## Exam Questions

2 a) Explain what is meant by a personal God.

*(1 mark)*

b) Choose one religion other than Christianity and explain what its followers believe about their God.

*(8 marks)*

3 a) What is a secular society?

*(2 marks)*

b) "Religion has no value in a secular society."

Do you agree? Give reasons for your answer, showing that you have thought about more than one point of view. Refer to religious arguments in your answer.

*(6 marks)*

4 a) Describe Christian beliefs about miracles.

*(3 marks)*

b) Explain what Jews/Muslims believe about the Torah/Qur'an.

*(6 marks)*

5 a) Give two examples of what a religious follower might consider to be their vocation.

*(2 marks)*

b) "Only religious people have vocations."
Refer to at least one religion in your answer.

i) Do you agree? Give reasons for your opinion.

*(3 marks)*

ii) Give reasons why some people might disagree with you.

*(3 marks)*

CHRISTIANITY

# Public and Private Christian Worship

Worship is the religious person's way of expressing their love of, respect for, and devotion to a god or gods.

## Sunday Worship in **Church** can take **Many Forms**

1) For Christians, Sunday is the 'Lord's Day' — this is when they celebrate the Sabbath. Most churches have their main service on a Sunday morning. It may be structured or spontaneous, and will usually include songs, Bible readings, and a sermon. The exact form of Sunday worship will vary between denominations.
2) In Roman Catholic, Orthodox, and most Anglican churches it will be structured and liturgical (i.e. it will follow a pattern laid down in writing — with set prayers, and readings).
3) Methodists and other nonconformists have structured but non-liturgical services, e.g. following the 'hymn sandwich' pattern, where the service consists of hymns alternating with things like readings, prayers and a sermon.
4) Roman Catholic and Orthodox Sunday services always include the Eucharist (called Holy Communion or, in the Roman Catholic tradition, Mass see p.114). Anglican churches usually include the Eucharist.
5) Pentecostals, House Churches and other independent Christian fellowships may have spontaneous, often charismatic worship (see p.106).
6) Some Christians hold church services in their own homes. Some because Christianity is prohibited in their country — others as they believe it's more like the simpler worship described in the New Testament.
7) Many Christians worship informally at home (not just on Sundays). This can be anything from saying Grace before a meal to singing worship songs with family and friends.

*There are several reasons for all this variety. Christians share the same basic beliefs about the importance of Holy Communion, the Bible, the sermon, the Holy Spirit etc., but they differ as to which matters most.*

## **Inside** A Typical Parish Church

Traditional Roman Catholic and Church of England churches are often very similar in layout:

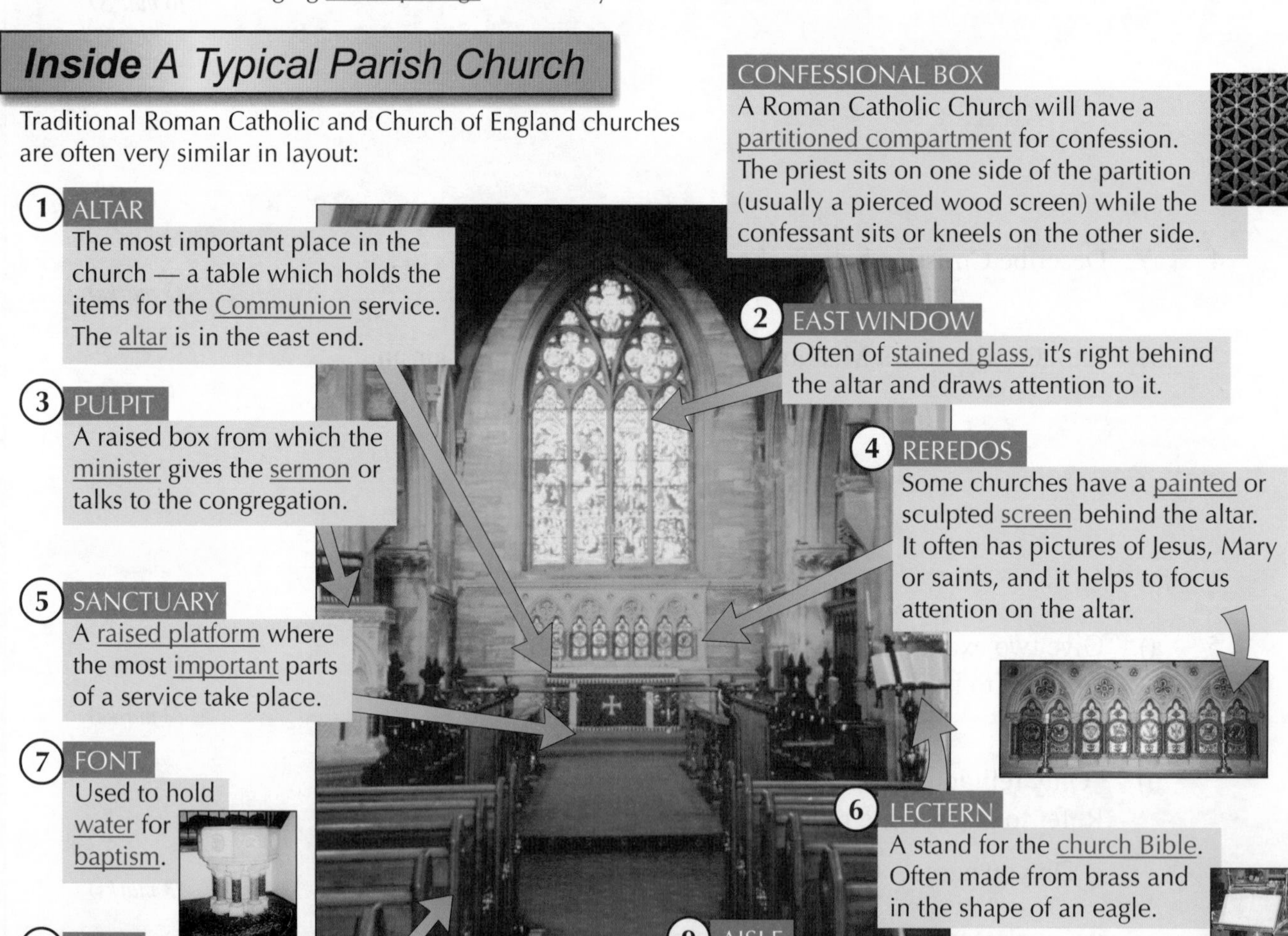


### Worship can be formal or informal...

Make sure you spend time learning what each little feature of a church is called and what it's used for.

# Symbolism in Christian Worship

CHRISTIANITY

Symbols are used within the Christian tradition to represent what's believed.
An obvious example is the symbol of the cross — used to represent the sacrificial death of Jesus Christ.

## Religious Architecture is often Symbolic

1. Cathedrals can be enormous, demonstrating their importance. They were historically built at the centre of the community to represent God's kingship on Earth. Inside, the focus of attention is always towards the altar (see p.92), where the main act of worship (the celebration of Holy Communion) takes place.

2. Orthodox churches are often in the shape of a cross, with a large dome on top symbolising Christ's presence, eternity and the nearness of heaven. Inside they are richly decorated with friezes and carvings.

3. Free Churches (e.g. Baptists) meet in simple halls where the pulpit is the focus of attention. This shows the importance to them of preaching from the Bible. Also in a Baptist church, the prominence of the Baptistry (a pool for baptism by total immersion) shows the central importance of baptism.

## Icons, Statues and Stained-Glass Windows are Symbolic

1. Icons are paintings (mostly saints) often found in Orthodox churches, and are often greeted with a kiss on entering the building. They're used to represent the presence of saints, and as a means to pray — 'prayers captured on wood'.

*Statues also represent the presence of the saints. In certain festivals a madonna (a statue of Mary) or another saint is paraded through the streets as an appeal to bless the community.*

2. Large cathedrals and churches are often decorated with colourful murals or frescoes, and many feature beautiful stained-glass windows depicting biblical stories. For centuries the finest work of leading artists was made for churches — all to offer to God the highest expression of worship, and to create a sense of awe.

3. The most well known Christian symbol is the cross which represents Jesus's crucifixion. However a cross isn't a crucifix unless it features a representation of Jesus. Crucifixes can be found in Roman Catholic and Orthodox churches, to remind them of Jesus's suffering — but empty crosses are found in Anglican, Baptist and Methodist churches to remind them of the risen Christ.

4. Another important symbol of Christianity from the earliest times is the fish. Jesus called on his followers to be *"fishers of men"* (**Mark 1:17**). The Greek word for fish 'ICTHYS' forms an acrostic (each letter becomes the first letter of a new word) for 'Jesus Christ, God's Son, Saviour' in Greek. It was a sign used by early Christians who were being persecuted.

## Church Music is also Symbolic

Church music is symbolic as it is used to praise God and to express belief. Mozart, Bach, Beethoven and many other great composers wrote music for worship — e.g. Handel's Messiah, Mozart's Requiem Mass.

1) Hymns have been part of Christian worship for many centuries — they're often derived from passages of scripture.
2) In some Protestant churches, choirs have an important role in leading the singing. There are many types, from Anglican schoolboys to Pentecostal gospel.
3) Many different musical instruments are used in worship — from pipe organs to brass bands and guitars. The music used in worship can be solemn and dignified or loud and lively depending on the type of church.
4) Dancing is common in Charismatic churches (see p.106) — it's seen as a sign of the Holy Spirit's presence.

## Symbolism plays a vital part in religious expression...

Christian beliefs are often expressed through ritual worship (e.g. baptism) — this is also a kind of symbolism.

JUDAISM

# Public and Private Jewish Worship

A Jewish place of worship is called a synagogue, although Jews more often use the word 'shul', or sometimes even 'Bet ha-Knesset' (House of Meeting).

## It's not what's on the **Outside** that matters...

There are no rules stating what a synagogue should look like on the outside — they can be plain or ornate, traditional or ultra modern. But you might recognise a synagogue from symbols on its outside walls, such as a menorah (a seven-branched candlestick), or a magen David (a six-pointed star/shield of David).

## ...it's what's on the **Inside** that's Important

The layout of the synagogue's Prayer Hall is based on that of the ancient Temple of the Jews. It faces Jerusalem, where the Temple stood, and is usually rectangular. All synagogues share the following four features:

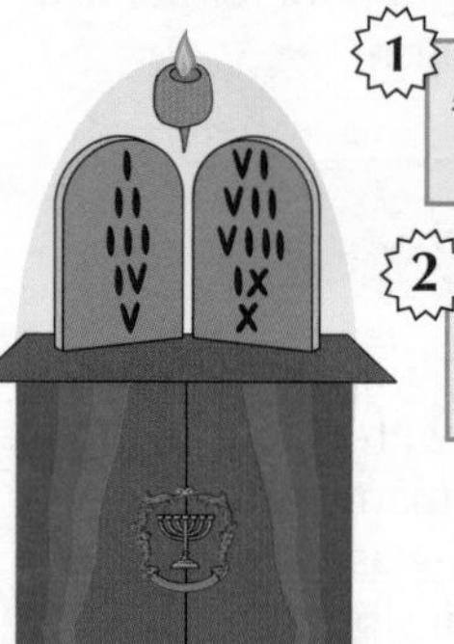

1. Aron Kodesh (the Ark) — this is the most important item of furniture, since it holds the Torah. It is a large cupboard or alcove, with doors or a screen, set on the wall facing Jerusalem.

2. Ner Tamid (Perpetual Light) — above the ark is a light which never goes out. It represents the menorah which was always kept alight in the Temple.

*There will be no 'pictures of God' (see next page).*

3. Sefer Torah (Scroll of the Torah) — parchment scroll. On each end is a wooden pole for winding it to the required passage. It must be handwritten by a sofer (scribe), and is usually decorated. It's kept inside the ark.

4. Bimah or Almemar — a raised platform with a reading desk, normally in the centre of the hall.

Also, some synagogues have a pulpit, and the Ten Commandments above the ark. Some have an organ (but on the Sabbath, all singing should be unaccompanied), and an Orthodox synagogue will have a gallery where women can sit.

## Shabbat (Sabbath) is Celebrated in the **Synagogue**...

The Sabbath is a day of rest to commemorate the 7th Day of Creation when God rested after making the Universe. It begins at sunset on Friday, and ends on Saturday evening when stars begin to appear.

There are 3 separate services in the synagogue on the Sabbath.

> The 4th Commandment instructs Jews to observe the Sabbath. *"Remember the Sabbath day by keeping it holy."* **Exodus 20:8**

FRIDAY EVENING Shabbat is welcomed as a queen or a bride with singing led by a chazan (cantor). No instruments are used — in memory of the destruction of the Temple with its instrumental music.

SATURDAY MORNING the main service of the week. The rabbi will read from the Torah and give a sermon. Also, seven men are called up to read or recite a blessing, and an eighth reads a portion from the books of the Prophets. In Orthodox synagogues, women sit separately from the men and take little part.

SATURDAY AFTERNOON this service includes a reading from the Torah, and three special prayers.

## *Shabbat is a holy day of rest and prayer...*

There are big similarities between all three of the faiths covered in this book. Each religion has a day or more a week set aside for special religious observance. Until the mid 1990s most shops in Britain weren't allowed to open on a Sunday (the Lord's Day). In Israel, government agencies don't open during Shabbat.

# Symbolism in Jewish Worship

Judaism

## ...and in the **Home**

1) To prepare for Shabbat, the house is cleaned and tidied, and all the food to be eaten on Shabbat is cooked in advance. Family members bathe or shower. At dusk, the mother of the family will light two candles and welcome the Sabbath by saying a blessing and gesturing with her arms.

2) At the beginning of the Shabbat meal, a sanctifying ceremony called kiddush takes place. It happens at home and at the synagogue, and includes the reciting of **Genesis 2:1-3** (God resting after creation). Wine is used to symbolise the sweetness and joy of Shabbat.

*The Mishnah (see p.88) lists 39 kinds of 'work' not allowed on the Sabbath.*

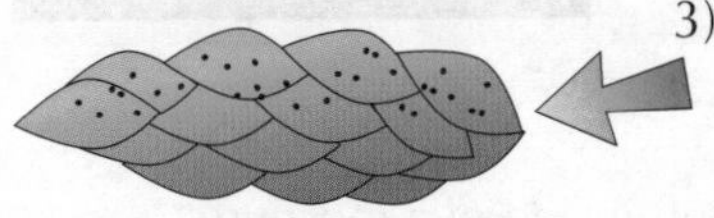

3) Challot are eaten — these are two plaited loaves which commemorate the double portion of 'manna' (miraculous food) which God provided the day before each Shabbat during the Exodus. They are blessed, cut and dipped in salt.

4) After the father has blessed his children, the Shabbat meal is eaten.

5) The havdalah ('division') ceremony marks the end of Shabbat, separating it from the six days ahead. Blessings are said over sweet-smelling spices, a cup of wine, and over a special plaited candle.

## ***Judaism** Has **Symbols** to Remind Them of God*

Since God is invisible, symbols are used by believers to help them focus on God in private prayer and in communal worship.

1. The mezuzah is a sign which is put in Jewish houses. It's a tiny parchment scroll containing the words of **Deuteronomy 6:4-9** and **11:13-21** in Hebrew. It must be handwritten by a trained scribe, and is put inside a case to keep it safe. There's one on the front door and every other door of the house except the bathroom and toilet. It constantly reminds the family of their duty to God.

2. Many Jewish men and boys wear a small cap called a kippah as a sign of respect to God. It reminds them that God's intelligence is vastly higher than ours.

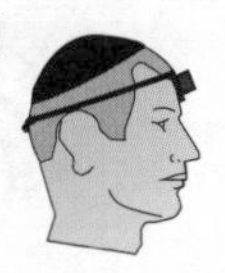

3. The Tefillin (or Phylacteries) are worn during morning prayers, except on the Sabbath and on festival days. They're two leather boxes, one worn on the upper arm (next to the heart), one on the head. Inside are tiny scrolls containing Torah passages. These remind Jews to serve God with head and heart — the command to wear them comes from **Deuteronomy 6:6-9**.

## *But **Jews** have **No Pictures** of God*

There are two reasons why Jewish art never tries to picture God.

1) No one knows what he looks like.

2) The 2nd of the 10 Commandments forbids it as idolatry.

*"You shall not make for yourself an idol in the form of anything in heaven above or on the earth beneath..."* **Exodus 20:4**

To avoid idolatry, no images of people are allowed in synagogues, as people are made in the image of God, The ban on idolatry also means three-dimensional sculptures aren't allowed.
Many synagogues won't have images of animals either, although the 'Lion of Judah' (a symbol of Judaism) can sometimes be found.

**Some Jews write 'G-d' instead of God**

In **Deuteronomy 12:1-4**, God tells the Jews to tear down the temples and wipe out the names of the gods they find written in the sacred places of other nations in Israel. But verse 4 warns them not to do the same to him. Many Jews take this as a warning never to erase the name of God — so they never write it out fully just in case.

## *Signs and symbols play an important part in worship...*

Jews don't have pictures of God and won't write down his name so they can't accidentally erase it. But, they do have symbols to help remind them of God. Make sure you know about the mezuzah, kippah and tefillin.

Islam

# Public and Private Muslim Worship

A mosque (or masjid) is more than a place of worship — it's also a centre of the community for Muslims. Masjid literally means 'place of prostration' (i.e. lying with the face down) — an act of submission to God.

## A **Mosque (Masjid)** is the Muslim House of Prayer

1) The Prophet Muhammad said that any clean place could be used for worship.
2) Some mosques are extremely simple, others are very grand, but all have a dome representing the universe.
3) Most mosques will have at least one minaret. This is a tall tower from where the muezzin (mu'adhin in Arabic) calls the adhan (call to prayer).

### **Inside** the Mosque

"Muhammad"

"Allah"

1) Beautiful mosaic tiles often decorate both the outside and inside of a mosque.
2) There are no pictures of Muhammad or Allah, since no one is allowed to draw them, and pictures of other living things are usually banned, to avoid idolatry.
3) The ban on images means that richly coloured Arabic calligraphy (writing) is often used to decorate mosques with words from the Qur'an and the names of Allah and Muhammad. The faith of the calligrapher is expressed in writing — this helps the believer focus on the meaning of the words. Calligraphy is one of the most respected arts in the Islamic world.
4) The colour green is traditionally used in mosques. This is believed to be because it was Muhammad's favourite colour (he's thought to have had a green turban and banner), and because it symbolises life.
5) Shoes must be left at the door, and every mosque must have somewhere for Muslims to wash before prayer.
6) There are no seats, but the whole floor is usually covered with rich carpet.
7) There is little in the way of furniture, but you will see a pulpit (called a minbar), where the imam (a respected person) will lead prayers from — especially on Fridays.
8) Muslims face Makkah when they pray, and a special niche (called the mihrab) in the 'direction-wall' shows the direction in which Makkah lies.

Apart from prayer, a mosque is used as a Madrasah (a mosque school), where Muslims learn the general principles of Islam, as well as how to carry out Muslim practices and recite the Qur'an.

*Regular daily prayer is an important part of being a Muslim (see p.98). It's one of the five Pillars of Islam (see p.82).*

Home life also has an important role in Islam — this is where many of the rules of Islam are kept.

- Most Muslim households have a copy of the Qur'an.
- It's where children first learn and witness Islamic values.
- It is also the centre of religious life for many women, who are not obliged to attend the mosque.

## **Tawhid** is the Belief in the **Oneness of Allah**

1) Islam teaches that nothing is remotely like Allah, and nothing can be compared to him.
2) The worst sin for a Muslim would be to believe that God was not supreme — this concept is called Shirk. (Shirk is the opposite of Tawhid.)

*Muslim beliefs about Allah...*
Allah is beyond time and space. He is the Almighty One, the Compassionate and the Merciful. All men and women owe their creation, and continued existence, to Allah — the One and Only Creator.

*And see page 82 for more basic Muslim beliefs about God.*

## *You need to learn about mosques — inside and out...*

The mosque and daily worship are central to an Islamic community. Some Muslims carry a special compass so they can pray in the right direction, even when they're nowhere near a mosque.

# Prayer and Meditation

GENERAL & CHRISTIANITY

Prayer is at the centre of many people's faith. Whereas worship involves all the things people do to express their faith, prayer is specifically the 'talking to God/Allah' part.

## *Prayer Puts People In Touch with their God*

1) Prayer is when believers mentally or vocally communicate with their god, or gods.
2) Prayer comes in many different forms: most branches of Christianity, Judaism and Islam have set prayers that people say when they are engaged in their main acts of worship.
3) But prayer also has a private dimension where the individual believer communicates with their god in their own words.
4) Some prayers have set words — these include the Lord's Prayer in Christianity and the Shema in Judaism.
5) Some religions require specific movements for some prayers — such as the Muslim Salah prayers (see next page), which require believers to take various positions including prostrating themselves with their hands, knees and foreheads placed on to the ground.

## *Prayer can be a **Powerful** Thing*

1) There's a strong tradition in Christian prayer of asking for things from God. When believers feel that God grants their requests this is known as an 'answered prayer'. Some believers think answered prayers are proof that God exists.
2) However this presents the problem of 'unanswered prayers' when God doesn't grant a believer's request.
3) Some Christians argue that God answers all prayers in his own way and in his own time. Others would argue that God has bigger plans that we cannot understand — He moves in mysterious ways.
4) Jesus himself on the night of his arrest prays: *"My father, if it is possible, may this cup be taken from me. Yet not as I will, but as you will."* (**Matthew 26:39**). The "cup" may represent suffering.
5) Roman Catholics and Orthodox believers pray to saints to ask for their 'intercession' (help) with God. They believe that the Saints can join in our prayers to God, making them more effective.
6) Protestant churches believe that Jesus is the only mediator between us and God, so we don't need the Saints' help. Some argue that we shouldn't pray to Saints, as no-one does in the Bible.

## *Private Prayer draws a **Believer** Closer to God*

Christian prayer is a conversation with God, and should take place both in church and in private. The whole point of prayer is for the believer to draw close to God to communicate with him and hear what he's saying — this deepens their faith. Different Christians use different methods to accomplish this:

**The 'Quiet Time'** — time spent alone with God, perhaps reading the Bible and praying.

**Meditation** — a form of prayer where the believer clears his or her mind of distracting thoughts and concentrates on God's nature or work. It may involve repeating a prayer over and over again.

**Contemplation** — true Christian contemplation is not merely deep thinking — it's intimate wordless prayer in which the believer senses God's presence strongly.

**The Rosary** — used by Catholics, this is a string of beads arranged in groups. As the beads are moved through the fingers, prayers are said, e.g. the Lord's Prayer, Ave Maria (Hail Mary) and the Gloria.

**Icons** — Orthodox Christians use icons (sacred pictures of saints) to help them focus on God. Although they may light a candle in front of the icon or kiss it, they don't pray to it.

Many parents pray with their children, believing this encourages them to grow up as praying Christians. And many Christians believe praying while ill brings God's healing or helps them accept their suffering as part of God's plan.

## *Prayer is a way of talking to God...*

Make sure you know the different types of prayer and why people pray.

JUDAISM & ISLAM

# Prayer and Meditation

The Jewish holy day is the Shabbat (Sabbath), but in Judaism, prayer is important every day of the week.

## Jews have Three Special Times for Daily Prayer

1) Prescribed daily prayers happen at three special times — in the morning, afternoon and evening.
2) At these times, men will try to attend the synagogue and become part of a minyan — a group of at least ten men, which is the minimum needed for a service. Women (traditionally because of their domestic commitments) are trusted to pray at home.
3) As well as the normal daily prayers, there are also special prayers for getting up, going to bed, before and after eating... in fact, pretty much every event in life, good or bad, can be a reason to pray.
4) The Jewish prayer book is known as the Siddur, which sets out the time of day for different prayers.
5) When praying, Jewish men will often wear a kippah (see p.95).
6) Some Jews wear tefillin (or phylacteries) while praying (see p.95). This fulfils the commandment in **Deuteronomy 6:8** — *"Tie them* [the commandments] *as symbols on your hands and bind them on your foreheads."*

## Prayer is a Pillar of Islam

*See page 82 for more about the Five Pillars.*

You can't be a Muslim without praying in the way Muhammad did. Regular prayer keeps Allah in a Muslim's mind. It also keeps Muslims aware of their duty to obey Allah.

1) Muslims should pray five times a day — at sunrise, early afternoon, late afternoon, after sunset, and late at night.
2) The muezzin makes the call to prayer (adhan) from the minaret of a mosque. The call to prayer begins *"Allahu Akbar..." (God is Greatest)*.
3) Ideally prayer should take place in a mosque. If this isn't possible, a prayer mat should be used to make a prayer place.
4) Wudu (washing exposed parts of the body three times before prayer) is important, so that a Muslim is pure and clean when approaching Allah.
5) A Muslim should face Makkah (Muhammad's place of birth) when praying. The direction of Makkah is called the qiblah. A compass can be used to find the qiblah (which in England is roughly southeast).
6) There is a set ritual for prayer — each unit of prayer is known as a rak'ah (and the rak'ah may be repeated several times at each prayer session). Each rak'ah involves standing, then kneeling, then putting your forehead to the ground as a sign of submission.
7) If several Muslims are praying in one place, then they all do the ritual together as a sign of unity.
8) Friday prayers are called Salat-al-Jum'ah (or just Jum'ah) — it's a community occasion, and at least 40 people should be there, all praying together.

*Women and men pray separately — so people keep their mind on Allah rather than on the opposite sex.*

Salah is compulsory prayer. Extra prayers are called du'a, and Muslims can do these at any time. In du'a prayers, beads can be used — 99 beads for the 99 names of Allah.

**Benefits of Prayer**

1) Keeps you in close contact with Allah and stops you forgetting him.
2) Expression of solidarity — doing exactly the same as all other Muslims.
3) Moral and spiritual discipline.

**Problems with Praying in 'non-Muslim' Countries**

In non-Muslim countries it can often be hard to pray at the right time, e.g. when you have to go to school or work. This is one of the ways in which life is more complicated for Muslims if they live in a country where Islam is not the way of life of most people.

## Muslims pray five times a day...

You can see why religion is such a big part of the lives of Jews and Muslims when they have to pray however many times a day. I guess that's one of the main points of prayer — keeping your god in your mind throughout the day. Just don't forget — it's three times for Jews (on ordinary weekdays) and five times for Muslims.

# Food and Fasting

GENERAL

Food is an important part of everyone's life — but some religions have special rules about food.

## *Food is Important in Many Religions*

1) One of the main ways in which cultures (religious or not) express themselves is through food. This is especially true at special times of year — i.e. during festivals.
2) Christians, Muslims and Jews all believe that God is the creator, and so ultimately, all food comes from Him.
3) Permanent prohibitions (bans) of certain foods are a common feature of many religions, although Christianity is an exception. Most cultures avoid certain food that others may eat anyway, e.g. frogs' legs or dog meat.
4) Fasting (not eating for a period of time) is a part of many religions either as atonement (see below), or as a way to focus the mind on spiritual matters.

## *Fasting — Not Vital in Christianity*

1) Christians believe fasting can help you draw closer to God, but there are no longer any compulsory fasts for Christians, or special foods they must eat or avoid. However Roman Catholics shouldn't eat meat on Ash Wednesday and Good Friday, and they should fast for an hour before the Eucharist (Holy Communion).
2) Lent (February/March) commemorates the 40 days and nights of Jesus's fasting in the wilderness after his baptism. Few Christians today fast during Lent, but many still give up certain luxuries. Lent ends on the day before Easter.
3) Festival foods (e.g. Christmas pudding, hot-cross buns) tend to be more cultural than religious in origin.

- Before Lent begins, rich foods should be eaten up, and Mardi Gras carnivals may be held ('carnival' means 'farewell to meat'). In some countries, like the UK, many people still eat pancakes on Shrove Tuesday (the day before Lent) — so it's often called Pancake Day.
- Whether religious or not, many people celebrate Easter (March/April) with Easter eggs, whether with hard-boiled and decorated versions of the real thing, or with chocolate versions, as a symbol of new life.
- Historically Christian countries often have special meals for Christmas (although some countries eat them on Christmas eve). In the UK 'Christmas Dinner' usually consists of roast turkey with stuffing and then Christmas pudding.

*See page 115 for more on Christian festivals.*

4) Don't forget that most Christian denominations celebrate the Eucharist (or Mass or Holy Communion) with bread (usually a communion wafer) and wine. This food and drink represents (and in some denominations is believed to become) the body and blood of Christ.

## *Kashrut — the Jewish Food Laws*

1) Observant Orthodox Jews follow a special diet based on the Kashrut (Jewish food laws).
2) Permitted food is called kosher — everything else is terefah ('torn').
3) These laws are an example of statutes laid down by God to test Jews' obedience, and to mark them out as different from other nations.
4) To be kosher, a mammal must have cloven (split) hooves and chew the cud. Fish with fins and scales are kosher, but no other seafood is. Some birds are also kosher.

*In Judaism, food is associated with happiness — so fasting shows grief or repentance. Judaism teaches that true repentance can atone (i.e. make amends) for any past transgression — 'the gates of repentance are always open'.*

5) Animals and birds must be specially slaughtered with one cut across the throat using a razor-sharp blade. Blood must not be eaten, and meat and dairy products must not be eaten together. Foods that aren't meat or dairy may be eaten with either.

## *Learn which foods are kosher...*

Eating is something everyone has to do — so it's no wonder that it pops up as a topic in pretty much every religion. Religious people have lots of special foods and fasts — and you've got to learn them all.

JUDAISM & ISLAM

# Food and Fasting

## Jews *Fast* for Some *Festivals*...

1) Yom Kippur (the Day of Atonement) is the most important fast in the Jewish calendar. Taking place ten days after the start of the Jewish New Year (Rosh Hashanah), it involves prayer and fasting for 25 hours from half an hour before nightfall on the eve of Yom Kippur, through to half an hour after nightfall on Yom Kippur itself.
2) Not only do Jews refrain from eating during Yom Kippur, they also don't drink — not even water. Yom Kippur is the day when Jews ask God to forgive the sins they committed over the past year. They abstain from food and drink the better to focus on spiritual rather than physical matters.

## ...and Eat *Special Food* at *Others*

1) One of the most important Jewish feasts of the year is Pesach (Passover). It commemorates the night before the Exodus — when Moses led the Israelite slaves from Egypt to freedom. In Egypt, the angel of death killed the first-born sons of the Egyptians, but passed over the Israelites.
2) Yeast is forbidden — all bread must be unleavened. The Seder (Passover meal) involves the symbolic arrangement and eating and drinking of matzah (a cracker-like unleavened bread), wine, salt water, bitter herbs, karpas (a vegetable), roast or hard-boiled egg, and a roasted lamb bone which isn't eaten.
3) During the Shavuot festival in early summer, Jews traditionally eat dairy products like cheesecake.
4) For Hanukkah, a wintertime festival, Jews traditionally eat fried foods like latkes (potato pancakes) and doughnuts, to celebrate the story of a day's worth of oil burning for eight days during the rededication ceremony for the Temple in Jerusalem.

## Muslims Fast During *Ramadan*

1) Muslims must fast between sunrise and sunset during the month of Ramadan in the Muslim calendar.
2) This fasting means no food, no drink, no smoking and no sex. Ramadan is a time of both physical and moral self-discipline, and a time of total obedience to Allah.
3) It's supposed to help Muslims understand hunger, and makes them more willing to help others.
4) It's also a time to show publicly that Allah matters more than physical needs.
5) Sawm (fasting during Ramadan) is one of the most important obligations for a Muslim.
6) Eid ul-Fitr marks the end of Ramadan. There are special prayers, and Muslims enjoy rich meals with their families.

There are exceptions to the normal Ramadan rules:
1) Children don't have to fast until they're about 12 years old.
2) People can be excused for medical reasons. Those who are ill (and women having their period) are excused. And it's okay to take medicine which has to be regular, e.g. antibiotics.
3) If you're on a journey, you can be excused. But you have to make up the missed days later.

7) Eid ul-Adha is the festival of sacrifice. It commemorates Ibrahim's willingness to sacrifice his son to Allah. Sheep and goats are sacrificed at the festival, and the meat is shared among the poor.

## The *Shari'ah* says Things are Either *Halal* or *Haram*

**HALAL means 'allowed'** **HARAM means 'forbidden'**

You need to know these two Arabic words. Think of the letter L — haLaL is aLLowed. And HARaM can HARM.

## *Food Laws — No Pork, No Blood* at all, No animals that *Eat Meat*

1) The basic rules are no pork, no blood at all, and no animals that eat meat.
2) This means it's very important how an animal is killed — it must be done by slitting the neck and allowing all the blood to drain out. Meat from animals killed like this is halal, i.e. allowed.
3) Food preparation is also important — no animal fat can be used (but vegetable oil is okay).
4) Intoxicants, e.g. alcohol, are also forbidden (see p.77).

# Christian Funeral Rites

GENERAL & CHRISTIANITY

Every religion has a special way of dealing with the dead.

## *Funerals are a Way to Say* ***Goodbye***

1) While many people never get Christened or have a Bar Mitzvah, nearly everyone gets a funeral.
2) Going back through history, people have always made special provision for their dead — e.g. by mummifying them, burying them, cremating (burning) them or with other rituals, e.g. burial at sea.
3) While UK law only specifies that the body has to be properly disposed of (e.g. buried, cremated) most people, with a religious faith or without, will hold some kind of ceremony.
4) Funerals are seen as a chance to say goodbye to the dead, and to remember and celebrate their lives.
5) Most funerals in Britain are organised by professionals known as funeral directors or undertakers.
6) Mourning is a deep sorrow for someone who has died. Many societies have a period of mourning after a funeral, when loved ones say special prayers for the deceased, remember their lives and forgo pleasures (e.g. music, bright colours, sex). At the end of that period, mourners try to move on with their lives.

## ***Christian Funerals*** *are* ***Sad****, but with a Note of* ***Hope***

Funeral services vary according to denomination, but all Christian funerals contain a note of hope.
For many this doesn't mean wishful thinking — it means confident expectation based on God's promises.

1) The coffin is carried into the church, and the verses on page 11 from John 11 are often read. There are hymns, other Bible readings and prayers. The priest (or someone else) often gives a short sermon about Christian belief in life after death, and may also talk about the life of the person who has died.
2) Of course there will be sadness too, particularly if the person died young or very suddenly.
   There are prayers for the bereaved (bereavement is the loss of someone close to you through their death).
   The congregation will express their sympathy for the family and close friends of the deceased.
   Black clothes are often worn, though some Christians consider this inappropriate and may even ask guests not to dress in this way.
3) It doesn't matter whether the body's buried or cremated — Christians believe that at the Resurrection they will have new 'spiritual bodies', not their old ones. There's another short service at the graveside or crematorium, then afterwards often a meal for family and friends.

**Roman Catholic Requiem Mass**

A Roman Catholic funeral includes Holy Communion (the 'Requiem Mass').
The purpose of a Requiem Mass is to pray for the soul of the dead person. The priest wears white vestments, and the coffin is covered with a white cloth (a pall). The coffin is sprinkled with holy water and the priest says, *"In the waters of baptism (name) died with Christ, and rose with him to new life. May s/he now share with him in eternal glory."* The coffin is later sprinkled again, and also perfumed with incense.

## *Funeral Customs help* ***Support*** *the* ***Bereaved***

1) Christian funeral services have a great deal to say about the hope of eternal life. The bereaved person is encouraged to believe that one day she or he will be reunited with the deceased.
2) In the days following the funeral, family and friends often try to contact those who were closest to the deceased, and encourage them to talk through their grief.
3) Usually the priest or vicar will also try to visit, and may offer counselling, or suggest someone who can. There are several stages to the process of grief, and it can help to talk to someone who understands this.

### *It's not all bad news...*

Christians try not to see death as depressing — after all, they believe the person who died is going to Heaven (probably). Make sure you've learnt the different funeral customs for Christian funerals.

JUDAISM & ISLAM

# Jewish and Muslim Funeral Rites

Jews and Muslims also have rituals surrounding death.

## *Judaism has Customs to **Comfort** the **Bereaved***

There are many rituals in Judaism concerned with death. They're designed to help bereaved people accept what has happened, give expression to their grief, receive comfort, and come to terms with their loss.

1) Jewish families gather together to be near a loved one who is dying, while the dying person should spend his/her last moments confessing sins and reciting the Shema (see page 81).
2) After the death, each member of an Orthodox family will make a small tear in their clothing — a symbol of grief and shock. This is less common in Reform Judaism.
3) The dead person must not be left alone, and must be buried (not cremated) as soon as possible, preferably within 24 hours. Reform Jews often allow longer, so that the family has more time to organise the funeral.
4) The body is ritually bathed and wrapped in a plain linen shroud, before being placed in a plain, unpolished, wooden coffin — in death rich and poor are equal. This is done by a Chevra Kaddisha (burial society).
5) At the funeral service in the synagogue, psalms are read and a prayer is said praising God for giving life and for taking it away. The rabbi might make a short speech about the deceased.

### ***Mourning** Continues for **Thirty Days** After Death*

1) The first week after the funeral is called shiva (seven). The immediate family stay at home and are visited by relatives and friends who pray with them three times a day and offer comfort. They do not cut their hair, shave, listen to music or have sex. The men recite a prayer called the kaddish. Everyone is encouraged to talk about the person who has died.
2) The first month after the funeral is called sheloshim (thirty). During this time life returns gradually to normal, and male mourners go to the synagogue to recite the kaddish. Anyone who has lost a parent remains in mourning for a whole year.
3) The anniversary of death is called yahrzeit. It is usually on the first yahrzeit that the headstone is erected above the grave. Every year a candle is lit for 24 hours and men say the kaddish.

## *'**Allah**' should be the **Last Word** a Muslim Hears*

A Muslim hopes not to die alone, but with relatives and friends around, who will:

1) Keep them company and look after them.
2) Ensure last-minute business is settled, so the dying one is not distracted by things to do with this life.
3) Pray, and recite *'There is no God but Allah,'* so that the person may be helped to concentrate on God. Ideally, the name of Allah should be the first thing a Muslim hears at birth, and the last thing at death.

### *Bodies are **Buried** Facing **Makkah***

1) After a person has died, the body is washed, as a sign of respect.
2) The body is then wrapped in a clean white shroud.
3) Funeral prayers (Janazah prayers) are said, praying that the dead person may be judged mercifully and gain a place in Paradise.
4) The body is buried in a simple grave, lying on its right side with the face towards Makkah.
5) A period of mourning is kept for three days, finishing with Qur'an reading and prayers for the dead person. Some Muslims do this after 40 days as well.

> It's said that graves are visited by two angels to question the deceased and work out whether they're fit for the next life.

## *Learn the different funeral rites...*

Make sure you know the funeral rites for Jewish and Muslim funerals.

# Warm-Up and Worked Exam Question

## Warm-up Questions

1) Name two symbols that are used to represent: a) Christianity, b) Judaism.
2) What is the minaret of a mosque used for? *(Islam)*
3) In a place of worship, what is:
   a) the nave? *(Christianity)*, b) Aron Kodesh? *(Judaism)*, c) the mihrab? *(Islam)*
4) Explain why some Christians pray to Saints but others don't. *(Christianity)*
5) Where and how often do followers of these religions pray? a) Christianity, b) Judaism, c) Islam.
6) Explain why certain foods are not allowed in Judaism.
7) What is mourning?

## Worked Exam Question

Now it's time to check that you've absorbed the information in this section — and to practise using it to answer exam questions. The first question's been done for you, so you can see the sort of thing you're aiming at.

1 a) What is Shabbat?

*The Jewish day of rest. It commemorates the seventh day of creation when God rested after making the Universe.*

*(2 marks)*

b) Explain how Jews use symbols to reflect their beliefs.

*At the Shabbat meal, plaited loaves called Challot are eaten to commemorate the double portion of manna which God provided the day before each Shabbat during the Exodus. Ceremonies involving blessings and arm gestures are used to symbolically separate Shabbat from the rest of the week.*

*Say what the symbolic object or action is AND what idea it represents.*

*Many Jewish men and boys wear a cap called a kippah as a sign of respect to God. The Tefillin are worn during most morning prayers. They are leather boxes worn on the upper arm and head. These remind Jews to serve God with head and heart.*

*Try to include symbolism from different aspects of Jewish life.*

*The Ner Tamid is a light in the temple that never goes out. It symbolises the menorah which was always kept alight in the Temple in Jerusalem.*

*(6 marks)*

*For questions worth 6 marks and up, you're likely to get more marks for a well-organised, well-written answer.*

# Exam Questions

*Answer these questions for whichever religions you're studying.*

2 a) Name two key features of a church/synagogue/mosque.

*(2 marks)*

b) Describe how religious symbolism is used in architecture.

*(3 marks)*

3 a) What are icons?

*(2 marks)*

b) Explain why some Christian churches are decorated with images.

*(3 marks)*

c) What are the main elements of Christian Sunday worship?

*(3 marks)*

4 a) State two purposes of a funeral service.

*(2 marks)*

b) Choose one religious tradition and explain the most important funeral rituals from that tradition.

*(8 marks)*

5 a) Explain how having a religious faith might influence someone's diet.

*(4 marks)*

b) Explain Christian/Jewish/Muslim beliefs about fasting.

*(6 marks)*

6 a) What is prayer?

*(2 marks)*

b) "Prayer is the most important part of religion."

Give two reasons why a religious believer might agree or disagree with this statement.

*(4 marks)*

# Beliefs and the Creeds

Worship offered to Jesus is what distinguishes Christianity from all other monotheistic (one-god) religions.

## Christians Believe in God as Unity and Trinity

1) Christians believe in one God — God as Unity.
2) They believe that God is omnipotent (all-powerful), omnipresent (everywhere) and omniscient (all-knowing), that God is divine, supreme, totally good and totally perfect, and that God has given us free will.
3) Christians also believe in the Trinity...

## The Trinity is Explained Nicely in the Nicene Creed

1) The Christian idea of the Trinity is perhaps best expressed in the Nicene Creed:

*"We believe in one God, the Father, the almighty, maker of heaven and earth... We believe in one Lord, Jesus Christ, the only son of God... Of one being with the Father... We believe in the Holy Spirit... The giver of life... Who proceeds from the Father and the Son..."*

*A 'creed' is a statement of religious beliefs.*

2) Christians might describe the Father as the creator and judge, the Son (Jesus) as the human incarnation of God (and the Messiah, or saviour), and the Holy Spirit as the presence of God in the world — inspiring, guiding and comforting them. (There's a load more detail about this on the next page.)

## The Apostles' Creed — a Summary of the Christian Faith

The Apostles' Creed summarises the basic Christian teachings about Jesus:

1. **Jesus is the Christ** — 'Christ' isn't a surname — it means the same as 'Messiah', i.e. 'Anointed One of God'.
2. **The Incarnation** — This was the act by which God became a human being. Note that Christians don't believe Jesus was 'half God and half man' — he was fully both.
3. **The Virgin Birth** — The Gospels say that Jesus was born of a virgin — Mary became pregnant through the influence of the Holy Spirit. This is why Christians say "God's Son", or "God the Son".
4. **The Crucifixion** — It was Jesus's death on the cross which won his people forgiveness of sin.
5. **The Resurrection** — Jesus rose from the dead on Easter Day, and is still alive today.
6. **The Ascension** — After the resurrection Jesus 'ascended into Heaven' (not necessarily 'in the sky').

1) The Apostles' Creed also includes important teaching about God the Father and the Holy Spirit.
2) The Holy Spirit is God's influence in the world, and is often pictured as fire, or as a dove, or thought of as a wind.

*After the Ascension, God sent his Spirit down upon Jesus's followers in 'tongues of fire'.*

*At Jesus's baptism the Spirit descended on him in the form of a dove.*

For Christians, the statements in the creeds are matters of faith — firmly-held beliefs, without (and without need for) logical proof.

### The nature of God — I thought I'd keep it nice and simple...

There's a lot of big ideas on this page, and it's really important that you get your head round them. Christians believe in one God who exists as three persons — the Father, the Son (Jesus) and the Holy Spirit. They believe that Jesus was fully God and fully human, that he died, was resurrected and still lives in heaven.

# The Trinity

So, back to this Trinity business. It's really important to Christians, so you'd best know a bit more about it.

## Christians Believe in the **Father**...

"In the beginning God created the heavens and the earth." **Genesis 1:1**

1) For many Christians, God the Father is the God of the Old Testament.
2) The title 'Father' is a mark of respect for God, and is used by Jesus in the Gospels: *"...when you pray... pray to your Father, who is unseen. Then your Father, who sees what is done in secret, will reward you."* (**Matthew 6:6**).
3) In **Genesis 1**, the Bible describes God as the Creator of Heaven and Earth, who created the world in six days. Some Christians believe this account literally, while others think that it should be understood symbolically.
4) To most Christians, belief in God as the Creator is important as it means that the world itself must be a good thing since he chose to create it, and that life is God's gift to us. Some Christians take their belief in the Creator to mean that we have a responsibility to look after the environment, as it was made for us (see p.57).
5) Many Christian traditions teach that God the Father will be our Judge after death. Since Christians believe God is all-knowing, everything they say, do or think is important as it will be judged by God.

## ...the **Son**...

1) Christians believe that Jesus is the incarnation of God in human form, and that God sending Jesus down to us shows how much he loves the world.
2) They believe Jesus is the Christ or Messiah ('anointed one') prophesied by Isaiah in the Old Testament.
3) Christians believe that Jesus provides a model for Christian behaviour in obedience to God the Father. The Gospels contain a record of his life and teachings, and are an important source of guidance for Christians on how they should live their lives.
4) Jesus is sometimes described as the 'lamb of God'. This is a reference to the lambs offered as sacrifices to God in the Jewish Temple. Christ is seen as a sacrifice on behalf of all humanity.

*Jesus Offers Christians Salvation from Sin*
Christians believe that through his suffering and death, Jesus won forgiveness for the sins of all people. They believe that Jesus was perfect (without sin), but that God placed all the sins of the world on him at his crucifixion: *"...the LORD has laid on him the iniquity of us all."* (**Isaiah 53:6**). Christianity teaches that his sacrifice paid for our sins, so long as we have faith in him (more about this on page 116). Christians believe that Christ's victory over the power of sin and death was revealed in his resurrection.

*As Jesus suffered, many Christians believe they have a duty to help those who are suffering.*

## ...and the **Holy Spirit**

1) Christians believe that the Holy Spirit is the presence of God in the world, who descended on Christ's disciples after his Ascension and continues to guide the actions of the Church.
2) Some Christians feel that the Holy Spirit also guides them personally in being good Christians.
3) Charismatic Christians believe that the Holy Spirit can descend on them during worship, just as with Christ's disciples. For example they might begin to 'speak in tongues' (unknown languages) or shake uncontrollably.
4) Different beliefs about the Holy Spirit are what initially separated the Orthodox and the Roman Catholic Churches during the Great Schism. Catholics (and from them Protestants) believe that the Holy Spirit descended from God the Father and God the Son, whereas the Orthodox Christians believe that the Holy Spirit is the product of the God the Father alone.
5) For Roman Catholics the most important action of the Holy Spirit is in guiding the Church. They believe that the Holy Spirit is how God continues to influence history through the Church.

Roman Catholic beliefs about the Trinity are detailed in the catechism — a series of statements laying down the official teachings of the Church.

## *Three into one doesn't go in maths — but this is RS...*

Remember, Christians don't believe in three Gods — they're just different forms of the same God.

# Christian Traditions and the Virgin Mary

There are significant variations among Christians' beliefs, but they share some kind of 'relationship with Christ'.

## Three Main Traditions — Roman Catholic, Orthodox and Protestant

There have been a couple of major splits in the history of the Christian Church.

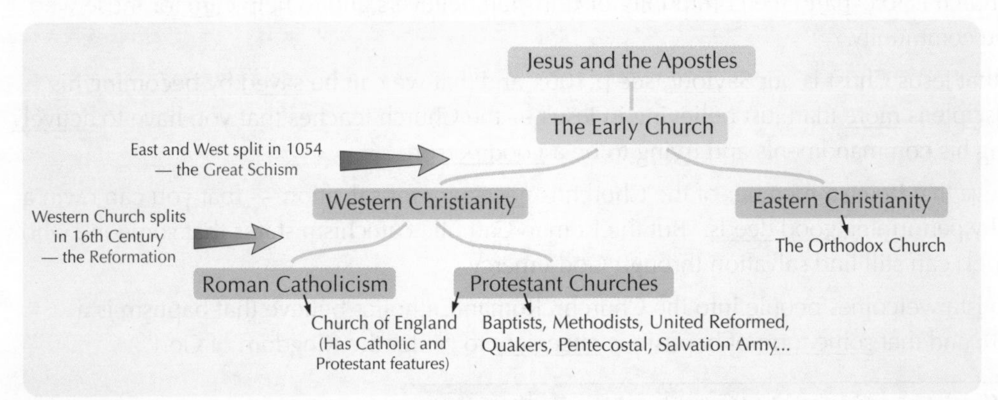


*In the Great Schism, the Pope and the Orthodox Patriarch excommunicated each other from their churches.*

*The Reformation began when Martin Luther challenged the authority of the Pope.*

**Roman Catholics**

1) Roman Catholics are all those Christians who accept the authority of the Pope. They are the largest Christian group in the world.
2) They believe in the seven sacraments as 'vehicles of God's grace' (see page 113).
3) They respect the authority of the Bible, Church tradition and the Magisterium (p.109).

**Protestants**

1) Protestants base their beliefs and practices on the ideas of the Reformation.
2) The Reformers stressed the importance of the Bible rather than Church tradition or the teachings of the Pope.
3) Members of the Protestant clergy are usually referred to as ministers.
4) The different groupings within Protestantism are known as denominations. In England and Wales, Protestant denominations that are not part of the 'Anglican Communion' are often called 'Nonconformists'. These include Methodists, Baptists, Pentecostals, The Society of Friends (Quakers) and the Salvation Army.

*The Church of England has both Roman Catholic and Protestant features. Anglicanism is the worldwide 'communion' of churches in fellowship with the parent Church of England.*

**Orthodox Christians**

1) Orthodox Christians are found mainly in Eastern Europe, Russia and Greece.
2) They believe that their clergy are in direct succession from the Apostles (see p.109).
3) They also have seven sacraments, and honour (but don't worship) icons — pictures of saints.

## The Virgin Mary is Very Important to Roman Catholics

1) Mary is very important to Christians because she gave birth to Jesus.
2) She is also seen as the model for Christian living, because she cooperated fully with God's will.
3) Roman Catholicism teaches that she was born without original sin, meaning she had none of the flaws that all other humans have — this is known as the Immaculate Conception.
4) Roman Catholics also believe she remained a virgin all her life, and after she died she was taken up to Heaven in the Assumption. They don't believe that Mary died a normal death — instead she's believed to have been taken directly up to Heaven.
5) Catholics don't worship Mary, but they do pray to her and ask her to pray for them (for example in the '*Ave Maria/Hail Mary*'). She is also known as 'Mother of God'.
6) Protestants generally believe that Mary is worthy of great respect. But they don't believe in praying to her, as they see this as a form of idolatry — i.e. worshipping something other than God.

## Christians are grouped into different traditions...

There are at least 20,800 denominations worldwide, so don't think that the above list is all there is to know. But at the same time, don't feel as though you need to know everything about all 20,800 — that would be a pretty tough assignment. Though not for God, obviously, because he's omniscient.

# The Role of the Church

The 'Church' traces its roots back to its founder, Jesus Christ. It's basically a community of believers. Those who profess faith in Jesus as God's promised Messiah become part of that community.

## The Church — More than a Building

1) The mission of the Church is to expand the community of Christian believers and to help care for those who are already part of the community.
2) The Church teaches that Jesus Christ is our Saviour (see p.106), and that we can be saved by becoming his disciples. Being a disciple is more than just believing in Jesus — the Church teaches that you have to actively follow him by keeping his commandments and trying to be a good person.
3) Many Christians believe that being a member of the Church is necessary for salvation — that you can't win a place in heaven just by performing good deeds. But the Roman Catholic catechism states that someone who's never heard the Gospels can still find salvation through God's mercy.
4) The ceremony of baptism welcomes people into the Church. Roman Catholics believe that baptism is a sacrament (see p.113), and that some form of baptism is necessary to "enter the Kingdom of God".

## *Saint Paul* Called the Church the *Body of Christ*

1) St Paul taught that the community of believers was the "Body of Christ" on Earth, with Christ as its head.
2) Christians who have died remain part of the faith community. The Church, made up of all Christians living or dead, is referred to as the Communion of Saints.
3) Christians believe the Church is 'holy' — sacred or belonging to God.
4) Despite its fragmentation into various traditions and denominations, the Church claims a spiritual unity. The word 'catholic' (small 'c'), meaning universal, is used to describe the community of all Christian believers.

## The Church has Various **Functions** in the **Community**

Most communities in the UK have access to at least one church. The role and function of local church communities is to put the Christian faith into action. They do this in the following ways:

i) By providing a regular pattern of worship — most churches hold a Sunday service every week, and may also have other acts of communal worship throughout the week.
ii) By providing 'rites of passage' — e.g. baptisms, confirmations, weddings, funerals...
iii) By teaching Christian beliefs as part of regular services, Sunday schools or Bible classes.
iv) By ministering to the sick, e.g. visiting and praying for parishioners in hospital.
v) By supporting groups that campaign for justice and peace.

## The Roman Catholic Church has a **Powerful Influence**

*The Pope has a massive influence over Roman Catholics — e.g. over the issues of abortion and contraception.*

Mimmo Chianura/Rex Features

1) The teachings of the Roman Catholic Church on moral issues (such as abortion, sexuality and social responsibility) continue to have a strong influence on its followers.
2) Church leaders are held in respect, and their pronouncements are adhered to by faithful followers.
3) The Church also offers guidance to those who believe they may be called by God into a specific vocation e.g. the ordained ministry.
4) The Church also influences social and political development all around the world, through its involvement in peace and justice movements.

## Churches — 'big-C ' are communities, 'little-c' are buildings...

Yep — so don't go assuming that when the exam asks a question about the Church, it's talking about that building down the road that rings its bells once a week. There's a wee bit more to it than that.

# The Authority of the Church

For Roman Catholics, the only authority higher than the Church is God.

## For **Roman Catholics**, the Church is the **Supreme Authority**

Roman Catholics consider the authority of the Church to be absolute on matters of faith.
This position of power is based on three main beliefs.

### The *Apostolic Tradition*

*'Apostolic' just means 'of, or relating to the Apostles'.*
*For Roman Catholics, the Church's link to the Apostles is very important.*

1) The Apostolic Tradition is a body of teachings and ritual practices, which the Roman Catholic Church believe was handed down through the early Church from the Apostles.
2) The Gospel authors themselves explain that they do not provide a complete record of Jesus's life and teaching: *"Jesus did many other things as well. If every one of them were written down, I suppose that even the whole world would not have room for the books that would be written."* (**John 21:25**).
3) Catholics believe this means that the traditions of the Church have as important a role to play in true Christian faith as the Bible — this means that not everything that Catholics believe will necessarily be taken from the Bible. In contrast, most Protestant denominations try to base everything on scripture.

### The *Apostolic Succession*

1) The Apostolic Succession is what Catholics believe makes a Church. It's the fact that new bishops were ordained by bishops who were ordained by bishops, going back in direct succession to the original Apostles as chosen by Christ.
2) This fact is so important that the Catholic Church does not recognise Protestant Churches as true Churches because of their break with this succession.
3) The Pope is believed to be a direct successor of St Peter — 'the first Pope'. Catholics view the Pope as the most important figure in the Church because Christ singled out St Peter: *"And I tell you that you are Peter, and on this rock I will build my church, and the gates of Hades will not overcome it."* (**Matthew 16:18**)

*Churches that believe they were originally founded by the Apostles describe themselves as apostolic.*

### The *Magisterium*

1) The Magisterium is the authority of the Pope and his bishops to teach correctly in all matters of faith and morals. Roman Catholics believe this authority is given by the Holy Spirit. The Church has the final say in the interpretation of scripture and tradition.
2) When the Pope and the bishops agree on a point of doctrine it becomes part of official Church teaching — and Catholics are then supposed not only to follow the teaching, but also to believe in it fully.
3) The Pope can make official statements on his own on questions of faith and morals, and these are believed to be infallible (they can't be wrong). But this doesn't happen very often — the last time was in 1950.
4) The firm beliefs of the Catholic Church are known as dogmas. Most of them are set out in the Roman Catholic catechism (see p.106).

## **Protestant Churches** have less **Authority**

1) Different Protestant Churches hold different views on the importance of Church hierarchy.
2) For example, Congregationalists believe each individual church is responsible for its own organisation. But Presbyterians send elders from each church to form councils which have authority over the churches.
3) Protestants tend to place far greater emphasis on a believer's own faith and understanding of the Bible according to their own conscience — and far less on the authority and teachings of the Church. This is one of the reasons why there are so many different Protestant denominations, as people often left old Churches and set up new ones, because they disagreed on an aspect of Church teaching.

### *This page is supremely authoritative...*

Arguments about the importance and authority of the Church played a key part in the Reformation — when the Protestants split from the Roman Catholic Church. So Protestants will have very different views on this stuff from Catholics. Make sure you know both sides, so you can answer a question about it in the exam.

# The Role of the Clergy

This is a page full of bishops and priests and stuff.

## *The **Roman Catholic** Church has a **Hierarchy**...*

The Roman Catholic Church is arranged in a hierarchy, with the Pope at the top.

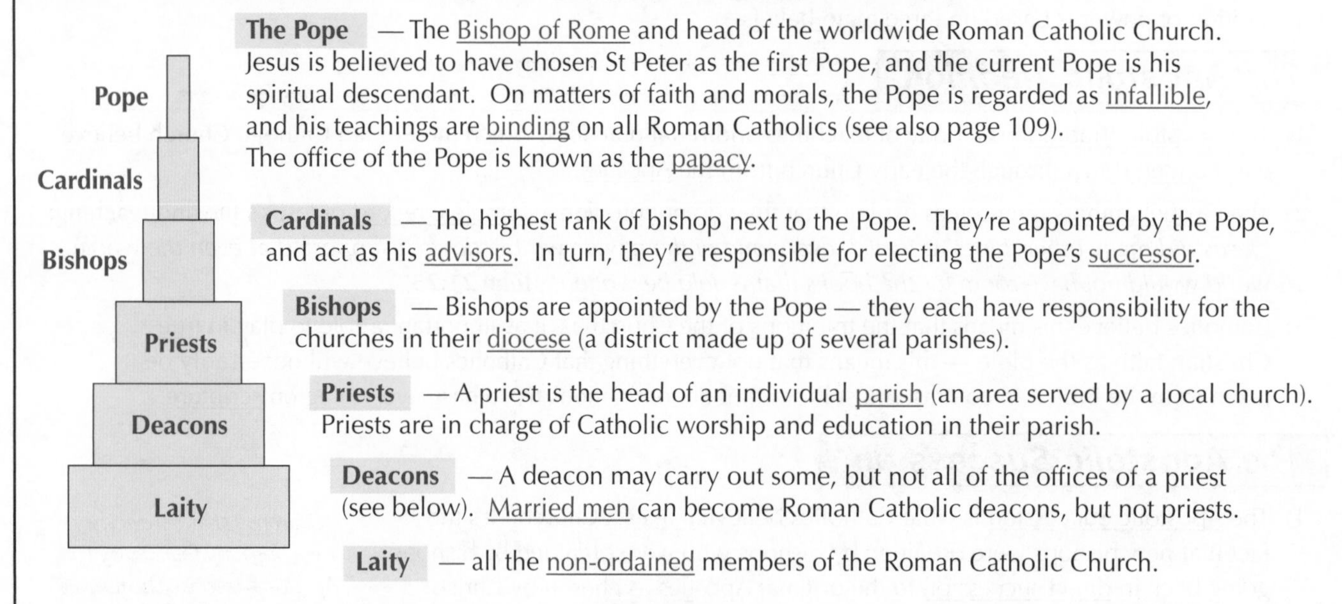


**The Pope** — The Bishop of Rome and head of the worldwide Roman Catholic Church. Jesus is believed to have chosen St Peter as the first Pope, and the current Pope is his spiritual descendant. On matters of faith and morals, the Pope is regarded as infallible, and his teachings are binding on all Roman Catholics (see also page 109). The office of the Pope is known as the papacy.

**Cardinals** — The highest rank of bishop next to the Pope. They're appointed by the Pope, and act as his advisors. In turn, they're responsible for electing the Pope's successor.

**Bishops** — Bishops are appointed by the Pope — they each have responsibility for the churches in their diocese (a district made up of several parishes).

**Priests** — A priest is the head of an individual parish (an area served by a local church). Priests are in charge of Catholic worship and education in their parish.

**Deacons** — A deacon may carry out some, but not all of the offices of a priest (see below). Married men can become Roman Catholic deacons, but not priests.

**Laity** — all the non-ordained members of the Roman Catholic Church.

1) The office of deacon (and those above it in the hierarchy) can be held by men (and only men) who have been ordained, i.e. officially admitted into the clergy.
2) The rite of ordination is one of the sacraments (see p.113), and it can only be performed by a bishop.
3) A Roman Catholic priest has a number of roles within the parish.
4) His main roles are to lead the celebration of the Mass (only a priest or bishop can perform the Liturgy of the Eucharist, see p.114) and to hear confession (see p.113).
5) It's also his job to preach the Gospel, administer the sacraments of baptism, marriage and anointing the sick (see p.113) and to offer support and guidance to the people of the parish.
6) A Roman Catholic deacon will often assist the priest of a large parish. Deacons may carry out any of the duties of a priest, apart from celebrating Mass, hearing confession or anointing the sick.

## ***Roman Catholic** Priests must be **Celibate***

1) In the Catholic Church, to become a priest a man has to be unmarried and stay celibate (not have sex). Catholics believe that this allows priests to focus fully on their spiritual duties.
2) They base this on the teachings of Paul that *"It is good for a man not to marry"* (**1 Corinthians 7:1**) and Jesus's remark that some *"have renounced marriage because of the kingdom of heaven"* (**Matthew 19:12**).
3) In recent years there has been a fall in the number of men wanting to become priests. Some Catholics blame this on the celibacy rule.
4) Protestants argue that celibacy is not stated as a qualification for priesthood in the Bible. Some have argued that celibacy is too difficult for many and so becomes a distraction rather than an aid to spiritual life.
5) Anglican priests and Protestant ministers are allowed to marry either before or after they're ordained. Some denominations encourage ministers to marry, to set a good example for the congregation.
6) In the Orthodox tradition, married men can be ordained as priests (but not bishops) — but they can't get married once they've been ordained.

### *It'd be a cardinal sin not to learn this page...*

I bet you thought vicars would get a mention. Well, here you are. 'Vicar' is a general title that's come to be used to refer to any parish priest. 'Minister' is also a general title — used to describe anyone who's been ordained. And the clergy consists of anyone who's been ordained. Lots of words for the same kind of thing.

# Warm-Up and Worked Exam Question

## Warm-up Questions

1) What are the six beliefs stated in the Apostles' Creed?
2) What was the Great Schism?
3) State two beliefs that set Roman Catholics apart from Protestants.
4) What is meant by the Immaculate Conception?
5) What are a) Cardinals, b) Deacons?
6) Explain why Roman Catholics don't believe that the Bible is the only source of religious authority.

## Worked Exam Question

Read through this worked example carefully, then have a go at the practice exam questions on the next page. You really do need to know the picky little details to do well on Roman Catholic Christianity exam questions — there are hardly any marks to be picked up by waffling (no matter how good you are at waffling).

1 a) Describe Roman Catholic teachings about the Magisterium.

*The Magisterium is the authority of the Pope and his bishops to teach correctly in all matters of faith and morals. Roman Catholics believe this authority is given by the Holy Spirit. When the Pope and his bishops make an official statement on a point of doctrine it becomes part of Church teaching.*

*(3 marks)*

*Use the special terms, e.g. doctrine, wherever possible.*

b) Explain the significance of "Apostolic Succession" to a Roman Catholic.

*Roman Catholics believe that the authority of the Pope and his bishops is due to Apostolic Succession. The bishops are direct successors of the original apostles, whose authority was given to them by Christ. The Pope is the direct successor of St Peter, who was given authority over the other apostles by Jesus.*

*(3 marks)*

*These are 'Explain' questions — so you need to do more than just define the terms.*

c) Explain what Roman Catholics believe about the Holy Spirit.

*Roman Catholics believe that the Holy Spirit is the presence of God in the world, and that the Holy Spirit descended from God the Father and God the Son. They believe the Holy Spirit continues to guide the actions of the Church. Some Roman Catholics feel that the Holy Spirit also guides them personally in being good Christians.*

*Remember — there are beliefs that only some followers of a religion hold.*

*(3 marks)*

# Exam Questions

2 a) Explain what Christians mean when they refer to Jesus as "the lamb of God".

*(2 marks)*

b) Explain Christian teachings about salvation.

*(3 marks)*

3 a) Explain what Christians mean by 'the ascension'.

*(2 marks)*

b) Explain Roman Catholic teachings about the Trinity.

*(6 marks)*

4 a) What is meant by the laity?

*(1 mark)*

b) State two roles of a Roman Catholic priest.

*(2 marks)*

c) "Priests should remain celibate."
Refer to Roman Catholic Christianity in your answer.
i) Do you agree? Give reasons for your opinion.

*(3 marks)*

ii)Give reasons why some people may disagree with you.

*(3 marks)*

5 a) Why is the Virgin Mary important to Roman Catholics?

*(3 marks)*

b) Describe Roman Catholic teachings about the Church.

*(6 marks)*

# The Seven Sacraments

Roman Catholic and Orthodox Churches believe in seven sacraments.

## The **Seven Sacraments** — Vehicles of God's Grace

God is thought to communicate his grace (unearned favour) directly through sacraments, whether or not the recipient understands what it all means. The sacraments are:

1. **Baptism** Baptism marks a person's official entry into the Church. It symbolises the start of a new life and the washing away of sin. Those who regard baptism as a sacrament see no problem with baptising infants. They believe that this cleanses the baby from original sin (see p.4).
2. **Confirmation** In this ceremony a Christian renews the vows made on his or her behalf at baptism.
3. **Reconciliation** This involves confession of a sin, followed by contrition, penance and absolution.
4. **Eucharist** In Holy Communion (see p.114), the believer receives Christ into him- or herself afresh.
5. **Ordination** This is the rite in which people are made deacons, priests or bishops (see p.110).
6. **Marriage** When a couple are joined in Holy Matrimony they receive a special blessing.
7. **Anointing the Sick** This may be for healing, or to prepare a dying person for the next life.

## **Confirmation** helps Strengthen a Person's **Faith**

1) Most Churches have a Confirmation rite. For Roman Catholics, it is considered a sacrament. It is believed to strengthen the ties of the confirmed to the Church and to God.
2) In Catholic Confirmations, the bishop anoints the believer's forehead with holy oil called chrism. This oil has been consecrated (made holy) with a blessing from a bishop.
3) Catholics get confirmed around the age of 13 or 14, when they're old enough to understand what it means. They have to show that they understand their faith — usually by attending a course of religious instruction.

## **Reconciliation** makes up for **Sin**

1) Reconciliation through confession is how Roman Catholics obtain forgiveness for the sins they commit.
2) Confession is where a believer admits to a priest any sinful things that they've done. To prepare for this, a believer must think seriously about the sins they've committed.
3) The priest will give a penance (a certain number of prayers to be said, or an action to be done) and will then pronounce absolution (God's forgiveness). For confession to be effective the believer needs to be genuinely sorry and make a commitment not to sin again — this is known as contrition.
4) Confession and reconciliation are important. All Catholics are supposed to confess at least once a year, but are recommended to do it more regularly. If a Catholic commits a serious (mortal) sin they should confess as soon as possible — Catholics believe that if they die unreconciled, they will go to Hell.

## Catholics Believe in **Anointing the Sick**

1) Catholics believe in anointing the sick — this is where a priest or a bishop anoints a seriously unwell person with the oil of the sick (oil, usually scented with balsam, that has been blessed by a bishop).
2) If someone is facing death it will be administered as part of the Last Rites, along with a final confession and a final Eucharist (known as the viaticum).
3) Catholics believe that, through this sacrament, the Holy Spirit renews the sick person's faith and strength to cope with their illness and accept their suffering. The anointing is also believed to link the person's suffering to the suffering of Christ, allow their sins to be forgiven and to heal them, if that is God's will.

### *Big Cats Rarely Eat 'Orrible Maggoty Apples...*

Try this way of remembering the initial letters of the seven sacraments. It's a good 'un.

# Mass

The Mass is the Roman Catholic service that includes the Eucharist (Holy Communion).

## Holy Communion Commemorates the Last Supper

1) At the Last Supper, Jesus said that the bread and wine on the table represented his body and blood. The disciples were to eat and drink in remembrance of him whenever they ate together.
2) Virtually all Christians recognise the importance of Holy Communion (also called the Eucharist), but most see it as largely commemorative — it reminds worshippers of the Last Supper and Jesus's sacrifice.
3) However, Roman Catholics believe that the bread and wine actually become the body and blood of Christ, by the power of the Holy Spirit. This is known as transubstantiation, and it is through this that Jesus takes up residence in his people. This is why it's vital for Roman Catholics to attend Mass regularly.

## There are Four Key Features of a Catholic Mass:

### Penitential Rite

This is a joint confession of sin and a request for God's mercy and forgiveness in the form of a prayer said by the whole congregation. It's followed by the reciting of the 'Kyrie' prayer, either in Greek or in English. *"Kyrie, eleison (Lord have mercy) Christe, eleison (Christ have mercy) Kyrie, eleison (Lord have mercy)".*

### Liturgy of the Word

A 'liturgy' is a well-defined pattern of rituals, set prayers and readings.

The penitential rite is followed by the liturgy of the word. This consists of readings from scripture, usually including a section from one of the Gospels, followed by a homily (a short sermon based on the readings). This is followed by a joint recitation of either the Nicene Creed or the Apostles' Creed (see p.105).

### Liturgy of the Eucharist

The liturgy of the Eucharist is the most important part of the Roman Catholic Mass — it is the point at which Catholics believe that the bread and wine are transformed into the body and blood of Christ. The bread and wine are usually brought in by a procession, and transubstantiated during a series of prayers including the Institution Narrative, which describes Christ's words and actions during the Last Supper.

### Rite of Communion

This begins with everyone saying the Lord's Prayer, followed by the sign of peace, where everyone shakes hands or hugs those around them. Following this, the congregation come forward to receive the bread and wine. Finally there is the concluding rite, which is a series of prayers that brings the Mass to a close. Any leftover consecrated bread and wine must be consumed by a priest, or placed in a ciborium (a lidded chalice) inside a 'safe' called a tabernacle.

## Non-Catholics also have a Eucharist

There are a wide variety of beliefs about the importance of the Eucharist, and what actually occurs during the service, for different denominations.

1) Lutherans, Methodists and most Anglicans believe that Holy Communion is more than just an 'intellectual' commemoration of the Last Supper, it's a re-enactment. They believe that there is a 'real presence' of Christ in the bread and wine. But they don't believe that transubstantiation occurs.
2) Reformed (Calvinist) Churches believe that the bread and wine are symbolic of a spiritual reality and are physically unchanged, but that the performance of the Eucharist does achieve 'spiritual nourishment'.
3) Quakers and the Salvation Army don't celebrate the Eucharist or any other sacraments, seeing them as unnecessary or inessential symbols for the inward acceptance of God's grace.

## *Mass — it's a weighty subject...*

While there are a variety of opinions as to what happens to the bread and wine during the service, Holy Communion is one of the few rites that nearly all Christian Churches have in common.

# Festivals and Church Worship

According to the Bible, no time of year is any more sacred than any other. However, certain times of year are used by Christians to commemorate, give thanks for and celebrate specific aspects of their faith.

## Christian Festivals Occur **Throughout the Year**

### ADVENT and CHRISTMAS — December

Advent marks the start of the Christian year, and begins 4 Sundays before Christmas.
It's a period of preparation for Christmas and for Christ's Second Coming. Advent candles are lit in homes and churches, and children may use Advent calendars to count off the days until Christmas. Christmas celebrates the Incarnation — when God's Son came to Earth as a human being. We don't know the exact date of his birth, but we celebrate it on December 25th.

Customs vary around the world, but often date from pre-Christian times (e.g. Christmas trees). In many Roman Catholic churches there's a 'Midnight Mass' to welcome Christmas Day, and a crib (nativity scene).
But some Christians think that the giving of expensive presents takes away the focus of what Christmas is supposed to be about. And others feel that it has retained too much pagan influence.

### LENT — February / March

Lent commemorates the 40 days and nights of Jesus's fasting (going without food) in the wilderness after his baptism. On the day before Lent (Shrove Tuesday), Roman Catholics confess their sins and are 'shriven' (absolved from sin). Rich foods should be eaten up before the start of the fast and Mardi Gras carnivals may be held.

On Ash Wednesday (the first day of Lent) ash is put on believers' foreheads to show that they are sorry for their sins. Lent ends on the day before Easter.
For Roman Catholics, Lent is traditionally a sombre time where the focus of worship is on the suffering of Jesus. Catholics are obliged to abstain from meat on each Friday of Lent, and to fast (limit themselves to one main meal and two small meals a day) for a minimum of two days — Ash Wednesday and Good Friday (see below).

### HOLY WEEK — March / April

This is the final week of Lent, lasting from Palm Sunday (the Sunday before Easter, recalling Jesus's triumphal entry into Jerusalem) until the day before Easter. It commemorates Jesus's final week on Earth.
Maundy Thursday recalls the Last Supper, and Good Friday Jesus's crucifixion. There are special services, especially on Good Friday between noon and 3pm — the hours when Jesus was dying on the cross.

### EASTER SUNDAY — March / April

This commemorates Jesus's resurrection. Special services are held — Roman Catholics hold an Easter Vigil the night before. Easter is the most important festival of the year for most Christians, since it celebrates the victory of Jesus over death. It starts a fifty day period of focusing on the actions of the risen Christ.
But some Christians dislike the modern use of symbols (e.g. eggs and Easter bunnies) that are believed to be associated with pre-Christian festivals.

## The **Altar** is the **Focus** of a **Roman Catholic Church**

1) The main features of a Roman Catholic Church are on page 92 — go and have a look.
2) In Roman Catholic churches, the focal point of the building is the altar. This reflects the 'liturgical' nature of their services and the importance of the Eucharist (see p.114).
3) In Roman Catholic churches, you'll also tend to find statues, e.g. of the Virgin Mary and painted or sculpted scenes called the 'Stations of the Cross'. These fourteen scenes depict the last hours before the death of Jesus, and are used to help Catholics pray and meditate on the sufferings of Christ — usually during Lent.

### *Holy Days (or holidays) — celebrations of religion...*

There's huge variety in the way festivals are celebrated, and many customs are cultural rather than Christian (e.g. Easter bunnies). Make sure you learn what the festivals celebrate and why, not how things are done.

# Love and the Christian Faith

Love is central to the Christian faith.

## God showed his Love by Sending Jesus

One of the most frequently quoted verses from the Bible is:

> *"For God so loved the world that he gave his one and only Son, that whoever believes in him shall not perish but have eternal life."* **John 3:16**

1) Christians believe that God expressed his love for us by sending us his son — who, although he was perfect, was punished so that our sins could be forgiven (see p.106).
2) This reconciliation between God and humanity is known as the atonement.
3) Christians believe that we must trust and love God and accept Christ as our saviour.
4) Then if we repent of our sins (are sorry, seek forgiveness and try hard not to repeat them) we will be forgiven. And doing so will lead to our salvation — we will be accepted into eternal life.

## Jesus Taught Us Not Just to Respect — but to Love

1) For Jesus, respect wasn't enough — he wanted his followers to love.
2) When asked which was the most important commandment in Judaism (i.e. all the laws given to the Jews in the first five books of the Bible), he gave this answer...

> *"'The most important one,' answered Jesus, 'is this... Love the Lord your God with all your heart and with all your soul and with all your mind and with all your strength. The second is this: Love your neighbour as yourself.'"* **Mark 12:29-31**

## Love is a Key Concept in Christianity

1) Love is what the Christian faith is all about, but this isn't always as simple as it might seem. Christians have developed the concept of *agape* — a selfless love, unconditional, always serving and always caring.
2) In **Matthew 25:31-46**, Jesus talks of separating out those who will be saved from those who won't (p.53). He explains that salvation will come to those who demonstrate love by helping people in need.
3) In another example, a man asks Jesus who his 'neighbour' is, since he's commanded to 'love his neighbour'. Jesus replies with the parable of the Good Samaritan (**Luke 10:25-37**) — see p.37.
4) This parable argues that compassion — the feeling of pity for and the desire to help those who suffer — is more important to God than being high up in the religious hierarchy.

## Local Churches Show Love of God and Others

1) Most local churches try to take an active role in the community.
2) A church's main function is to help its congregation express their love of God through regular religious services for people in their local area (parishioners).
3) Some local churches demonstrate their love for others by getting involved in campaigns on social issues, e.g. by raising money to help the poor and underprivileged, or encouraging people to buy Fair Trade products.
4) Many churches have youth groups and Sunday Schools to encourage young people to get involved in the Church and its activities.

### All you need is love...

Churches get involved in all sorts of activities: choirs, coffee mornings, Bible study groups, fund-raising... all to express love of God and other people. Who'd have thought a jumble sale could be an expression of love.

# The Sermon on the Mount

The Sermon on the Mount is a summary of Jesus's teachings on how Christians are supposed to live.

## *The **Sermon on the Mount** — the Christian Ideal*

The Sermon on the Mount is one of the most important summaries of Jesus's moral teaching found in the Gospels. It appears as a collection in **Matthew 5:1-7:29**, but much of the same material is also in Luke.
Some say that the Sermon on the Mount preaches an ideal, which no one can live up to. But others argue that Christians can still aspire to this ideal, though no one can be totally perfect (this side of the grave, anyway).

### *Jesus Reinterprets the Law of Moses **(Matthew 5:17-48)***

1) In the Sermon, Jesus reinterprets the Law of Moses — the rules given by God in the Old Testament.
2) Jesus takes these laws and makes them more strict and more internal. Where the Law of Moses calls for people not to kill, Jesus orders us to go further and not be angry with each other. Where the Law of Moses orders us not to commit adultery, Jesus warns that looking upon someone lustfully is sinful in itself. Jesus takes commandments about actions and makes them about intentions and emotions.
3) Jesus speaks about anger, adultery, divorce, vows, revenge and love for our enemies: *"If someone strikes you on the right cheek, turn to him the other also."*

### *Displaying Religion **(Matthew 6:1-18)***

It's in this part of the Gospel that Jesus teaches his followers the Lord's Prayer — "Our Father in heaven, hallowed be your name..."

1) Jesus orders his followers to do their praying, giving to charity, and fasting quietly and without trying to impress other people.
2) Jesus says that those who do good things in secret will be rewarded by God. But that those who deliberately do good work in front of a crowd, known as 'displaying religion', have already had their reward in the effect it has on their audience.
3) Jesus calls those who display religion hypocrites — people who act out beliefs they don't really hold, or whose actions don't match what they say.
4) Most modern Christians take this to mean that, while prayers, charity and fasting don't need to be done in private, they should be done for God alone, with no thought of trying to impress others.

### *Christians and Money **(Matthew 6:19-34)***

1) Jesus orders his followers not to seek material riches (*"treasures on earth"*), or even material security, but rather spiritual riches (*"treasures in heaven"*). He says *"You cannot serve both God and Money."*
2) He tells his followers that it's wrong to even worry about material things : *"Look at the birds of the air; they do not sow or reap or store away in barns, and yet your heavenly Father feeds them. Are you not much more valuable than they? Who of you by worrying can add a single hour to his life?"*
3) Most Christians don't take these verses to mean that we shouldn't save money, but rather that our main concern should be with spiritual things and helping other people.

### *Christians and Judgement and The Golden Rule **(Matthew 7:1-12)***

1) Jesus warns his followers *"Do not judge, or you too will be judged."* He uses the image of someone trying to remove a speck of sawdust from another man's eye when they have a plank in their own.
2) Most Christians interpret this as meaning they should strictly judge their own moral state before looking at other people's, and that they must be charitable and forgiving of other people's failings.
3) Jesus then states what's known as the Golden Rule:

> *"do to others what you would have them do to you, for this sums up the Law and the Prophets."*

Many Christians use the Golden Rule as a moral rule of thumb (see p.53).

## *Don't pass judgement on others — that's the examiner's job...*

The Bible's a long book (you've probably noticed) — but Matthew 5, 6 and 7 give you the gist of Jesus's teachings.

# Christian Values and Vocation

Jesus was a Jew, so his values were grounded in Jewish belief — the laws found in the Old Testament.

## The *Ten Commandments* were Given to *Moses*

The most famous laws in the Old Testament are the Ten Commandments given to Moses in **Exodus 20**.
There's a full list of the Commandments on page 49.
Most Christians believe that it's necessary to try to stick to the Ten Commandments.
The Roman Catholic Church teaches that observance of them is necessary for salvation.

## The Commandments are about *Respecting God*...

The first three commandments are about showing respect to God.

1) The first calls for monotheism. Worshippers of God mustn't worship anything else — including idols.
2) The second commandment demands respect for the name of the Lord. Not only does this ban using "God" or "Jesus" as swear words, but also using God's name to back up a lie or in a dishonest manner.
3) Different Christian groups place greater or less emphasis on the third commandment of observing the Sabbath. This is God's instruction to take one day out of the week and keep it holy. Traditionally, the Sabbath was a day dedicated to God and family on which no work was allowed to be done.
4) For most Christians, including Roman Catholics, the Sabbath day is Sunday. Sunday is the Lord's Day, since this was the day of Christ's resurrection.
5) In the UK, laws against working on a Sunday have gradually been relaxed as society has become less religious. An organisation called Keep Sunday Special campaigns for stricter rules on Sunday trading — both to help religious people keep the Sabbath, and to secure a day that families can spend together.

## ...and *Other People*

The last seven commandments are about showing respect for other people.

1) Some Christians believe that the fourth commandment, which calls for the honouring of your father and mother, includes respect not only for extended family members but also for those placed in positions of responsibility and authority, such as teachers.
2) The fifth commandment, not to kill, is interpreted in different ways. The Roman Catholic Church is willing to make exceptions for killing in war — but some groups, like the Religious Society of Friends (Quakers), are pacifists and are against fighting and killing under any circumstances.
3) Many modern Bibles translate the commandment as *"You shall not murder"*, which allows for killing in war and capital punishment. They argue this is more in keeping with the rest of the Old Testament.
4) Roman Catholics take the commandment not to kill to include a ban on abortion.
5) The sixth, seventh and eighth commandments ban adultery (cheating on your partner), theft and lying.
6) The last two are perhaps the subtlest of the commandments. You don't have to actually do anything to break them — you break them just by lusting after a married woman (or man), or yearning for something that belongs to someone else. These commandments are closely linked to the sin of envy.

## You can *Respond to God* Through a *Vocation*

1) Some people feel that they've experienced a call from God to lead a Christian life. This 'calling' is known as a vocation (see p.83).
2) It can be a job, but isn't always.
3) For example, some people feel called to serve the Church by taking holy orders (being ordained) as a deacon, priest or bishop. Others are drawn to full-time worship of God as part of a religious order (see next page). Most Christians with a vocation believe that God has created them with the right talents for it.

### *Number 11 — You shall learn this page...*

It's always a good idea to know the rules — that way you won't break them accidentally. But if in doubt, 'respect' is a good place to start. If something feels disrespectful, you probably shouldn't be doing it.

# Religious Communities

Christians believe that love is all-important, whatever your vocation, but it can be expressed in different ways.

## Religious Communities Worship Full Time

1) A religious order is a group of monks or nuns who live by the same 'rule'.
2) An order who live together in a monastery or convent are called a religious community. Religious communities express their love of God by fully committing to a life of worship.
3) Members of religious orders usually make vows dedicating their lives to God (a bit like in a marriage).

**MEMBERS OF MOST RELIGIOUS ORDERS TAKE THREE VOWS**

**Poverty** — Members have no personal possessions. These are given to the community or the poor.

**Chastity** — Members abstain from sexual relationships to better focus on a life of prayer.

**Obedience** — Members follow the rules of the community, and promise to obey superiors in the order.

4) These three rules are known as the evangelical counsels. They're generally believed to be only for those with this specific religious calling.

## There are Two Main Types of Religious Community

1) APOSTOLIC orders stress service to the poor, sick or destitute, and their members work 'in the world'. Members of these orders are said to live the active life. Mother Teresa's *'Missionaries of Charity'*, and the *'Franciscans'* are good examples.
2) CONTEMPLATIVE orders are dedicated to prayer and study. These orders are usually enclosed religious communities, where members live together and rarely (if ever) leave their monasteries. *'The Carmelites'* and *'Poor Clares'* (for women), and the *'Carthusians'* or *'Cistercians'* (for men) live the contemplative life.
3) Someone who lives as a monk or nun in a religious community is said to live a monastic life.

## Religious Communities Express their Love of God...

1) Those in contemplative orders aim to remove themselves from the world and dedicate their lives to God through prayer, and to living together in peace.
2) Monks and nuns pray at a number of specific times during the day — starting from early in the morning (around 4:30 a.m.) through into the late evening. The rest of their time will usually be spent studying scripture or working — many religious orders make things to sell to fund the community.
3) Members of apostolic orders also dedicate time to prayer and study — but this fits into their work 'in the world' rather than being their sole focus.
4) Some Protestants don't agree with religious communities based on vows, since this idea isn't mentioned in the Bible, so most orders are Roman Catholic.

## ...and Other People

1) Those in apostolic orders go out into the community to try to help people and to advance their faith. For example, the Roman Catholic Society of Jesus (Jesuits) are famous for their work in education.
2) Mother Teresa's Order of the Missionaries of Charity work to relieve the suffering of the poor all over the world — see page 20.
3) Members of contemplative orders will pray for other people and offer spiritual guidance to visitors.

### *Religious communities dedicate themselves to God...*

Most Christians believe that they should seek to discover their vocation — the thing that God's calling them to do. For some people, that means joining a religious community and dedicating their lives to worship.

# Christian Charities in the UK

Christians, like all people with a religious faith, try to act in a way that's consistent with their beliefs. For many this means getting involved in charity — giving time and money to help people in need.

## Christians have a Duty to Help **Relieve Poverty**

> *"Rich nations have a grave moral responsibility towards those which are unable to ensure the means of their development by themselves..."*
> **from the Catechism of the Catholic Church: paragraph 2439**

1) All Christian denominations have become more concerned over the last few decades with a fairer distribution of wealth.
2) A key question for all Christians is whether wealth ultimately belongs to God, and should therefore be for the good of everyone.
3) Many Christians are concerned about whether or not they should be wealthy. Jesus spoke of giving up wealth to help the poor, but the Roman Catholic Church is a very wealthy organisation.
4) Financial charity is an important part of Christianity (see p.20).
5) Jesus also said that we have an obligation to love each other, and that if we help those who need it, it is as if we are helping Jesus himself (see p.53).
6) A number of Christian organisations exist to tackle poverty — both in the UK and on a global level. Those who work internationally include Christian Aid (see p.20) and CAFOD.

## **The Passage** Helps the **Homeless** in London

1) The Passage is a Roman Catholic organisation set up to help the homeless.
2) It was started in 1980 by Westminster Cathedral together with an apostolic religious order (see previous page) called the Daughters of Charity of St Vincent de Paul.
3) The Passage runs a hostel (i.e. temporary accommodation) in London for homeless people, with priority given to the most vulnerable.
4) Although The Passage does provide a Roman Catholic chaplaincy service if requested, it doesn't carry out any deliberate evangelical work — it doesn't try to convert people to Roman Catholic Christianity.
5) It also offers medical care, skills training and advice to help homeless people get jobs and build new lives for themselves.

## **Church Action on Poverty** Campaigns for the Poor

1) Church Action on Poverty is a national ecumenical charity (i.e. made up of representatives from different denominations) that works to reduce poverty in the UK.
2) They encourage churches to get actively involved in helping the poor.
3) They campaign on a number of issues, including securing rights for asylum seekers and trying to get a raise in the minimum wage.
4) They also try to help people in poverty have an influence on the decisions that affect them, e.g. decisions made by local government.

### "Let us not love with words... but with actions and in truth..."

(**1 John 3:18**) This page is one of the best adverts for Christianity. Regardless of your religious beliefs, it's difficult to argue with any group that gets out into the world and actually spends its time helping people. As Jesus says, "a tree is recognised by its fruit" — and there's some pretty good fruit right here.

# Warm-Up and Worked Exam Question

## Warm-up Questions

1) Name the seven sacraments.
2) What is a) the liturgy of the word? b) transubstantiation?
3) What is Ash Wednesday? How do Roman Catholics mark this day?
4) What name is given to the reconciliation between God and humanity brought about by Jesus's sacrifice?
5) Describe Jesus's teachings on displaying religion.
6) State three commandments, given in Exodus 20, that are about respecting God.
7) What are the Evangelical Counsels?

## Worked Exam Question

You know what to do by now — read the worked example, then try the following practice exam questions. You may not feel very much agape towards them, but they'll do you good in the long run. Don't forget — check out the number of marks each question is worth. It'll help you know how much to write.

1 a) Explain what Christians mean by 'agape'.

*A selfless love that is unconditional, always serving and always caring.*

*(2 marks)*

*To get both marks, give a full definition. Don't just say "a type of love".*

b) Explain how Jesus's teachings on love might make a difference to the life of a Roman Catholic.

*First say what Jesus's teachings on love are...*

*Jesus taught that the most important commandment was to love God, and the second most important was to love your neighbour as yourself. Therefore, Roman Catholics are likely to express their love of God through attending Mass and through private prayer. They may express their love for other people by helping those who suffer, or giving to charity, either financially or by donating their time.*

*(4 marks)*

*...then explain how they'd affect a Roman Catholic's actions.*

c) Explain how Jesus reinterpreted the Law of Moses in the Sermon on the Mount.

*Jesus reinterpreted the Law of Moses to make it stricter and more internal. E.g. where the Law of Moses calls for people not to commit murder, Jesus orders us not to feel anger towards others, and where the Law of Moses orders us not to commit adultery, Jesus warns that looking lustfully at someone is a sin.*

*(3 marks)*

# Exam Questions

2 a) What is 'Lent'?

*(2 marks)*

b) "All Christians should give something up for Lent."

Refer to Roman Catholic Christianity in your answer.

(i) Do you agree? Give reasons for your opinion.

*(3 marks)*

(ii) Give reasons why some people may disagree with you.

*(3 marks)*

3 a) Describe the important features of a Roman Catholic Mass.

*(6 marks)*

b) Explain what different Christians believe about Holy Communion.

*(6 marks)*

4 a) What is the contemplative life?

*(2 marks)*

b) Explain how one Roman Catholic organisation helps relieve poverty and suffering in the UK.

*(3 marks)*

5 a) How might Roman Catholics use the 'Stations of the Cross'?

*(2 marks)*

b) "Confirmation is a much more important sacrament than baptism."

Do you agree? Give reasons for your answer, showing that you have thought about more than one point of view.
Refer to Roman Catholic Christianity in your answer.

*(6 marks)*

# The Nature of Discipleship

Christianity sees Jesus as the Son of God — and so his story is pretty important.

## The Gospels — Good News, but Not Biographies

1) The Gospels were written to preserve the story of Jesus after the apostles died.
2) They also pointed to the coming of the 'kingdom of God'. The 'kingdom of God' is the rulership of God in people's lives. In the Gospels, it either refers to the total acceptance of God in someone's heart, or to the final Kingdom after Judgement Day.

*"Jesus went into Galilee, proclaiming... 'The kingdom of God is near. Repent and believe the good news!'"* **Mark 1:14-15**

3) An early Christian wrote that Mark was the 'interpreter of Peter', but that he hadn't known Jesus personally. Mark may have used early collections of Jesus's words and actions, or he may have got information from Peter (see pages 125 and 131 for more about Peter.).

## The *Calling of the Disciples* — Jesus Gathered Followers

1) The word 'disciple' means 'follower', and is often used to refer to one of Jesus's followers from the Gospels. But it can also be used more generally to mean any Christian.
2) Mark tells us that Jesus called as his first disciples: Simon, Andrew, John, James and Levi.

The Calling of the First Disciples (**Mark 1:14-20**)
As Jesus walked by the Sea of Galilee, he came across four fishermen: Simon (who he later called Peter or 'rock'), Andrew, and the 'sons of Zebedee' — James and John.

*"'Come, follow me,' Jesus said, 'and I will make you fishers of men.'"*

They all abandoned their nets and followed Jesus.

The Calling of Levi (**Mark 2:13-17**)
Jesus called a tax collector, Levi, to follow him. He had dinner with Levi and other people the Pharisees called 'sinners':

*"...they asked his disciples: 'Why does he eat with tax collectors and 'sinners'?' On hearing this, Jesus said to them, 'It is not the healthy who need a doctor, but the sick. I have not come to call the righteous, but sinners.'"*

3) Jesus didn't choose to call well-educated, religious men, e.g. the Sadducees (Jewish priests) or Pharisees (teachers of the Law). Instead he called common fishermen to learn from him and serve God.
4) He also called Levi to be a disciple — a tax collector. Tax collectors were strongly disliked by most Jews, because they worked for the occupying Romans. (According to the Gospel of Matthew, Levi is Matthew the Apostle.)
5) Most modern Christians believe these two passages show that anyone can be a follower of Jesus. It doesn't matter what your background is, or how much you've sinned in the past. Anyone who repents and follows Jesus is welcome.

## The *Mission of the Disciples* — Go Out and Preach

1) Over time, Jesus called other disciples to him until he had 'the Twelve' (later known as the apostles).
2) He sent the disciples out in pairs to tell the people of Israel the good news of the kingdom of God.

The Sending Out of the Twelve (**Mark 6:7-13**)
Jesus sent his disciples out with authority over evil spirits. They were to take a staff — but should not take bread, money, a bag or an extra coat. Where they were made welcome, they were to stay in that place until they left town. Where they were not made welcome, they were to shake the dust from their feet as a marker to others.

*"They went out and preached that people should repent. They drove out many demons and anointed many sick people with oil and healed them."* **Mark 6:12-13**

3) The disciples were told to trust in God and He would provide for them during their mission (through the charity of others). Many Christians believe that they should be prepared to do the same.
4) This passage also carries a message to Christians today about giving charity. They should be among the people who would welcome the apostles, rather than those who turn them away.

# The Costs of Discipleship

## *Jesus Said there were **Costs** of Being a **Disciple***

### *True **Family*** ...a disciple's true family is his fellow believers.

> *"Then Jesus' mother and brothers arrived. Standing outside, they sent someone in to call him... 'Who are my mother and my brothers?' [Jesus] asked. Then he looked at those seated in a circle around him and said, 'Here are my mother and my brothers! Whoever does God's will is my brother and sister and mother.'"* **Mark 3:31-35**

1) Some Christians interpret this as Jesus rejecting his physical family in favour of his 'spiritual' family — that he was telling his disciples to forget blood ties and find a new family in God.
2) Many modern Christians are uncomfortable with these ideas, and feel that you should love and respect your family whatever their beliefs
3) Others interpret the 'true family' teachings as expanding, not replacing, a Christian's family. In following Jesus, you become part of a worldwide family of believers.

### *True **Greatness*** ...a disciple must be the servant of all.

1) In **Mark 9:33-37**, the disciples argue on the road through Galilee to Capernaum about who among them is the greatest.
2) They tried to hide their argument from Jesus, but he responded by saying that true greatness comes through serving others:

> *"'If anyone wants to be first, he must be the very last, and the servant of all.'"* **Mark 9:35**

3) Putting yourself last like this involves a great deal of self-sacrifice (putting other people's needs before your own). Although most Christians see this as an ideal, it can be a very hard teaching to follow.

### *The **Rich Man*** ...a disciple must follow the commandments faithfully and give all he has to the poor.

1) In **Mark 10:17-31**, a wealthy man asks Jesus, *"what must I do to inherit eternal life?"*
2) Jesus said he must do two things: follow the commandments (the ten laws in Exodus 20) and give his wealth to the poor.

> *"'...sell everything you have and give to the poor, and you will have treasure in heaven.'"* **Mark 10:21**

> *"'How hard it is for the rich to enter the kingdom of God!... It is easier for a camel to go through the eye of a needle than for a rich man to enter the kingdom of God.'"* **Mark 10:23-25**

3) He told his disciples that it was desperately hard for a rich person to enter the kingdom of God, although everything is possible for God.
4) He went on to tell the disciples that whatever they gave up now, they'd get a hundred times as much, both now and in the future, i.e. you may face hardship now, but there's eternal life in the end.
5) This story causes big problems for some modern Christians. If a person sells everything they have, they're left with no way of looking after themselves — and so become a burden on other people.
   And how rich is too rich? In the developed world, are we all too rich to enter the kingdom of God?
   Also, many modern Christians fail to keep all the commandments (e.g. most Christians do work of some sort (gardening, cleaning, paying bills, etc.) on Sunday, the Christian Sabbath — *"Remember the Sabbath day by keeping it holy... On it you shall not do any work..."* **Exodus 20:8-10**)

### *The **Parable** of the **Tenants*** ...discipleship is dangerous.

1) In **Mark 12:1-12**, Jesus tells a parable about the dangers and responsibilities faced by God's servants:

> A man left his vineyard in the hands of tenants. He sent servants to collect the rent that was due — but all were beaten or killed by the tenants. In the end he sent his own son, but the tenants killed him too so that the vineyard would become theirs. The owner responded by killing the tenants and giving the vineyard to others.

2) This parable is told to the chief priests and the Pharisees — they are compared to the tenants who would kill the son (Jesus) for their own ends. The vineyard owner represents God.
3) This parable also warned the disciples that they risked persecution and death for carrying God's message. The same warning applies to some Christians today — in some parts of the world, people are still discriminated against, beaten or even killed for their faith.

# The Problems of Discipleship

Jesus's disciples were only human. They didn't always understand, and sometimes they failed.

## The Disciples *Couldn't* Cast a *Spirit* from a Boy

1) When the disciples were sent out to preach in **Mark 6** (see p.123), Jesus gave them authority over evil spirits. They were expected to heal and perform exorcisms in Jesus's name, just as Jesus did himself.

*The Boy with an Evil Spirit* (**Mark 9:14-29**)
The disciples attempted to cure a boy with an evil spirit but failed. When Jesus arrived, he called the people an *"unbelieving generation"*, and told the father that the boy could only be healed if he showed faith. The father replied that he believed, but needed help to have enough faith. Jesus cast the spirit out, and told his disciples that the demon could *"come out only by prayer"*.

*"...the boy's father exclaimed, 'I do believe; help me overcome my unbelief!'"* **Mark 9:24**

2) So according to Mark, the disciples failed because the people didn't have faith, and hadn't been praying for the miracle. Jesus was able to drive out the demon because the father exercised what little faith he had.

## The *Sower* — Should Only *Some People Get It*?

1) According to **Mark 4:1-20**, Jesus told a story about a farmer sowing seed:

*The Parable of the Sower* (**Mark 4:1-20**)
A farmer scattered seeds across the ground. Some fell on the path and were eaten by birds. Some fell in shallow soil, and grew up quickly, but died because the plants had no roots. Some fell among thorns and the plants were choked. But some fell on good soil and *"produced a crop, multiplying thirty, sixty, or even a hundred times"*.

2) This is a rare example of Jesus using allegory in his parables — the story is entirely symbolic, with the seeds and the soils representing the word of God and the hearers of the Gospel respectively.
3) Mark says that Jesus followed the parable with the call, *"He who has ears to hear, let him hear"*, and then delivered one of the most controversial passages in the Gospels to the disciples (**Mark 4:10-12**):
   - He said that he spoke in parables so that the crowds wouldn't understand him.
   - He didn't want the crowds to understand, because *"otherwise they might turn and be forgiven!"*
4) Jesus was disappointed with his disciples, because they needed him to explain the parable — they had failed to understand. But Jesus went on to explain it to them, and only to them (**Mark 4:13-20**).

## More Failures: *Rivalry*, *Gethsemane*, Peter's *Denial*

It wasn't easy being a disciple of Jesus. Mark highlights, in particular, the failings of those closest to Jesus — James and John (the sons of Zebedee) and Simon Peter.

*Rivalry and Service* (**Mark 10:41-45**)
James and John asked Jesus to let them sit at his right and left hands in heaven. Jesus told all the disciples that they shouldn't want to *"lord it"* over other people, and repeated what he'd said earlier about true greatness (see p.124): *"...whoever wants to become great among you must be your servant, and whoever wants to be first must be slave of all. For even the Son of Man did not come to be served, but to serve..."*

*Prayers at Gethsemane* (**Mark 14:27-42**)
Jesus told the disciples that they would all abandon him, and he predicted Peter's denial. All the disciples swore they'd never disown him. Jesus then took Peter, James and John to keep guard while he prayed in the garden of Gethsemane. Three times he went to pray for an hour. Each time, when he returned, he found all three disciples asleep.

*Peter's Denial* (**Mark 14:66-72**)
After Jesus was arrested, Peter was asked three times if he was with Jesus. Three times, he denied it: *"He began to call down curses on himself, and he swore to them, 'I don't know this man you're talking about.'"* — then he broke down in tears when he realised that Jesus had been right.

*These stories cause problems for some modern Christians. If the disciples (even Peter, the first Bishop of Rome) couldn't obey Jesus, and repeatedly failed him, what chance do they have? On the other hand, the humanity of the disciples can help Christians to cope with their own failings. Jesus loved his disciples despite their shortcomings — he didn't expect perfection from them, just as he doesn't expect it from us.*

## *Sometimes Jesus's followers seemed to lack faith or understanding...*

Reading Mark, it's easy to see Peter as a failure. He questioned Jesus, didn't seem to understand a lot of the time, fell asleep at Gethsemane, ran away when Jesus was arrested and denied knowing him three times. But it was Peter who first recognised Jesus as the Christ, and who led the Church following the resurrection.

# Jesus in Conflict with Jewish Law

There's evidence of conflict all through Mark's Gospel. And some of the most memorable parts of the Gospel are where Jesus argues about the Law (the laws handed down by God in the Torah) with the Pharisees.

## *The **Pharisees** and **Scribes** were **Experts** in the Law*

1) The Pharisees were a Jewish sect who studied the Law of Moses, and were dedicated to keeping the Jewish faith alive. They believed that obedience to the Law was all important.
2) The scribes were religious lawyers. They made copies of the Torah, and so knew the Law very well.
3) Jesus was often in conflict with the Pharisees and scribes for breaking laws or traditions. For example, Jesus dined with sinners (**Mark 2:13-17**) and his disciples didn't fast (go without food as sign of devotion to God) (**Mark 2:18-20**). Jesus explained that his followers would only fast once he was dead.

## *Jesus **Forgave** and **Healed** a **Paralysed** Man*

*The Paralysed Man* (**Mark 2:1-12**)
A paralysed man was brought to Jesus. Jesus saw the faith in the man and those who had brought him, and forgave the man for his sins. Some teachers of the Law (scribes) thought this was blasphemy, since they believed only God could forgive sins. Jesus asked whether it was easier to forgive sins or cure a paralysed man. The man got up and walked, proving that *"the Son of Man has authority on earth to forgive sins"*.

*"Which is easier: to say to the paralytic, 'Your sins are forgiven,' or to say, 'Get up, take your mat and walk'?"* **Mark 2:9**

## *He said **People** were More Important than the **Sabbath**...*

The Sabbath (Saturday) is the Jewish day of rest, when Jews aren't supposed to do any work.

*Picking Grain on the Sabbath* (**Mark 2:23-28**)
The Pharisees accused the disciples of working on the Sabbath when they picked grain. Jesus reminded them that even King David broke the Law when he was hungry and in need, by eating bread meant only for priests. He said *"the Sabbath was made for man, not man for the Sabbath"*.

*The Man with the Shrivelled Hand* (**Mark 3:1-6**)
Jesus cured a man with a shrivelled hand in a synagogue on the Sabbath — the Pharisees saw this healing as work, and so forbidden.
Jesus asked, *"Which is lawful on the Sabbath: to do good or to do evil, to save life or to kill?"*
The Pharisees' stubbornness distressed Jesus.

In both cases, Jesus justified working on the Sabbath on the grounds that human need should come before religious laws, and that preventing or repairing harm is always a good thing.

## *...and **Challenged** Traditions*

Mark tells us that Jesus challenged the traditions of ritual cleanliness (laws on food and washing that prevented anything 'unclean' entering a Jew's body) and corban (a gift dedicated to God).

*Ritual Cleanliness* (**Mark 7:1-8 and 7:14-23**)
The Pharisees had elaborate laws about washing before eating in order to stay ritually clean. Jesus argued that it's not what goes into a man that makes him unclean, but rather, what comes out of him.

*"What comes out of a man is what makes him 'unclean'. For from within, out of men's hearts, come evil thoughts, sexual immorality, theft, murder, adultery, greed, malice, deceit, lewdness, envy, slander, arrogance and folly."* **Mark 7:20-22**

According to Jesus, following these rituals didn't make you a good person in the eyes of God. Your motives and actions were much more important.
These views would have caused major conflict within the Jewish community at the time. But many Christians believe that putting people's welfare before strict religious rules, and always trying to be a good person, should be the basis for good community cohesion.

*Corban* (**Mark 7:9-13**)
Jesus argued that the Jews were more concerned with their own traditions than God's word. The example he gave was that of corban. The priests allowed people to leave their parents destitute, which goes against God's Law, if they were giving everything to the Temple as a gift to God (corban).

## *Learn some quotes from Mark's Gospel*

There isn't room here to put in the full texts from the Gospel, so make sure you read all the relevant bits yourself.

# Jesus in Conflict with Authority

It wasn't just lawyers that Jesus fought with — he doesn't seem to have been a fan of authority in general.

## The **Saddducees** were a Group of **Priests**

1) The Sadducees were a group of priests who ran the Temple in Jerusalem (the building where burnt sacrifices were made to God). They believed in sticking very rigidly to the books of the Torah, and they didn't believe in the resurrection of the dead.
2) The chief priests feared Jesus and wanted him dead.

## Jesus Sparked Conflict when he **Entered Jerusalem**

*The Triumphal Entry* (**Mark 11:1-11**)
When Jesus entered Jerusalem at the end of his journeys around Israel, he entered as a King. He was carried on the back of a colt (a young horse) while the people cried: *"Hosanna!"* and *"Blessed is the coming kingdom of our father David!"*. Cloaks and palm branches were spread along the road for his horse to walk on.

*This is the event that Christians celebrate on Palm Sunday, the Sunday before Good Friday.*

*The Cleansing of the Temple* (**Mark 11:15-18**)
In the Temple courtyard in Jerusalem, Jesus found a market, with *"money changers"* and *"those selling doves"*. He overturned their tables and drove the traders out, saying they'd turned the Temple into *"a den of robbers"*.

*The Authority of Jesus Questioned* (**Mark 11:27-33**)
The chief priests and elders asked Jesus on who's authority he was acting. He replied with a question about John the Baptist: *"Answer me, and I will tell you by what authority... John's baptism — was it from heaven, or from men?"* Saying *"from heaven"* meant admitting they were wrong about John, but saying *"from men"* would anger the people (who believed John was a prophet). So they couldn't answer.

1) In each of these examples, the conflict is about authority. Jesus is implying that his authority is greater than the priests in the Temple, because he's acting for God — but he never actually says that.
2) Instead, he quotes scripture as he clears the Temple (in **Mark 11:17** he quotes Isaiah and Jeremiah) and traps his opponents with an unanswerable question.

## Jesus Argued about **Resurrection** and **Taxes**

*Marriage at the Resurrection* (**Mark 12:18-27**)
The Sadducees didn't believe in resurrection of the dead, and they tried to catch Jesus out with an awkward question. The Jews had a custom called levirate marriage, where if a man died childless, his brother must marry his widow. The Sadducees imagined a woman who married seven brothers in turn in this way. They asked Jesus: *"At the resurrection whose wife will she be, since the seven were married to her?"* Jesus replied that after the resurrection, people would be *"like the angels in heaven"*, and so wouldn't be married at all. In favour of resurrection, Jesus argued: *"He is not the God of the dead, but of the living."*

1) This story is quite significant for modern Christians. It shows that the idea of resurrection was around before Jesus, challenging the belief that life after death depends on a belief in Jesus Christ.
2) It describes life after the resurrection as very different from life on earth.
3) Also, the statement that God is God *"of the living"* implies that judgement and resurrection come at death, rather than people staying dead until the Last Day.
4) Another time, the authorities tried to catch Jesus out with a question about taxes to Rome:
5) This passage has been used to justify various different positions over the years, e.g. that Church and State should be separate, that Christians are obliged to obey State laws, or that money is an earthly thing that distracts you from God.

*Paying Taxes* (**Mark 12:13-17**)
Jesus avoided the trap of some Pharisees and Herod's men when they asked him whether it was right to pay taxes to Caesar. He asked them to bring him a coin and tell him whose picture was on it: *"'Caesar's,' they replied. Then Jesus said to them, 'Give to Caesar what is Caesar's and to God what is God's.'"*

## The two things you can be certain of — death and taxes...

Jesus was prepared to challenge authority when he felt it was necessary, but he was no anarchist. He didn't condone not paying taxes, and most of his anger was directed at what he saw as hypocrisy and impiety.

# Jesus in Conflict with His Followers

Mark doesn't record many arguments between Jesus and his followers, but there were a few.

## Jesus **Predicted** his **Passion** Three Times

1) The 'Passion' was the suffering of Jesus in the time leading up to (and including) his death.
2) He predicted his passion, and according to Mark, he told his disciples about it three times.

> *Jesus's Prediction of the Passion* (**Mark 8:31-33**)
> Jesus taught his disciples that he must suffer and die, but would be resurrected on the third day:
> Peter took Jesus to one side *"and began to rebuke him"* (by telling Jesus it would never happen to him — Mark isn't specific, but **Matthew 16:22** is).
> Jesus reacted angrily to Peter: *"'Get behind me, Satan!' he said. 'You do not have in mind the things of God, but the things of men.'"*

> *"He then began to teach them that the Son of Man must suffer many things and be rejected by the elders, chief priests and teachers of the law, and that he must be killed and after three days rise again. He spoke plainly about this..."* **Mark 8:31-32**

3) Jesus's reaction was very strong. Jesus didn't just tell Peter he was wrong, he compared him with Satan tempting Jesus away from his necessary fate.
4) Two more times before entering Jerusalem, Jesus predicted his suffering and death (in **Mark 9:30-32** and **Mark 10:32-34**). On these occasions, the disciples were described as *"afraid"* and *"astonished"*.
5) Modern Christians accept that the passion was an essential part of Jesus's ministry, and that it's through his sacrifice that Christians find salvation.

## The **Anointing** at **Bethany** Angered the Disciples

1) This is a slightly odd story — it doesn't fit very well with the rest of Jesus's teachings.

> *Jesus Anointed at Bethany* (**Mark 14:3-9**)
> A few days before his arrest, a woman 'anointed' Jesus by pouring an expensive jar of perfume over him.
> The disciples *"rebuked her harshly"* for wasting such a valuable thing. It could have been sold for *"more than a year's wages and the money given to the poor"*.
> Jesus's response was unexpected: *"'Leave her alone,' said Jesus... 'She has done a beautiful thing to me. The poor you will always have with you, and you can help them any time you want. But you will not always have me... She poured perfume on my body beforehand to prepare for my burial.'"*

2) 'Messiah' means 'anointed one', so some Christians believe she was expressing her faith that Jesus was the Messiah. Kings of Israel were anointed in a similar way, so this could also be a reference to his kingship.
3) Some Christians believe that the disciples' anger showed that they didn't believe Jesus would die — that only Jesus and the woman really understood what was going to happen.
4) But Jesus's response seems surprisingly selfish, particularly given **Mark 10:21** (*"Go, sell everything you have and give to the poor..."*).

## The Disciple **Judas** was Part of the Plot to **Kill Jesus**

1) In **Mark 14:1-2**, the *"chief priests and the teachers of the law"* plotted to arrest and kill Jesus in *"some sly way"* after the Passover feast. They didn't want to take him in public, because he had too many followers. And not during Passover because the people might *"riot"*.
2) One of Jesus's own disciples, Judas Iscariot, decided to betray Jesus to the Jewish authorities.

> *"Then Judas Iscariot, one of the Twelve, went to the chief priests to betray Jesus to them. They... promised to give him money. So he watched for an opportunity to hand him over."* **Mark 14:10-11**

3) That evening (**Mark 14:17-21**), Jesus predicted the betrayal: *"'It is one of the Twelve,' he replied, 'one who dips bread into the bowl with me... But woe to that man who betrays the Son of Man! It would be better for him if he had not been born.'"*

# The Last Supper, Judas and the Trial

It's a fairly famous story... you may just know something about this already.

## *The Last Supper — Jesus **Knew** he Would be Betrayed*

1) The Last Supper (**Mark 14:12-26**) is the last meal Jesus and the Twelve ate together. They were celebrating the Feast of Unleavened Bread — the first night of the Jewish Passover festival. Passover commemorates the release of the Jews from slavery in Egypt (**Exodus 12**), and is a very important festival.
2) During the feast, held in the 'upper room' of a man's house, Jesus predicted that one of the disciples would betray him (see previous page). Each disciple denied that it would be him.
3) Jesus then broke a piece of bread and said, *"Take it; this is my body."* He passed round a cup of wine and said, *"This is my blood of the covenant, which is poured out for many"*.
4) After the supper (**Mark 14:25-31**) Jesus felt that his death was near, saying *"I will not drink again of the fruit of the vine until that day when I drink it anew in the kingdom of God."* He then went with the Twelve to the Mount of Olives, where he predicted Peter's denial (see p.125).

This is a very important passage for modern Christians, as it's the origin of the Eucharist (Holy Communion — see p.114). Many Christians believe that they receive the saving power of Jesus into themselves by eating the bread and drinking the wine at the Eucharist. Holy Communion also reminds Christians of the 'new covenant' made with God through the death of Jesus. In **Luke 22:19**, Jesus adds, *"do this in remembrance of me"*. This phrase isn't part of Mark's Gospel, though, so there's nothing in Mark's account to suggest that Jesus was beginning a tradition.

## *Jesus **Prayed** at **Gethsemane***

1) That night, after the meal, Jesus went with Peter, John and James to the garden of Gethsemane to pray (**Mark 14:32-42**).
2) Peter, John and James were to keep watch while he prayed, but failed (see p.125).
3) Mark writes that Jesus was *"deeply distressed"* saying that his soul was *"overwhelmed with sorrow to the point of death"*. Jesus prayed for God to take the *"cup"* of his suffering from him, but only if that would fit God's plan. Jesus didn't want to die if he didn't have to, but would obey God.

*"'Abba, Father,' he said, 'everything is possible for you. Take this cup from me. Yet not what I will, but what you will.'"* **Mark 14:36**

4) These verses show Jesus's humanity, and so cause problems for some Christians. Some feel that if Jesus was God (as part of the Trinity), then he should know what was necessary, and not question his fate. Others think that, by praying to God, Jesus shows that he's separate from him.

## *He was **Betrayed**, **Arrested** and **Tried** by the **Sanhedrin***

1) Judas Iscariot arrived at Gethsemane to betray Jesus (**Mark 14:43-52**), accompanied by *"a crowd armed with swords and clubs, sent from the chief priests, the teachers of the law, and the elders"*.
2) Judas had arranged a signal with the crowd — the person he kissed was the one they should arrest.

The betrayal is a thorny subject for Christians. Many believe that Judas's treachery damned him to hell. He betrayed God and sent a good man to his death. But if Jesus's death was necessary for our salvation, then was the betrayal necessary too? And if Judas was destined to be the betrayer, could he have chosen not to be?

3) In **Mark 14:53-65**, Jesus was put on trial before the High Priest (the leader of the Temple) and the rest of the Sanhedrin (the Jewish supreme council). According to Mark, the court was simply *"looking for evidence against Jesus so that they could put him to death"*.
4) As far as Christians are concerned, this wasn't a real trial, and it had nothing to do with justice. The chief priests felt threatened by Jesus, and this show trial was their opportunity to get rid of him.
5) Various people testified falsely against Jesus, but their stories didn't agree with each other.
6) Jesus stayed silent — he didn't try to defend himself — until the High Priest asked Jesus directly, *"Are you the Christ, the Son of the Blessed One?"*

*"'I am,' said Jesus. 'And you will see the Son of Man sitting at the right hand of the Mighty One and coming on the clouds of heaven.'"* **Mark 14:62**

7) This was enough to condemn Jesus for the very serious crime of blasphemy — insulting God.
8) Then in the courtyard below, Peter was accused of being a follower of Jesus and denied it three times (see p.125).

# The Crucifixion and Resurrection

## The **Sanhedrin** Turned him Over to **Pontius Pilate**

1) **Mark 15:1-15** records the events of the morning after the trial, when Jesus was turned over to Pontius Pilate — the Roman governor of Judea. He had the power to sentence Jesus to death.
2) The priests accused Jesus of *"many things"* before Pilate, but again Jesus refused to answer the accusations. Pilate was *"amazed"*. The one thing Jesus did reply to was Pilate's question: *"Are you the king of the Jews?"* Jesus replied, *"Yes, it is as you say"*.
3) According to Mark, it was customary to release a prisoner to mark Passover, and Pilate asked the crowd if he should release Jesus. The crowd, having been *"stirred up"* by the chief priests, called for a man named Barabbas to be released instead. Barabbas had committed murder in a recent uprising.
4) Mark writes that Pilate knew it was *"out of envy that the chief priests had handed Jesus over to him"*. He writes that the crowd called for Jesus to be crucified, and that Pilate agreed to it to keep the crowd happy.
5) So according to Mark, the priests and the Jewish crowd were responsible for Jesus's death, not Pilate. This view was probably influenced by Mark's background. Mark was most likely living in Rome, where Christians were being persecuted by the Roman authorities. He might have felt it wise to paint the Roman Pilate in a good light.
6) Modern Christians tend to lay some of the blame for Jesus's death with Pilate. As a Roman governor, he had the power to refuse to do what the priests wanted, but he chose to go along with them.

> *"'Why? What crime has he committed?' asked Pilate. But they shouted all the louder, 'Crucify him!' Wanting to satisfy the crowd, Pilate released Barabbas to them. He had Jesus flogged, and handed him over to be crucified."* **Mark 15:14-15**

## Jesus was **Crucified** and **Died** at **Golgotha**

1) **Mark 15:21-39** records that Jesus was led to Golgotha (The Place of the Skull) where he was to be crucified — nailed to a cross to hang until he died. Simon of Cyrene carried his cross.
2) Jesus refused the drugged wine he was offered, and was crucified next to two robbers. A sign was fixed to Jesus's cross that read "The King of the Jews", to record the charge against him. Passers-by threw insults at Jesus, saying that he could save others, but couldn't save himself.
3) Christians believe that it was by dying on the cross that Jesus truly saved his followers from death.
4) They believe that God had placed all the sins of the world on Jesus while he hung on the cross. In his suffering, Jesus cried out, *"My God, my God, why have you forsaken me?"*
5) As he died, the curtain of the Temple tore in two. (This would have been a symbol of mourning to the Jews, who ritually tear their clothes when a loved one dies.) A Roman soldier said, *"Surely this man was the Son of God!"*
6) Joseph of Arimathea was allowed to take Jesus's body down from the cross for a decent burial (bodies were usually left on the cross). Joseph placed it in a tomb cut from the rock and rolled a stone over the entrance. Mark implies that this was done in a hurry, because it was getting close to the Sabbath.

## Then on the **Third Day** he was **Resurrected**

1) As soon as the Sabbath was over, **Mark 16:1-8** tells us that Mary Magdalene, Mary the mother of James and Salome went to Jesus's tomb to anoint his body.
2) They got there to find the stone rolled back and the tomb empty. A young man dressed in white was there who told them: *"He has risen! He is not here. See the place where they laid him. But go, tell his disciples and Peter, 'He is going ahead of you into Galilee..."*
3) The three women fled in terror and didn't say anything to anyone. The oldest copies of Mark end here.
4) Later copies of Mark go on to say that the resurrected Jesus appeared to Mary Magdalene, and then to the eleven remaining apostles. He told them to *"preach the good news to all creation"*.
5) Christians believe that Jesus's resurrection was physical, not just spiritual. The risen Jesus wasn't a ghost — he rose again in the flesh, showing his power over death (see **Luke 24:36-49**).

# Jesus's Baptism and Transfiguration

The start of Jesus's ministry was marked by his baptism by John the Baptist.

## Jesus was **Baptised** by **John the Baptist**

1) The first few verses of Mark describe the ministry of John the Baptist. John was baptising people in the river Jordan *"for the forgiveness of sins"*. The people confessed their sins and John immersed them in the river to symbolise the sins being washed away.
2) **Mark 1:9-11** describes Jesus going to John for baptism. This causes problems for some Christians, since if Jesus was really the son of God and without sin, why did he need to be baptised?
3) But whatever the reason was for him going to John — to encourage his followers to be baptised, or just to mark the start of his ministry — this is where Mark tells us that Jesus was the Son of God.

> *"As Jesus was coming up out of the water, he saw heaven being torn open and the Spirit descending on him like a dove. And a voice came from heaven: 'You are my Son, whom I love; with you I am well pleased.'"* **Mark 1:10-11**

## **Peter Confessed** his Faith at **Caesarea Philippi**

1) 'Confession' in this sense just means acknowledging something — Peter made a statement of belief.
2) In **Mark 8:27-33**, Jesus and his disciples were travelling towards the city of Caesarea Philippi when Jesus asked them, *"Who do you say I am?"* Peter replied, *"You are the Christ"*.
3) This was the first time one of Jesus's disciples had openly declared him to be the Christ or Messiah (see p.133). Jesus told them not to tell anyone who he was (this is often called the Messianic Secret).

*Matthew's Account of Peter's Confession is Important for Roman Catholics* (**16:13-20**)

In Matthew, Jesus responds to Peter's confession by offering him the *"keys of the kingdom of heaven"*:

For Roman Catholics, this passage marks the foundation of their Church, with Peter as the first Pope (Bishop of Rome).

> *"Blessed are you, Simon son of Jonah... I tell you that you are Peter, and on this rock I will build my church, and the gates of Hades will not overcome it. I will give you the keys of the kingdom of heaven; whatever you bind on earth will be bound in heaven, and whatever you loose on earth will be loosed in heaven."* **Matthew 16:17-19**

*'Peter' means 'rock' in Greek.*

Mark's account of the event doesn't include any mention of this, so Matthew's record is more important for Roman Catholic Christians today.

## Jesus Met with **Elijah** and **Moses** at his **Transfiguration**

1) **Mark 9:1-10** describes a miraculous event called the transfiguration, in which Jesus's appearance changed in front of Peter, John and James.

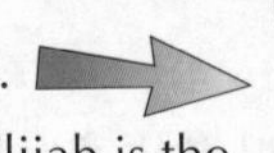

> *"...he was transfigured before them. His clothes became dazzling white..."* **Mark 9:2-3**

2) The prophets Moses and Elijah appeared, and were talking to Jesus. Elijah is the Old Testament prophet who is prophesied to return before the Messiah.
3) This is the most openly 'god-like' thing that Jesus is recorded as having done in Mark's Gospel. Some Christians are uneasy about it — they find it hard to reconcile Jesus the man with this sort of transformation.
4) While the disciples stood there terrified, a cloud came down and enveloped them. A voice from the cloud said, *"This is my Son, whom I love. Listen to him!"*, and then everything returned to normal.
5) As at the baptism, this is the voice of God himself declaring Jesus to be his son.
6) Jesus again told Peter, James and John not to tell anyone what they'd seen until after he'd risen from the dead.
7) But if Peter, James and John had witnessed this transfiguration, seen the prophets, and heard the voice of God, it's hard to understand why they struggled to accept the idea of Jesus's resurrection (**Mark 16:11-12**).

### *Who is Jesus...*

Jesus never actually says he is the Messiah, the Son of God, until his trial.

# Jesus's Miracles

According to Mark's Gospel, Jesus performed many miracles. These miracles showed that he had God's power, but they also demonstrated the importance of faith.

## Healing Miracles and Faith are Linked

Jesus exercised his own faith every time he performed a miracle. And he showed that people could be cured miraculously of both physical and mental illness — as long as they had faith.

*The Raising of Jairus's Daughter* (**Mark 5:21-43**)
Jairus, a synagogue ruler, begged Jesus to heal his daughter. When Jesus arrived, the girl was apparently dead already, but Jesus revived her. As in most of the healing miracles, faith is crucial. The sick girl's father demonstrated faith by asking Jesus for help.

*"Jesus told the synagogue ruler, 'Don't be afraid; just believe.'"* **Mark 5:36**

*The Healing of a Man with Evil Spirits* (**Mark 5:1-20**)
A man was possessed by many evil spirits that caused him to hurt himself: *"he would cry out and cut himself with stones"*. The spirits were so strong that the man could break the chains put on his wrists and ankles. The man ran to Jesus and fell on his knees in front of him, but the demons spoke through the man. They called Jesus *"Son of the Most High God"* and referred to themselves as *"Legion... for we are many"*. The demons begged Jesus to send them into a herd of pigs, rather than driving them from the country altogether. When the demons entered the 2000 pigs, they ran to the lake and drowned. Jesus told the man to spread the word about what he had done.

*Mark never tells us the name of the man, but you'll often hear him called "Legion" after the demons that possessed him.*

1) There are two ways of looking at these healing miracle stories — either as descriptions of real events, or as symbolic of Christian teachings.
2) Where the miracles seem to be treating what we'd now consider mental illness (e.g. Legion), most Christians see how faith could have a profound effect. But healing physical illness, or even death, through faith alone is harder for some modern Christians to accept.
3) Many Christians believe that the story of Legion is symbolic, where the man represents the whole of humanity being plagued by the many demons of sin.

## Jesus Controlled Nature — Inspiring Awe and Wonder

Mark also describes several nature miracles, in which Jesus shows his power over nature.

*Calming the storm* (**Mark 4:35-41**)
A storm broke out and threatened to sink the boat that Jesus and the disciples were in. Jesus calmly instructed the wind to die down, which it did. The disciples were filled with awe at what they saw: *"They were terrified and asked each other, 'Who is this? Even the wind and the waves obey him!'"*

*Walking on water* (**Mark 6:45-52**)
Jesus caught up with his disciples' boat by walking across the water. Although they'd just seen him feed the 5000, they were still shocked at his powers.

*Feeding the 5000* (**Mark 6:32-44**)
A crowd had gathered around Jesus and the disciples, but there were only 5 loaves and 2 fish to eat. Jesus gave thanks to God, broke the bread and the disciples passed the food round. All 5000 people had enough to eat, and there was enough food left over to fill 12 baskets.

*"Then he climbed into the boat with them... They were completely amazed, for they had not understood about the loaves; their hearts were hardened."* **Mark 6:51-52**

1) Taken at face value, these stories cause problems for some modern Christians.
2) In a world that follows the normal physical laws, you can't turn 5 loaves and 2 fish into enough food to feed thousands of people, or walk on water as though it was solid ground.
3) Some Christians believe that physical laws didn't bind Jesus, because he was the Son of God, and had God's power within him. Others prefer to view the stories symbolically. For example, the feeding of the five thousand can be seen to represent God providing for those who trust and have faith in him.

## Faith is good — but revision helps too...

In the story of Legion, the demons call Jesus the "Son of the Most High God". So Mark describes the demons as recognising Jesus for who he was, even if the people he was ministering to didn't.

# The Titles of Jesus

In Mark's Gospel, Jesus is called by a number of titles, each of which gives a clue to Jesus's identity.

## His **Followers** Called Jesus the **Messiah**

1) The words 'Messiah' in Hebrew, and 'Christ' in Greek, both mean 'anointed one'.
2) They come from the practice of consecrating kings and priests to God by anointing them with blessed oil.
3) In the Jewish scriptures, the Messiah is the promised King of Israel who will deliver the Jews from suffering, and usher in the 'messianic age' — an age of peace when everyone will worship God.
4) Christians believe that Jesus was the Messiah promised in the books of Isaiah and Zechariah.
5) The Gospels pick out events and actions that show Jesus fulfilling many of the messianic prophecies during his time on Earth. There aren't many examples of this in Mark's Gospel, but there are lots in Matthew, e.g. **Matthew 21:5** describes the Triumphal Entry (see p.127) as a fulfilment of **Zechariah 9:9**.
6) Christians believe that, during his life, Jesus only fulfilled some of the prophecies about the Messiah. And that he will return (the Second Coming) to bring in the messianic age, or the Kingdom of God.

## **Jesus** Called **Himself** the **Son of Man**

1) When Jesus refers to himself in Mark's Gospel, he uses the title 'Son of Man', e.g.

- healing the paralysed man (see p.126): *"...the Son of Man has authority on earth to forgive sins..."*
- in response to the request of James and John to sit at his side in glory (see p.125): *"...the Son of Man did not come to be served, but to serve..."*
- the prediction of his passion (see p.128: *"...the Son of Man must suffer many things..."*.
- at his trial before the Sanhedrin (see p.129): *"...you will see the Son of Man sitting at the right hand of the Mighty One and coming on the clouds of heaven."*

2) Many Christians see the title as a reference to Jesus's humanity. They believe that he lived, suffered and died as a man.
3) As a human, Jesus could atone for the sins of humanity (p.116).
4) It's likely that the title was also a reference to the prophet Daniel:

*"In my vision... there before me was one like a son of man, coming with the clouds of heaven... He was given authority, glory and sovereign power... His dominion is an everlasting dominion that will not pass away..."* **Daniel 7:13-14**

## Christians **Believe** Jesus is the **Son of God**

1) Christians believe that Jesus is the second person of the Trinity (see p.106) and the Son of God.
2) There's evidence for this in Mark's Gospel:

- The clearest evidence comes from Jesus's baptism and transfiguration, where the voice of God declared Jesus to be his Son (see p.131).
- Jesus prayed to God as his "Father".
- Jesus's miracles (see previous page) showed that he had the power of God.
- Jesus confirmed that he was the Son of God at his trial before the Sanhedrin (see p.129).
- Jesus rose from the dead (see p.130) — demonstrating his divinity.

3) But not everyone is convinced from Mark's account that Jesus was divine. He showed normal, human emotions at Gethsemane (see p.129), and up until his trial, he never claimed to be the Son of God.
4) Others don't trust the evidence of Mark's Gospel. It was probably written some time after Jesus's death, by someone who wasn't a first-hand witness of the things he's describing.

### Son of Man — or Son of God...

No person called Jesus the Son of God until his trial, because connecting yourself with God in that way was considered blasphemous by the Jews. But if you believe Mark's account, a supernatural voice said it twice.

# Warm-Up and Worked Exam Question

## Warm-up Questions

1) In Mark's Gospel, what is meant by a) a disciple? b) corban?
2) Describe the story of the Rich Man from Mark 10:17-31.
3) Who were the Pharisees?
4) Give three examples from Mark's Gospel of Jesus coming into conflict with the Jewish authorities.
5) Name four people or groups of people who were partly responsible for Jesus's death.
6) According to Mark, what happened at Jesus's baptism?
7) List two healing miracles and two nature miracles described in Mark's Gospel.

## Worked Exam Question

Right — this is the last lot of questions before the big sample exams. Read through the example below, then have a go at the questions on the next page. Once more with feeling...

1 Explain why the Parable of the Tenants *(Mark 12:1-12)* is important for Christians today.

*In the Parable of the Tenants, Jesus teaches about how the old religious authorities (represented by the tenants in the parable) would be replaced by those who truly sought God's will (represented by the new tenants).*

For this sort of question, don't waste time describing the parable in detail —you won't get marks for it.

*The parable serves as a warning that those who do not behave righteously will be punished in the end, just as the tenants were punished. This may be important for Christians today who feel that they are doing wrong. They should repent, because in the end there will be judgement.*

If the parable could be important to different Christians for different reasons, say so in your answer.

*For some Christians, the parable illustrates God's patience, forgiveness and love. Each time his servant was beaten or killed, God sent another. He didn't just give up on the tenants, but was patient with them.*

*The Parable of the Tenants is perhaps most important to Christians today as it shows that being a disciple is a difficult and dangerous thing. By carrying God's message, disciples risk persecution and death, just as the servants did. Simply being a Christian has been dangerous at many times in history and is still not a safe option in some parts of the world.*

*(8 marks)*

It can be good to leave your best point 'til the end.

# Exam Questions

2 a) What is the kingdom of God?

*(2 marks)*

b) From Mark's Gospel, describe Jesus's teachings on 'true greatness'.

*(3 marks)*

c) Explain why the calling and sending out of the first disciples is important to Christians today.

*(8 marks)*

3 a) Do you think it is important for Christians to keep the Sabbath? Give two reasons for your point of view.

*(4 marks)*

b) "Christians should always be prepared to challenge authority."

In your answer you should refer to Christianity.

(i) Do you agree? Give reasons for your opinion.

*(3 marks)*

(ii) Give reasons why some people may disagree with you.

*(3 marks)*

4 a) What is Gethsemane?

*(2 marks)*

b) Explain the significance of Jesus's death and resurrection to Christians.

*(8 marks)*

5 a) Who was Jairus?

*(2 marks)*

b) "Jesus was the Son of God."

In your answer you should refer to Christianity.

(i) Do you agree? Give reasons for your opinion.

*(3 marks)*

(ii) Give reasons why some people may disagree with you.

*(3 marks)*

# Do Well in Your Exam

General

You've learnt all the facts — now it's time to get those grades.

## The Basics — Read the Questions

1) Read the questions carefully.
2) If you've got a choice of questions, make sure you read them all before you pick one of them. Remember, you've got to answer all the parts of the questions you pick.
3) The more marks a question's worth, the longer you should be spending on it.
4) Be aware of how much time you're using. Make sure you leave plenty of time for the long-answer questions, and if you've got a bit of time left at the end, read through your answers.

## You get Marks for What you Know and How you Express It

In GCSE Religious Studies there are two Assessment Objectives — these are the skills you'll need to show to get marks in the exams. You get half your marks for each.

1) Describing and explaining what you know.
2) Making arguments backed up with well-thought-out reasoning — and understanding and explaining other people's opinions.

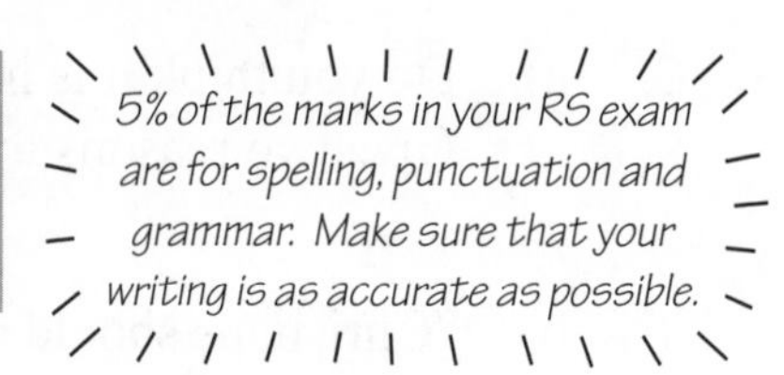


The exact format of your questions will depend on your exam board, but they're all along the same lines...

## There are Easy Marks for Knowing What Things Mean

You'll probably get questions asking you what important terms mean. They'll only be worth a mark or two, so keep your answers short and to the point — but make sure you define the term properly. Learn the terms from the glossary (see pages 174-176) that relate to the unit (or units) you're doing.

What is meant by **displaying religion**?

Good Answer: *Making a show of good deeds or religious observance to impress other people.*

Try to answer this sort of question in one sentence.

Not-so-Good Answers:

*In the Sermon on the Mount, Jesus says that we are to carry out acts of charity and worship in private, rather than in public. He says that praying loudly on street corners, or making sure people know when we give to charity is wrong, because we should be doing it for the benefit of God rather than an audience. We describe this fault as displaying religion.*

This is too long. You don't have time to write an essay on questions that don't offer many marks. Keep your answer short and to the point.

But this is just an example, not a definition, so it wouldn't get full marks. → *Praying in public.*

## You Might be Asked to Describe Religious Teachings

These are generally worth 3 or 4 marks, so you need to give a bit more detail than in the definition questions, but don't get carried away. They're not expecting you to write an essay.

Describe Islamic teachings about charity.

*Muslims are expected to help those in need. Zakah is one of the five pillars of Islam, which states that all Muslims should give a percentage of their yearly savings to the poor, regardless of how wealthy they are. Additional charitable acts, called Sadaqah, are also encouraged. Muslims believe that all possessions in the end belong to Allah, and so should be used for the benefit of everyone.*

Most religions teach that it's important to help the poor. Make sure you write about the teachings that are specific to the religion you've chosen.

# Do Well in Your Exam

GENERAL

Descriptions and definitions are all well and good, but it's when you start to explain things that the marks come thick and fast...

## *You Might Have to **Explain** the **Impact** of **Faith***

These are still fairly quick questions — worth about 4 marks each — but they take a bit more thinking about than the ones on the previous page. You get marks for explaining how religious beliefs might influence a person's actions, views and practices.

Explain how having a religious faith might encourage a person to get married.

*Islam places great importance on procreation and teaches that marriage is the best foundation for starting a family. Muslims also teach that the only right context for a sexual relationship is marriage — cohabiting is considered very sinful. So a Muslim who wants to have children is likely to get married first.*

Try to include some of the specialist language you've learnt.

## *Use **Good English** for **Longer-Answer** Questions*

1) For long-answer questions, you're still marked first and foremost on your understanding of the religion. However, you can get a better mark if you use better English. (On Edexcel exams, these questions are marked with an *.)
2) You need to be really careful about your spelling, punctuation and grammar, and write in paragraphs.
3) Structure your answer — you might want to sketch out a plan before you start.
4) The best marks will go to those who put in a number of reasons and/or develop their reasons well.
5) You'll also get marks for using the specialist language that you'll find in the glossary — learn what the words mean, how to use them, and how to spell them.

Choose **one** religion and explain its teachings about religious tolerance.

It won't hurt to remember a bit of scripture.

*It says in the Qur'an that Allah created everyone from a single soul so that we could "know each other", not so we could "despise each other." This suggests that there is a requirement for Muslims to be friendly to people of other faiths.*

*Muslims believe that Islam is the only true faith, and as such they may feel a responsibility to convert non-Muslims.*

*However the Qur'an states that those who follow other religions faithfully, especially Judaism and Christianity, shall be rewarded in the next life. This suggests that Muslims should respect people of other faiths.*

*Perhaps the most important reason why Muslims should want to live in harmony with Christians and Jews is the fact that they believe that they all worship the same God.*

Put your best point last.

Explain the use of symbolism in **two** different religious traditions.

Remember — all Christian traditions are not the same. Say which ones you're referring too.

You have to explain why religious people do what they do.

*The most common Christian symbol is the cross. It reminds believers of Jesus's suffering and resurrection. Christians will often put a fish symbol on the back of their cars to demonstrate their faith to others.*

*In Orthodox Christianity, churches are filled with icons that represent Jesus, Mary, angels and saints. Worshippers kiss the images, which they believe brings the presence of those who they represent into the church.*

*In Islam, images of Muhammad or Allah are not allowed. This is because such images are seen as creating the temptation to commit idolatry. For this reason Arabic characters are used to represent them.*

*All mosques have a dome to symbolise the Universe. Green is a commonly used colour in Islam, as it was believed to be Muhammad's favourite colour and represents life.*

## *Make sure you write clearly...*

The best way to prepare yourself for the exam is to practise doing exam-style questions under timed conditions. Make sure your punctuation, spelling and grammar are all correct — otherwise you'll lose marks.

GENERAL

# Do Well in Your Exam

For these questions, you have to have an opinion, and understand those of other people.

## If You're Asked for Your **Opinion** You'll Need to **Back It Up**

There's no right answer to this kind of question — only good answers that'll get you lots of marks and bad answers that won't. The difference between the two is that good answers give clearly developed reasons.

Do you agree with the UK ban on euthanasia? Give **two** reasons for your point of view.

*I don't believe that euthanasia is wrong in all circumstances because in cases where people have no quality of life, forcing them to continue living is just forcing them to suffer.*
*As a Christian I believe that we have a duty to help those who are suffering. In some cases, helping them end their suffering may be the best thing that we can do.*

Both of these answers are pretty good despite arguing different things from different perspectives.

Your reasons don't have to be religious, unless the question says they do.

*As a Muslim I believe that euthanasia is wrong in all circumstances because suffering is a test of our faith, and those who remain faithful will be rewarded after death.*
*Doctors and nurses have a duty to protect life, and to never harm their patients. They do not have the authority to decide when it is right for their patients to die.*

## You Have to Know **Both Sides** of the Big **Arguments**

1) In discussion questions, you get marks for writing what you think and for writing what people who disagree with you think. Aim to spend the same time and effort on each.
2) They're long-answer questions, so you'll usually be marked on your writing skills too (see p.137).
3) You'll be told to refer to a religion, so make sure you do or you'll lose marks.

*You might be asked to refer to a specific religion, e.g. Christianity, but that doesn't mean you must only write about Christian views.*

"Scientific advances make the existence of God less likely."
Discuss this statement. You should include different, supported points of view and a personal viewpoint. You must refer to at least one religion in your answer.

Remember to include your own personal response.

*I do not believe that scientific discoveries show that God is less likely to exist. I would argue that, although scientific discoveries have made it difficult to believe in some of the scriptures literally, they should be interpreted symbolically.*
*Some people would argue that the Big Bang theory removes the need to believe in God as a 'first cause', or creator, of the Universe. Many Christians do not find the scientific explanation of creation a problem. They would argue that although the Universe was not created exactly as described in the Bible, it does not mean that God was not involved. They believe that we should look for the spiritual lessons of the creation story, rather than treating it as if it were a scientific theory about the Universe.*
*People who believe that science has made the existence of God less likely, would argue that one of the most important proofs of God has been disproved. The argument from design — that the world is so complex it had to have a designer — could be said to have been disproved by the theory of evolution, which shows how complexity could have arisen without being externally guided.*
*Some Christians, known as creationists, reject scientific theories about evolution and geology, which go against the literal meaning of scripture. For them, no scientific discovery can make God's existence less likely, as any discovery that threatened to do so would be rejected.*

Make a clear reference to the religion(s) you're discussing.

Try to make the reasons why people disagree with you as good as the reasons for your own opinion.

Don't waffle — it just makes life harder for the person doing the marking.

## *Your opinion matters...*

Make sure you learn the different arguments for all sides of the key issues. It's not a bad lesson to take away from the exam — even if you believe something strongly, it's worthwhile knowing why other people don't.

# Practice Exams

Once you've been through all the questions in this book, you should feel pretty confident about the exam. As final preparation, here are some **practice exams** to really get you set for the real thing. There are **five** papers — one for each chunk of the book. Only do the papers that are relevant to your syllabus, and answer all the questions in the paper. The papers are designed to give you the best possible preparation for the differing question styles of the actual exams, whichever syllabus you're following. You can use the answers provided to work out a rough mark that'll give you an idea of how your revision is going.

## General Certificate of Secondary Education

# GCSE Religious Studies

| Centre name | | | | | |
|---|---|---|---|---|---|
| Centre number | | | | | |
| Candidate number | | | | | |

## Paper 1: Religion and Life

(Believing in God, Life and Death,
Marriage and the Family,
Religion and Community Cohesion)

| Surname | |
|---|---|
| Other names | |
| Candidate signature | |

**Time allowed**:
1½ hours

**Instructions to candidates**
- Answer **all** of the questions.
- Write your name and other details in the spaces provided above.

**Information for candidates**
- The marks available are given in brackets at the end of each question or part-question.
- There are also 4 marks available for correct spelling, punctuation and grammar in this paper.
- Marks will not be deducted for incorrect answers.
- There are **4** questions in this paper.
- There are no blank pages.

**Advice to candidates**
- Work steadily through the paper.
- Don't spend too long on one question.
- If you have time at the end, go back and check your answers.

Leave blank

**1 Believing in God**

(a) What is **agnosticism**? *(2 marks)*

(b) Do you think that suffering shows that God does not exist?
Give **two** reasons for your point of view. *(4 marks)*

(c) Explain how arguments from causation and design lead some people to believe in God. *(8 marks)*

(d) "No one can be a scientist and really believe in God."

Refer to at least one religion in your answer.

(i) Do you agree? Give reasons for your opinion. *(3 marks)*

(ii) Give reasons why some people may disagree with you. *(3 marks)*

**2 Life and Death**

Answer this question for whichever religion you've studied.

(a) What does the word immortal mean? *(1 mark)*

(b) State two things that a Christian/Jew/Muslim might believe about the soul. *(2 marks)*

(c) Describe Christian/Jewish/Muslim beliefs about Heaven/Gan Eden/Paradise. *(3 marks)*

(d) Why do many Christians/Jews/Muslims give to charity? *(6 marks)*

(e) "It is always wrong to take a life."

Discuss this statement. You should include different, supported points of view and a personal viewpoint.
You must refer to a religion in your answer. *(12 marks)*

**3 Marriage and the Family**

(a) What is **celibacy**? *(2 marks)*

(b) Do you agree with sex before marriage?
Give **two** reasons for your point of view. *(4 marks)*

(c) Choose **one** religion and explain why some of the followers of that religion agree with the use of contraception and others do not. *(8 marks)*

(d) "Children are best off with two parents who are married to each other."

Refer to at least one religion in your answer.

(i) Do you agree? Give reasons for your opinion. *(3 marks)*

(ii) Give reasons why some people may disagree with you. *(3 marks)*

Leave blank

**4 Religion and Community Cohesion**

Study the information below and answer the questions that follow.

(a) Explain what religious believers mean by 'equality'. *(2 marks)*

(b) Explain how having a religious faith may influence a person's views on gender equality. *(4 marks)*

(c) There can be only one true faith.

Give **two** reasons why a religious believer might agree or disagree with this statement. *(4 marks)*

(d) Explain from **two** different religious traditions the teachings about discrimination. *(6 marks)*

(e) 'Religious people are likely to be supportive of immigrants'.
Do you agree? Give reasons or evidence for your answer, showing that you have thought of more than one point of view. You must include reference to religious beliefs in your answer. *(8 marks)*

## General Certificate of Secondary Education

# GCSE Religious Studies

## Paper 2: Ethics and Society

(Morals and Responsibilities, Environment, Medical Ethics, Peace & Justice)

| Centre name | | | | | |
|---|---|---|---|---|---|
| Centre number | | | | | |
| Candidate number | | | | | |

| Surname | |
|---|---|
| Other names | |
| Candidate signature | |

**Time allowed:**
1½ hours

**Instructions to candidates**
- Answer **all** of the questions.
- Write your name and other details in the spaces provided above.

**Information for candidates**
- The marks available are given in brackets at the end of each question or part-question.
- There are also 4 marks available for correct spelling, punctuation and grammar in this paper.
- Marks will not be deducted for incorrect answers.
- There are **4** questions in this paper.
- There are no blank pages.

**Advice to candidates**
- Work steadily through the paper.
- Don't spend too long on one question.
- If you have time at the end, go back and check your answers.

*Leave blank*

**1 Morals and Responsibilities**

(a) What are **human rights**? *(2 marks)*

(b) Do you think that it is the Government's responsibility to protect human rights? Give **two** reasons for your point of view. *(4 marks)*

(c) Describe where a religious believer may look for moral guidance. *(8 marks)*

(d) "Sometimes doing the right thing involves breaking the law."

Refer to at least one religion in your answer.

(i) Do you agree? Give reasons for your opinion. *(3 marks)*

(ii) Give reasons why some people may disagree with you. *(3 marks)*

Leave blank

*Answer these questions for whichever religion you've studied.*

**2 Environment**

(a) What does the word 'conservation' mean? *(1 mark)*

(b) State two ways of reducing your impact on the environment. *(2 marks)*

(c) Describe Christian beliefs about using animals for the benefit of humans. *(3 marks)*

(d) Explain why Christians/Jews/Muslims are often concerned about environmental issues. *(6 marks)*

(e) "We should stop using genetic engineering."

Discuss this statement. You should include different, supported points of view and a personal viewpoint. You must refer to a religion in your answer. *(12 marks)*

**3 Medical Ethics**

(a) What is **infertility**? *(2 marks)*

(b) Do you think that new drugs should be tested on animals? Give **two** reasons for your point of view. *(4 marks)*

(c) Explain why some Christians agree with organ donation but others do not. *(8 marks)*

(d) "All types of fertility treatment should be widely available."

Refer to at least one religion in your answer.

(i) Do you agree? Give reasons for your opinion. *(3 marks)*

(ii) Give reasons why some people may disagree with you. *(3 marks)*

**4 Peace & Justice**

(a) What is a pacifist? *(1 mark)*

(b) State two Christian/Jewish/Muslim teachings about forgiveness. *(2 marks)*

(c) Describe Christian beliefs about justice. *(3 marks)*

(d) Explain why some religious believers agree with capital punishment but others are against it. *(6 marks)*

(e) "War is wrong."

Discuss this statement. You should include different, supported points of view and a personal viewpoint. You must refer to a religion in your answer. *(12 marks)*

General Certificate of Secondary Education

# GCSE Religious Studies

## Paper 3: Philosophy of Religion

(Deity and Revelation, Symbolism, Worship and Ritual)

| Centre name | | | | | |
|---|---|---|---|---|---|
| Centre number | | | | | |
| Candidate number | | | | | |

| Surname |
|---|
| Other names |
| Candidate signature |

**Time allowed:**

1½ hours

**Instructions to candidates**

- Answer **all** of the questions.
- Write your name and other details in the spaces provided above.

**Information for candidates**

- The marks available are given in brackets at the end of each question or part-question.
- There are also 4 marks available for correct spelling, punctuation and grammar in this paper.
- Marks will not be deducted for incorrect answers.
- There are **3** questions in this paper.
- There are no blank pages.

**Advice to candidates**

- Work steadily through the paper.
- Don't spend too long on one question.
- If you have time at the end, go back and check your answers.

*Leave blank*

**1 Deity and Revelation**

Answer this question for whichever religion you've studied.

(a) What do religious believers mean by the word 'revelation'? *(1 mark)*

(b) State two things that a Christian/Jew/Muslim might believe about God/Allah. *(2 marks)*

(c) Describe Christian beliefs about the Trinity. *(3 marks)*

(d) Explain the ways in which a Christian/Jew/Muslim may believe that God/Allah has revealed himself to them. *(6 marks)*

(e) "God/Allah can be found outside scripture."

Discuss this statement. You should include different, supported points of view and a personal viewpoint. You must refer to a religion in your answer. *(12 marks)*

Leave blank

**2 Symbolism**

Answer this question for whichever religion you've studied.

(a) What is meant by symbolism? *(1 mark)*

(b) How might Christians use icons? *(2 marks)*

(c) Describe Christian/Jewish/Muslim beliefs about representing religious figures in art. *(3 marks)*

(d) Explain the important features of a church/synagogue/mosque. *(6 marks)*

(e) "It should not matter to a Christian what their church looks like."

Discuss this statement. You should include different, supported points of view and a personal viewpoint. You must refer to Christianity in your answer. *(12 marks)*

**3 Worship and Ritual**

(a) Explain what religious believers mean by 'worship'. *(2 marks)*

(b) Explain how having a religious faith may influence someone who has been bereaved. *(4 marks)*

(c) It does not matter what happens to someone's body after death.

Give **two** reasons why a religious believer might agree or disagree with this statement. *(4 marks)*

(d) Explain from **two** different religious traditions the most important features of worship. *(6 marks)*

(e) "It doesn't matter what religious people eat."

Do you agree? Give reasons or evidence for your answer, showing that you have thought of more than one point of view. You must include reference to religious beliefs in your answer. *(8 marks)*

## General Certificate of Secondary Education

# GCSE Religious Studies

## Paper 4: Roman Catholic Christianity

**Time allowed**:

1½ hours

| Centre name | | | | |
|---|---|---|---|---|
| Centre number | | | | |
| Candidate number | | | | |

| Surname | |
|---|---|
| Other names | |
| Candidate signature | |

**Instructions to candidates**

- Answer **all** of the questions.
- Write your name and other details in the spaces provided above.

**Information for candidates**

- The marks available are given in brackets at the end of each question or part-question.
- There are also 4 marks available for correct spelling, punctuation and grammar in this paper.
- Marks will not be deducted for incorrect answers.
- There are **4** questions in this paper.
- There are no blank pages.

**Advice to candidates**

- Work steadily through the paper.
- Don't spend too long on one question.
- If you have time at the end, go back and check your answers.

*Leave blank*

**1 Festivals and Church Worship**

(a) What is Holy Week? *(2 marks)*

(b) Explain why the altar is often considered the most important part of a Roman Catholic Church. *(4 marks)*

(c) "Christmas is the most important time of the year for Roman Catholics."

Do you agree? Give reasons for your answer, showing that you have thought about more than one point of view. *(6 marks)*

Leave blank

**2 Beliefs**

(a) What is the 'the Incarnation'? *(1 mark)*

(b) State two religious authorities accepted by Roman Catholics. *(2 marks)*

(c) Explain the significance of the Christian belief in God as the Creator. *(3 marks)*

(d) What key differences in belief have separated the Roman Catholic Church from other Christian Churches? *(6 marks)*

(e) "We should listen to the Pope's opinion."

Discuss this statement. You should include different, supported points of view and a personal viewpoint. You must refer to Roman Catholic Christianity in your answer. *(12 marks)*

**3 Sacraments**

(a) Give two reasons why anointing the sick is important for Roman Catholics. *(2 marks)*

(b) Describe the sacrament of reconciliation. *(4 marks)*

(c) "Baptism is the most important sacrament."

Do you agree? Give reasons for your answer, showing that you have thought about more than one point of view. *(6 marks)*

**4 Values and Vocation**

(a) Explain how an understanding of the Sermon on the Mount might make a difference in the life of a Roman Catholic. *(3 marks)*

(b) Explain how a local church might express love for other people. *(3 marks)*

(c) "Christianity is irrelevant in the fight against poverty."

Do you agree? Give reasons for your answer, showing that you have thought about more than one point of view. *(6 marks)*

(d) (i) Explain the vows that members of religious orders usually make. *(6 marks)*

(ii) "People who choose the contemplative life are wasting their time."

Do you agree? Give reasons for your answer, showing that you have thought about more than one point of view. Refer to Christianity in your answer. *(6 marks)*

## General Certificate of Secondary Education

# GCSE Religious Studies

## Paper 5: St Mark's Gospel

**Time allowed**:
1½ hours

| Centre name | | | | | |
|---|---|---|---|---|---|
| Centre number | | | | | |
| Candidate number | | | | | |

| Surname | |
|---|---|
| Other names | |
| Candidate signature | |

**Instructions to candidates**
- Answer **all** of the questions.
- Write your name and other details in the spaces provided above.

**Information for candidates**
- The marks available are given in brackets at the end of each question or part-question.
- There are also 4 marks available for correct spelling, punctuation and grammar in this paper.
- Marks will not be deducted for incorrect answers.
- There are **4** questions in this paper.
- There are no blank pages.

**Advice to candidates**
- Work steadily through the paper.
- Don't spend too long on one question.
- If you have time at the end, go back and check your answers.

*Leave blank*

**1 Discipleship**

(a) Who were the **Sons of Zebedee**? *(2 marks)*

(b) Do you think Jesus was right to call Levi as a disciple?
Give **two** reasons for your point of view. *(4 marks)*

(c) Explain why Jesus's teachings about true family might cause problems for some Christians today. *(8 marks)*

(d) "The disciples failed Jesus."

In your answer you should refer to Christianity.

(i) Do you agree? Give reasons for your opinion. *(3 marks)*

(ii) Give reasons why some people may disagree with you. *(3 marks)*

Leave blank

**2 Conflict and Argument**

(a) Who were the Sadducees? *(1 mark)*

(b) What is meant by 'ritual cleanliness'? *(2 marks)*

(c) Why did the healing of the paralysed man lead to conflict? *(3 marks)*

(d) Explain the significance to modern Christians of Jesus's disagreements with the Jews over the meaning of the Law. *(6 marks)*

(e) "The woman at Bethany was right to anoint Jesus with perfume."

Discuss this statement. You should include different, supported points of view and a personal viewpoint. In your answer you should refer to Christianity. *(12 marks)*

**3 Death and Resurrection**

(a) What was the **Sanhedrin**? *(2 marks)*

(b) Do you think Judas was evil?
Give **two** reasons for your point of view. *(4 marks)*

(c) Explain why the Last Supper is important to Christians. *(8 marks)*

(d) "Pontius Pilate was responsible for Jesus's death."

In your answer you should refer to Christianity.

(i) Do you agree? Give reasons for your opinion. *(3 marks)*

(ii) Give reasons why some people may disagree with you. *(3 marks)*

**4 The Identity of Jesus**

(a) What is the **transfiguration**? *(2 marks)*

(b) Do you think Jesus was the Messiah?
Give **two** reasons for your point of view. *(4 marks)*

(c) Explain why Matthew's account of Peter's confession at Caesarea Philippi is more important to Roman Catholics than Mark's account. *(8 marks)*

(d) "Jesus fed 5000 people with five loaves and two fishes."

In your answer you should refer to Christianity.

(i) Do you agree? Give reasons for your opinion. *(3 marks)*

(ii) Give reasons why some people may disagree with you. *(3 marks)*

## Section One — Believing in God

### Page 8 (Warm-up Questions)

1 Two of, e.g. reading religious scripture, an answered prayer, miracles, a numinous experience.

2 A belief that God is all-powerful (all things are possible for him).

3 The Big Bang theory says that the Universe was created in a huge explosion of energy and matter.

4 All three.

5 E.g. people can't believe that a God who is good would allow suffering / people believe that God can't prevent suffering, so he mustn't be very powerful.

6 E.g. Songs of Praise
Positive, e.g. sharing other people's experiences of God can make viewers feel part of a larger Christian community / the themes covered can help lead to a deeper understanding of the Christian religion / viewers can take part in communal worship without having to go to church.
Negative, e.g. it's hard to feel personally involved in a service if you're watching it on TV / it might be seen to trivialise worship / people might find it boring.

### Page 9 (Exam Questions)

2 a) A numinous experience is a feeling of awe, in which a person can 'sense' the presence of God.

b) *For this question, you need to give your personal view and two reasons to back it up — develop them both for all four marks.*

Either: Yes, I think religious programmes make people more likely to believe in God. E.g. Because:

- Religious TV programmes allow viewers to share other people's experiences of God. This shows them how a belief in God has benefited others in their lives.
- Many programmes are interactive, which encourages people to take part in worship by praying or singing. This can give them a direct experience of God.

Or: No, I don't think religious programmes make people more likely to believe in God. E.g. Because:

- People who don't already believe are not likely to bother watching. As it doesn't mean anything to them they will find it boring.
- It's hard to feel personally involved when watching a TV program. Without the religious experience of joining in worship, they are unlikely to be moved enough to believe.

3 a) *All three faiths are similar in their response to the problem of unanswered prayers — so you should have a similar answer whichever faith you chose to write about.*

- God hears all sincere prayers and does answer them. We just sometimes cannot understand God's reply.
- Some believers think that since we can never know what God's plan is, we can't know what is best for us, so we have to just trust in him.
- Sometimes people might question their faith if their prayers are not answered. They might decide that God doesn't exist and reject their faith. Alternatively, they may decide that God exists but isn't powerful enough to help.

*This question is worth 6 marks — so you need to give a decent length answer. Think about all your points before you start writing. To get all six marks, you need to organise them sensibly.*

b) E.g. Yes, I agree that it isn't possible to prove that God/Allah exists.

- There is no scientific evidence for the existence of God/Allah. There are no tests that can be done to show He exists.
- Miraculous events are sometimes claimed to be proof of the existence of God. However, it's more likely there is a scientific explanation for them that we haven't worked out yet.
- It's an important part of faith that the existence of God/Allah cannot be proved.
- I believe that God/Allah doesn't exist. Therefore, trying to prove that he does is pointless.

However, some people may disagree because:

- They believe that God/Allah has revealed himself to them, through prayer, miracles or numinous experiences.
- They believe that the Universe must have been caused by something and that this first cause must have been God/Allah.
- They claim that religious scriptures are the word of God/Allah, and so prove his existence.

*State what you believe clearly — there's no right or wrong answer. But to get all the marks you need to give other points of view too, and* ***explain*** *your reasons fully.*

4 a) Evil caused by humans, e.g. murder.

b) *For this type of question you need to give several reasons, and explain some of them in depth. Also, use specialist terms when you can (but make sure you're using them correctly, or the examiner won't be impressed at all).*

Different Jews might respond to the holocaust in different ways, e.g.:

- Some Jews might conclude that there is no God.
An omnipotent, omnibenevolent God would not have allowed his 'chosen people' to suffer so badly.
- Some Jews might conclude that God exists, but lacks either the goodness or the power to intervene.
- Some Jews may think that that the Holocaust was a test of faith — if good people always got good things in life, everyone would be good for the wrong reasons. The Holocaust happened because God gave us free will, and God refuses to override this.
- Some Jews may believe that the most important thing is to keep practising Judaism, because otherwise Hitler will have won.
- Some Jews see those who died in the Holocaust as martyrs for the faith, and see their martyrdom as 'sanctifying the name of God'.

c) Christianity and Judaism:

- Evil entered the world as a result of Adam and Eve giving in to temptation in the Garden of Eden — this switch from a perfect world to one containing evil is known as 'The Fall'.
- After the Fall, every human being was born with a flawed nature, capable of causing suffering — this is the idea of original sin.
- God created humans with free will — it's up to us to choose whether we perform evil deeds or not.
- Some Christians believe in an evil, spiritual force known as the Devil or Satan who is working against God.
- Many Christians and Jews believe that suffering is a part of God's plan, which we cannot understand.
- A key Jewish idea about evil is found in the Book of Job.
Job endures terrible suffering of all kinds and he questions God. In the end Job comes to the conclusion that God is all-powerful and knows what he is doing.

Islam:

- Muslims believe that evil is a test of humanity's free will.
We have free will, so we can choose whether to give in to temptation or not. It's a test of faith.
- Islam teaches that if we choose to act against the will of Allah we will have to answer for it on the Day of Judgement.
- Some Muslims believe in a devil (called Iblis or Shaytan) who was cast out by Allah and tries to tempt us.
- Allah has reasons for allowing evil, which we cannot understand, so suffering must be accepted.

*You'll only get all six marks here if you use religious terms extensively — so you've really got to know your stuff.*

5 a) The Universe and the life in it works so intricately that it can't have come about by chance. There must have been a designer, and the designer was God.

b)(i) E.g. No, I disagree with this statement.

- All the scientific evidence, e.g. fossils/continual expansion of the Universe, points to other theories, e.g. evolution/the Big Bang.
- The Roman Catholic Church accepted the Big Bang Theory in 1996. Many Christians, Jews and Muslims accept the scientific theories and say that the accounts of Creation in religious texts are symbolic descriptions/a way for us to understand Creation.

(ii) But some people may agree with the statement because, e.g.

- The Bible (the first chapter of Genesis) states that God created the Universe and everything in it in six days.
- Some Orthodox Jews and some Christians take the Bible literally, and believe it to be the Word of God, and so an accurate account of what happened.

*If you agree with the statement, then you'd swap the reasons to part (i) and part (ii) over. Always try to develop your points as much as possible.*

## Section Two — Matters of Life and Death

## Page 17 (Warm-up Questions)

1 A vision experienced by someone close to death, usually an 'out-of-body' experience.

2 A place, or state of existence, where sins are punished before the soul can move on to Heaven. This is a Roman Catholic belief.

3 E.g. Heaven is a place of great beauty and serenity where you spend an eternity with God. Hell is a place of pain and torment.

4 An era of perfect peace and prosperity, brought about by the Messiah.

5 Akhirah

6 Someone taking their own life. Attempted suicide is no longer illegal in the UK.

## Page 18 (Exam Questions)

2 a) *You could answer this question from the point of view of Orthodox Judaism, Reform Judaism or a combination of the two, e.g.*

- Orthodox Jews forbid cremation. They believe that the physical body will be resurrected, intact, in the messianic age. Cremation destroys the body, meaning it can't be resurrected.
- Reform Jews believe that the body is simply a vessel for the soul, and reject the idea of physical resurrection. It doesn't matter what is done to the physical body after death. So Reform Jews accept cremation.

b)(i) E.g. No, I disagree with the statement.

- According to Jewish teachings, all people who live good lives will obtain eternal life. Jews believe that all the righteous dead (including non-Jews) will be resurrected in the messianic age.
- If there is a God and he is fair, he would judge people on their moral behaviour in life. If religious people are only good because they think it will get them eternal life, then this is not as virtuous as a non-religious person who does the right thing expecting no reward.
- Muslims believe that Allah is merciful and compassionate, so some Muslims believe that even non-believers may be sent to Paradise (al'Jannah).

(ii) Some people may disagree with me because, e.g.

- Most Christians believe that only those who follow Jesus will have eternal life in Heaven. Living a good life is not considered enough, because no human can live perfectly enough to deserve heaven.
- In John 11, Jesus said *"He who believes in me will live, even though he dies..."*
- Many Muslims believe that only those who obey Allah will go to al'Jannah.

*It's always good to quote bits of scripture — so make sure you have a few up your sleeve to pull out.*

3 a) The soul is the spiritual part of a human that isn't part of the physical world.

b) Two from: Christianity —

- Christianity teaches that the soul lives on after death, and that the body will be resurrected for Judgement Day, just as Jesus was resurrected after his crucifixion.
- Christians believe that God will judge you, and you'll go either to Heaven, or to Hell.
- Heaven is a paradise where you'll spend eternity with God — as long as you believe in Jesus, have followed his teachings and have lived a good life.
- Hell is a place of torment and pain.
- Roman Catholics also believe in a place, or state of existence, called Purgatory. Here sins are punished before the soul is able to move on to Heaven.

Islam —

- Muslims believe we are being tested during life, and the way we act determines what happens to us after we die.
- We remain in the grave after death in a state called barzakh (the 'cold sleep') until the Day of Judgement. The soul is judged after death.
- The reward for those who have followed Allah will be entry into al'Jannah — the Qur'an refers to al'Jannah as 'gardens of delight', filled with flowers and birdsong.
- Those who don't believe in Allah, or have committed bad deeds, will go to Jahannam for eternity. The Qur'an describes Jahannam as a place of scorching fire, hot winds and black smoke.
- But Allah is also merciful, so many of those who have lived sinful lives may not be sent to Jahannam.

Judaism —

- Orthodox Jews believe that the physical body will be resurrected, intact, in the messianic age. Reform Jews believe that it is only the soul that lives on.
- Many Jews believe the afterlife is spent in places called Gan Eden ("Garden of Eden" or Paradise) and Gehinnom (a bit like Purgatory — a place of punishment).
- Some have a spiritual view of Gan Eden (as a closeness to God) and of Gehinnom (a chance to see the harm caused in life).
- Only if you've lived a blameless life will you be sent straight to Gan Eden when you die.
- Most souls are first sent to Gehinnom for punishment and purification, which lasts no longer than 12 months, before ascending to Gan Eden.

4 a) *For this question, you need to give your personal view and two reasons to back it up — develop them both for all four marks.*

Either: Yes, I agree with abortion. E.g. Because:

- A woman has a right to choose what happens to her body. The foetus can't exist independently, so must be considered part of the woman.
- I think abortion should be allowed when the mother's physical or mental health is at risk, or when the child would be seriously disabled. Without abortion, many more children would be unloved, or suffer through disabilities, and the mental and physical health of mothers would suffer too.

Or: No, I don't agree with abortion. E.g. Because:

- All life is sacred and belongs to God, so only God should decide to start or end it. This is the sanctity of life argument.
- Abortion is murder. Murder is considered wrong both in religious scriptures and in the law. You would be punished for killing a person after birth, and it is just as bad to kill a foetus.

b) *Remember — not all people of a religion will think the same way. For the six marks on offer here, include more than one view.*

- Allah creates all life, so abortion is generally seen as wrong.
- But the mother's life is considered more valuable than the potential life of the child, so abortion is always permitted to save the life of the mother.
- Many Muslims believe abortion is permissible within the first 120 days if the baby would be born with a serious defect. After 120 days, abortion is only allowed to save the life of the mother.
- Some Muslim women argue that they should be free to choose what happens to their bodies. Those that disagree claim that in the Qur'an it says that unborn children will want to know why they were killed.

5 a) Killing someone painlessly in order to relieve suffering.

b) *Read the instructions carefully for this question — there are quite a few things you have to do to get full marks.*

*First, say if you agree:* E.g. No, I don't agree with the statement.

*Then give some reasons, referring to religious arguments, e.g.*

- Euthanasia may be compassionate if someone does not have any quality of life, or has no hope of improvement. Many Christians argue that death may be considered a blessing, and that compassion is an important part of Christianity.
- There could be strict controls in place to make sure that euthanasia was only carried out at the request of the person in pain — either directly, or through written instructions a bit like a will. If it's done genuinely to help, then whoever does it shouldn't be punished.

*Show that you've thought about other people's points of view, e.g.*

- Euthanasia is the deliberate ending of someone's life. Whatever the justification, many people consider this murder, and so prohibited by God.
- If euthanasia was allowed, it would be very difficult to police, e.g. someone might kill an elderly relative to get their inheritance. Also, some people may feel under pressure to volunteer for euthanasia so as not to be a burden.

## Page 24 (Warm-up Questions)

1 E.g. war, which prevents people from working the farms / drought or flood, which damages crops.

2 E.g. unemployment, gambling, alcoholism.

3 Any help freely given, e.g. financial donations, visiting the sick, working for free.

4 E.g. Christian Aid has over 40 member organisations in the UK and Ireland. It raises money through donations and charity events. Christian Aid's work is mostly in development projects, using the skills of local people. They have set up projects to improve sanitation, education and healthcare to help poor people get themselves out of poverty. They also aim to change government policy to help reduce the suffering of the world's poor, e.g. through debt relief and fairer trade.

5 The Jewish practice of giving 10% of their wealth to the poor.

6 Aid given by Muslims in addition to the compulsory Zakah, e.g. extra money or an act of compassion.

## Page 25 (Exam Questions)

2 a) Usury is charging interest (particularly a high rate of interest) on a loan.

b) E.g.

- Any profits are made at the expense of others, so gambling is considered an unfair way of making money. In Islam, it is strictly forbidden.
- Gambling can be addictive, leading to social problems for the gambler, e.g. being unable to support themselves or their family, or resorting to crime to pay.

*The first few parts of a question ease you in gently. They're a place to pick up a few fairly easy marks.*

c) They might not apply for jobs they consider immoral, e.g.

- They might avoid working for a company that exploits people (e.g. by using child labour).
- They might avoid occupations that directly harm people (e.g. weapons dealing) or the environment (e.g. unsustainable logging).
- They might avoid occupations that are sexual in nature, or avoid working for companies that use sexually suggestive advertising.
- They might avoid occupations that encourage gambling.
- Some (particularly Muslims) might avoid working for companies that charge interest on loans, e.g. Western banks.
- Muslims would avoid jobs that involve making or selling alcohol.

d) *It's important not to just start ranting in this type of question. You need to organise your reasons carefully and explain them. And don't forget to think about how someone else might see the situation.*

No, I don't agree.

- There are people in the Bible who are both wealthy and faithful to God, e.g. Joseph of Arimathea was a rich council member who retrieved the body of Jesus from the Roman authorities and arranged his burial.
- In the Jewish books of the Kings, King Solomon was one of the great kings of Israel, who rebuilt the Temple in Jerusalem: *"King Solomon was greater in riches and wisdom than all the other kings of the earth." (1 Kings 10:23)*
- Muslims believe that all wealth belongs to Allah, and that personal wealth is a gift from Allah.
- Wealthy, religious people can help people by giving money to charity, e.g. Zakah in Islam is 2.5% of a person's wealth.

But some people might disagree:

- Religions teach that it is important to be charitable and help those less fortunate than themselves. So while poverty exists, some people might argue that religious people should give away everything they don't actually need.
- Luke 3:11 says: *"The man with two tunics should share with him who has none, and the one who has food should do the same."*

3 a) E.g. two from:

- Rapid population growth means there are too many people to be taken care of.
- Wars are common, which kill some working people and prevent others from working safely. They also destroy buildings and crops, which are expensive to replace.
- Some raw materials are sold for very low prices so workers aren't paid enough to live on.

*A lot of RS relates to what's going on in the world. If you can't remember what it said about poverty in your RS book, then use your general knowledge — think about what you've seen on the news for example.*

b) Either: Yes. E.g. because:

- All wealth ultimately belongs to God, so people have an obligation to share their money with the poor. Otherwise they are depriving the poor of what they're owed.
- Christianity teaches that you mustn't use your money in a way that might harm you or others, e.g. gambling is strongly disapproved of.

Or: No. E.g. because:

- Most people work hard to earn their money. If they could not choose how to spend it, e.g. if they were forced to give it to charity, then there would be no incentive for anyone to work hard and nothing would get done.
- Most people already have to pay taxes to the government. These taxes are used to help support less fortunate people. People should be able to choose how to use the money they have left, whether it be donating to charity or buying luxuries.

*Remember, you don't just have to use religious arguments when you're answering these questions.*

c)
- Christians believe that it is not wealth that is a problem, but the love of wealth. E.g. "*...the love of money is a root of all kinds of evil*", and *"No one can serve two masters... You cannot serve both God and Money"*.
- There were people in the Bible who were both wealthy and faithful to God, e.g. Joseph of Arimathea.
- The Bible teaches that you shouldn't be selfish with wealth, and that Christians have a duty to care for others. E.g. *"Go, sell everything you have and give to the poor, and you will have treasure in heaven"*.
- Christians believe that money must be earned and used responsibly, in a way that doesn't harm other people.

*This type of question is a great place to show examiners that you really know the details about a religion. It's good to refer to specific bits from religious texts.*

4 a)
- The person may feel that the film puts a 'wrong' message across. E.g. glamorising abortion or suicide.
- They might feel that it insults their religion, or gives it a 'bad name'.

b) They might agree because, e.g.
- They realise that by having to respond to any criticism, their faith may be deepened, because they'll have thought about the reasons for their beliefs.
- They believe in freedom of speech being a fundamental human right. They realise that everyone is entitled to air their own opinion, even if it's wrong from a religious viewpoint.

They might disagree because, e.g.
- Religious people are entitled to hold their own views on matters of life and death, and shouldn't have to defend them. If the media is free to say whatever it likes, it could cause unnecessary offence.
- Media representations of these issues are sometimes seen to be biased or exaggerated. This is unfair, as it can give religion a 'bad name'.

*Don't forget — develop both of your reasons. You won't get four marks for two short sentences.*

## Section Three — Marriage and the Family

### Page 34 (Warm-up Questions)

1 Living together in a sexual relationship without being married.

2 There has been a growth in the number of single-parent families and re-constituted families (where people with children from previous relationships find new partners). More children are born outside marriage, and more marriages end in divorce.

3 Christianity and Judaism (Islam allows men to have up to 4 wives).

4 The joining of a same-sex couple with the same rights and responsibilities as in a civil marriage.

5 The Roman Catholic Church teaches that the use of contraception is a grave sin, since it denies the human obligation to 'be fruitful and increase in number'.

6 Three of, e.g. homosexuality, rape, prostitution, celibacy, incest, marriage, infidelity.

### Page 35 (Exam Questions)

2 a) E.g. Marriage is the only proper context for sex. Marriage is the only proper situation in which to raise children.

b)
- Marriage is a lifelong union/a contract between two people, involving commitment and responsibility.
- Marriage involves submission/devotion to your partner.
- The joining of husband and wife reflects the union of Jesus with his followers.
- Marriage is for procreation.
- Marriage is a faithful relationship.
  One of the Ten Commandments demands this.

*You're asked for Christian beliefs here — so try to get some specific ones from that religion in. Don't just go for general waffle about why religious people usually think marriage is good.*

3 a)
- Most faiths teach that the only proper context for sex is within marriage, so they may decide to wait until they're married.
- They may believe that sex should have a special status and shouldn't be treated casually.
- Religions teach that self-control and sexual restraint are important.

*Always try to develop some of the points you make.*

b) (i) E.g. No, I don't agree.
- Homosexual relationships can be as committed, and filled with mutual love and support as a relationship between a man and a woman. They should be allowed to be blessed like a marriage.
- God created everyone, and if he created some as homosexuals, then this is his will. Homosexuality is seen in other species, so must be a natural alternative to heterosexuality and should be accepted by religious believers.
- Society has changed from the time when most religious scriptures were written. Religious attitudes need to change to reflect this.

(ii) Some people may disagree because, e.g.
- Religious texts suggest that homosexual sex is wrong.
  E.g. *"Because of this, God gave them over to shameful lusts... Men committed indecent acts with other men, and received in themselves the due penalty for their perversion."*
  Therefore, religions should not give their approval to homosexual relationships.
- Some religious people think that marriage is the only proper context for bringing up children. They think it would be unfair for any children that the homosexual couple might have or adopt. So marriage is the only type of relationship that should be blessed religiously.

*Don't forget what the statement is actually saying. It's not saying that homosexual relationships are wrong, or that civil partnerships shouldn't be allowed — it's saying that civil partnerships shouldn't receive religious blessings. You probably haven't learnt a big list of reasons for and against this, so you might have to apply what you know about related matters.*

4 a) E.g. Yes, I do, because:
- It might not have been the divorcee's fault that their first marriage ended, e.g. their husband/wife might have committed adultery. The Bible even permits divorce and remarriage in such circumstances (Matthew 19:8-9).
- Religions teach forgiveness. If someone broke their marriage vows first time round, they should be forgiven and allowed a second chance.

Or, no I don't because, e.g.
- Roman Catholicism teaches that marriage is a sacrament. God joins two people together for life, and this cannot be undone. Marrying again while your first spouse is alive is the same as adultery.
- Marriage is supposed to be a life-long commitment. If divorcees are allowed to marry in church, this could be seen as condoning divorce.

b) *You're asked to explain the key features in this question — so don't just list them.*
- The opening statement often explains the purpose of marriage.
- Hymns symbolise the couple starting their life together with the help of God and the religious community.
- Prayers and readings are a traditional part of Christian worship. They remind the couple of the seriousness of their vows.
- The couple exchange rings as a physical symbol of the vows and of lifelong commitment.
- The couple take vows in front of witnesses and God, which indicates the seriousness and sacredness of marriage.

5 a) Adultery is when a married person has sex with someone who isn't their spouse.

*It's for questions like this that you need to learn the terms in the glossary. They might only be worth 2 marks — but they might make all the difference between one grade and another.*

b) Either: Yes. E.g. because:
- Actors often become role models, especially for young people, so it seems likely that they would copy the behaviour they see on TV.
- Explicitly portraying promiscuous behaviour on the TV surrounds people with it, and encourages them to think of this behaviour as the norm.

Or: No. E.g. because:
- People know the difference between reality and fiction. Most people are not impressionable enough to copy the behaviour that they see on TV.
- TV programmes also show the negative effects of adultery and promiscuity. They are just as likely to deter people from doing these things as to encourage them.

## Section Four — Religion and Community Cohesion

### Page 46 (Warm-up Questions)

1 People of all races living and working together peacefully.

2 Men and women have separate areas for prayer. Only men can form a minyan and read from the Torah. Only men can become rabbis.

3 Three of, e.g. they may have poor English, so need an interpreter while they learn the language / they may have a poor understanding of UK laws and customs / they may have suffered physically, mentally or emotionally in their home country and so be traumatised / they may face discrimination from local people. E.g. the Boaz Trust works to help failed asylum seekers. They offer food, shelter and legal help to make an appeal.

4 a) Christianity teaches that the only way to get into Heaven is through Jesus, so some Christians believe they have a duty and sacred right to convert people.

b) Muslims are happy to accept converts, but don't usually go out looking for them. Converting *from* Islam to a different faith is considered a very grave sin.

c) Jews have no real desire to convert people. Orthodox Jews tend not to accept converts at all. Reform Jews will often accept converts after a period of study (usually about 18 months).

5 Missionaries spread the message of Christianity all around the world in an attempt to convert people.

6 Hatred and fear of Islam.

### Page 47 (Exam Questions)

2 a) Community means the people living in a certain place, or a group of people with the same religious or cultural characteristics.

b) Either: Yes, I think the media encourages community cohesion.

- It educates people about other faiths and races so that they can understand each other better.
- Religious leaders often appear in the media following trouble caused by racial or religious intolerance. These leaders usually appeal for calm and often give a truer representation of a faith than people might otherwise have seen.

Or: No, I don't think the media encourages community cohesion.

- The media emphasises the strain placed on resources by immigrants. This can make people prejudiced against immigrants.
- The media can give an unbalanced picture of a religion. This can cause hatred and fear in communities. E.g. media coverage of Islam following the London bombings in 2005 is likely to have contributed to Islamophobia.

*For this question, think about how the media might make people feel towards others in the community — either positively, or negatively, depending on your point of view.*

3 a) Judging something or someone for no good reason, or without full knowledge of a situation.

b) Judaism:

- The Book of Genesis suggests that all of humanity comes from the same source and is, therefore, equal before God.
- Other messages of tolerance found in the Torah are "*When an alien lives with you in your land, do not mistreat him... Love him as yourself...*" and "*Do not abhor an Edomite, for he is your brother. Do not abhor an Egyptian...*"
- Scriptures show that God does not want the Jews to turn their backs on non-Jews, but to be *"a light for the Gentiles"*.
- The story of Ruth promotes racial harmony: Ruth is very loyal to her Israelite mother-in-law, and becomes devoted to God. This bloodline eventually produces King David. The message is that good things happen to those who are nice to people from other lands.
- Jewish religious leaders, e.g. Lord Jonathan Sacks, often promote racial harmony.

Islam:

- Islam teaches that all people were created by Allah, and were created equal (although not the same). He intended humanity to be created with differences. But this just means we're all individuals.
- Muslims all over the world are united through the ummah — the community of Islam. This promotes racial harmony, as no one is excluded or discriminated against.
- Hajj demonstrates equality. Those on pilgrimage all wear simple white garments, showing everyone's equal before Allah — wealth, status and colour don't matter.
- The fact that all Muslims should pray five times a day at set times, and face Makkah whilst doing so, also demonstrates unity and equality.
- Some Muslim religious leaders promote racial harmony.

4 a) *This is the great thing about Religious Studies. You get to air your opinion, and no one argues with you. But you really need to develop those reasons to get the four marks on offer here.*

Either: Yes, because:

- A mixed-faith marriage will be unlikely to work because the husband and wife will be pulling in opposite directions rather than being unified in their beliefs.
- Any children of a mixed-faith marriage will be given conflicting messages on religion and so are less likely to be brought up as observant members of either religion.

Or: No, because:

- The only thing that matters is that the people involved love each other. If this is so, any religious differences can be overcome.
- Some faiths are inclusive. E.g. Judaism and Islam teach that people of other religions can be righteous if they live morally good lives. The Qur'an even suggests that Jews and Christians may be sent to Paradise on Judgement Day. This means the husband and wife may welcome each other's faith.

b) E.g. No, I disagree, because:

- Women have proved themselves capable of going out to work and performing just as well as men. Men should be expected to take on an equal share of the housework and childcare.
- Bibical references to the different roles of men and women just reflected society at that time, rather than how it should be.
- Jesus treated men and women equally, and women are found amongst Jesus's followers.
- Men and women have an equal obligation to Allah in terms of pilgrimage, fasting and prayer, therefore, they should have equal responsibilities elsewhere.

Some people may disagree with me because, e.g.

- The Bible talks about wives submitting to their husbands. *"Wives, submit to your husbands as to the Lord. For the husband is the head of the wife as Christ is the head of the church..."* This implies they should have different roles in the home.
- In most countries, men and women traditionally have had different roles in the home. This is just the way things are.
- Women go through pregnancy and are the ones who can breastfeed. These things may interfere with them going out to work, so they may well have some different roles.
- God created two sexes, so he must have intended there to be differences between them.

*Structuring your answer is important to maximise your marks. One way of doing it is to talk about the reasons for one point of view first, and then the reasons for another point of view.*

5 a) Christianity:

- Christians generally believe that people have the right to practise any faith.
- But they argue that Christianity is the only true faith, and that it's only through following the teachings of Jesus Christ that people can reach God: "*I am the way and the truth and the life. No one comes to the Father except through me.*"

- Many Christians believe that it is their duty to convert people of other faiths to Christianity. The Catechism of the Roman Catholic Church makes this clear: "*...the Church still has the obligation and also the sacred right to evangelise all men*".
- But Christian inclusivists believe that there's at least some truth in what other religions say about God.

Judaism:

- Judaism teaches that it is the only true faith for Jews to follow, but is tolerant of other faiths.
- People of any religion are generally deemed to be righteous if they follow the Noahide Code — moral laws given to Noah after the flood that prohibit idolatry, murder, theft, sexual immorality and blasphemy.
- So there's no real desire to convert people, although Reform Jews will accept converts.
- Their respect for other religions means that Jewish participation in interfaith groups, e.g. '*The Council for Christians and Jews*', is common.

Islam:

- Muslims believe that Islam is the only true faith — although there is an acceptance that all righteous people will be favoured by Allah, as he knows all we do.
- Muslims believe that men like Adam, Ibrahim (Abraham), Musa (Moses) and Isa (Jesus) were all Prophets of Allah. So the Torah and the Bible are also holy scriptures revealed by Allah (albeit edited from their original form), and therefore they do contain some truth.
- But some Muslims argue that Islam shouldn't have anything to do with other faiths, and some Muslims feel they have a mission to lead non-Muslims to Allah.

*Remember — within any religion, there'll be a range of views. These matters are rarely black and white, so make sure you show that you understand this.*

b) (i) E.g. No I don't agree.

- Some people will suffer abuse and torture in their own country. We should let them in to protect them.
- Christians, Jews and Muslims all agree that human beings should be treated fairly and humanely. It would be cruel to send immigrants back to their home country to suffer.
- Some immigrants bring skilled labour into the country, and they are often willing to do jobs that local people are not prepared to do.

(ii) Some people may disagree with me because, e.g.

- There are lots of people without jobs in this country. Immigrants take jobs, so some people think that letting in more new people will worsen unemployment.
- Some people feel that immigrants place a strain on social services and health care resources.
- Some people believe that immigrants are not prepared to fit in with our customs. They worry that this will cause our culture and traditions to change.

## Section Five — Morals and Ethics

### Page 54 (Warm-up Questions)

1 Three of, e.g. religious scripture, the example of great teachers and/or prophets, conscience, the teachings of religious institutions (e.g. the Catechism of the Roman Catholic Church / Shari'ah).

2 An inner feeling of what's right and what's wrong.

3 You shall have no other gods before me. You shall not bow down before idols. You shall not misuse the name of the Lord. Observe the Sabbath and keep it holy. Honour your father and mother. You shall not murder. You shall not commit adultery. You shall not steal. You shall not give false testimony. You shall not covet (your neighbour's wife or anything else that is your neighbour's).

4 a) Jewish commandments

b) A Muslim belief that Allah has appointed humans as vice-regents or trustees of his creation.

5 E.g. All human beings deserve to be treated fairly and with respect because all humans are created in the image of God.

6 E.g. voting, protesting, joining a pressure group, joining a political party.

7 Jesus taught that loving God and loving others are the two most important commandments. Christians have a responsibility to put this love into action by caring for and helping others.

### Page 55 (Exam Questions)

2 a) A list of what someone believes to be right and wrong.

b) *For this sort of question, you're marked on your English as well as your religious knowledge — so write in full sentences, use the right religious terms and organise your answer so it's easy to follow.*

E.g.

- Jesus challenged authority. Christians can follow Jesus's example by challenging rules that they see as cruel or unnecessary.
- Jesus taught that love was more important than laws or traditions. Christians can follow his example by being loving and charitable.
- Jesus set an example of self-sacrifice, both during his life and in his death. Christians can follow his example by putting other people's needs before their own.

c) E.g. I disagree — there are many sources of moral guidance.

- Sacred texts were written a long time ago, so they don't have the answers to all modern ethical questions.
- Some people follow religious traditions — they see them as the living interpretation of religious texts.
- Many religious believers trust the teachings of religious leaders, e.g. the Magisterium, Rabbinical writings or fatwas.
- Some people believe that our conscience is the 'voice of God', so we should always use it as a moral guide.
- Some people base their moral judgements on Situation Ethics. Sacred texts do not always support the most loving action.

However, some people may agree with the statement because, e.g.

- They believe that sacred texts are the direct Word of God and so should be followed to the letter.
- They believe that religious traditions and teachings that aren't found in sacred texts are the work of humans, who have failings.
- They believe that your conscience is the product of your upbringing, and so not necessarily trustworthy.

*Give as many different points of view as you can. Explain them all clearly, and don't forget to give your **own** opinion too.*

3 *For this question, you need to give your personal opinion — there isn't a right or wrong answer. But to get full marks you need to give two developed reasons why.*

Either: Yes. E.g. Because:

- All people are equally valuable and equally entitled to respect, because all humans are created in the image of God.
- All humans should be free to think and behave in the way that they feel is correct, e.g. to please God.

Or: No. E.g. Because:

- Some people may choose to exercise a right, e.g. the right to freedom of expression, in a way that's hurtful or harmful to other people.
- 'Human rights' are an idea invented by the Christian West, and they may not all be appropriate to other societies, e.g. Arab societies are quite different.

4 a) *This one isn't actually about religion directly — sneaky.*

- Political parties are groups of like-minded people who put forward candidates for election to parliament. They campaign for election based on social, economic and environmental policies.

- Once in power, the ruling party can bring about changes in society, e.g. by setting taxes, deciding what to spend money on and passing laws.
- Pressure groups are organisations that try to influence government decisions or people's behaviour on a particular issue, e.g. abortion.
- Pressure groups can bring about social change directly (by encouraging people to change their behaviour) or indirectly (by encouraging government to pass new laws).

*This is an 8 mark question, so you need to get in plenty of detail and explain all your ideas clearly.*

b)(i) E.g. Yes, I agree with the statement.

- It's important for everyone to take up their opportunity to influence the decisions that are being made that affect their lives, otherwise they can't complain if they don't like something.
- Democracy can bring about social change, and Christians believe they have a responsibility to try to make the world a more fair and loving place.

(ii) But some people may disagree with me, e.g. because

- It's impossible for an individual to affect society, so it doesn't matter whether people take part in democracy or not.
- Religious people should try to change society through their own actions, by setting an example for others, rather than through politics.

*What's the old saying — "never talk about politics or religion"? Well, whoever said it had clearly never sat a Religious Studies exam.*

5 a) The teaching of Jesus that you should: *"do to others what you would have them do to you".*

b) *You need to write about a particular passage from the Bible, so including a quote or two will help.*

- The Parable of the Sheep and the Goats is a parable of Judgement Day — Jesus teaches that people will be split into the good (sheep) and the bad (goats). The sheep will go to Heaven and the goats to Hell.
- The sheep will be those that have fed the hungry, clothed the naked, cared for the sick, etc.
- Caring for any person is the same as caring for Jesus himself *"whatever you did for one of the least of these brothers of mine, you did for me".*
- The goats will be those who didn't help others. The parable teaches that not helping a starving person is the same as leaving Jesus to starve.

## Page 63 (Warm-up Questions)

1 Three of, e.g. increasing amounts of greenhouse gases in the atmosphere are making the Earth warmer (global warming), which could lead to flooding and climate change / agricultural and industrial chemicals pollute rivers and lakes, harming plants and animals / toxic waste on the land (e.g. nuclear waste) can kill plants and animals and cause cancer in humans / air pollutants can cause acid rain / particulates in the air can cause health problems / CFCs damage the ozone layer / natural resources will run out.
People can reduce their impact by, e.g. farming organically, removing pollutants from waste water and gas before they're emitted, recycling, using less energy.

2 Mending the world.

3 Humans are generally considered more important than animals, but animals must be treated with mercy and care as God's creations.

4 All the human beings on the planet, or the ways of acting and feeling that all humans share, which separate us from other animals.

5 Three of, e.g. artificial insemination by the husband — sperm from the husband is injected directly into the wife's womb / artificial insemination by donor — sperm from a sperm donor is injected directly into the wife's womb / IVF — eggs are fertilised in a test tube and then placed into the mother's womb / egg donation — a form of IVF in which a different woman's egg is used / surrogacy — where a different woman bears the child for the couple.

6 Two of, e.g. possible reduction in biodiversity, crops may be unsafe, 'superweeds' may be created, there could be unforseen problems, a reduction in the gene pool could lead to problems with disease, some people see genetic engineering as 'playing God', genetic engineering of plants and animals may lead to the engineering of humans.

## Page 64 (Exam Questions)

2 a) Taking care of the Earth as custodians of creation (so it can be passed on to the next generation).

b) *You're not getting marks here for having the right opinion — you're getting them for the reasons you give to back your opinion up.*

Either: Yes. E.g. Because:

- There's only a certain amount of each natural resource in the Earth, so if we don't conserve them, they won't be there for future generations.
- We shouldn't abuse God's creation by taking too much from the Earth.

Or: No. E.g. Because:

- It's more important for people to have a good quality of life, and to do that we have to use up natural resources.
- The resources were created by God for humans to use, so we should make full use of them.

c) E.g. They might agree because:

- According to Genesis Chapter 2, God created all the plants and animals to help man.
- They believe that God gave humans dominion over the Earth and everything on it: *"You made him ruler over the works of your hands; you put everything under his feet."*

E.g. They might disagree because:

- They believe that God created humans as stewards, to take care of the rest of His creation, *"The Lord God took the man and put him in the Garden of Eden, to work it and take care of it".*
- They believe that everything on Earth is interdependent, so while using up resources or harming the planet might provide short-term benefits, it will be harmful to humans in the long term.

*This is a four mark question, so make sure you've developed both your points.*

3 a) Two of, e.g. food, scientific experiments, hunting, zoos and circuses.

b) E.g. yes, I agree.

- Christianity teaches that animals should be treated with kindness because they are part of God's creation.
- The Noahide laws forbid cruelty to animals — animals are here to help us, not to be abused.
- Muslims believe that all creatures should be treated with compassion — so cruelty to animals is forbidden, as is using animals purely for human pleasure (e.g. hunting for sport).
- Jews and Muslims believe that if an animal is to be slaughtered for food, it should be done as humanely as possible. The animal is killed with a single cut across the throat with a sharp blade to bring a quick death.

But some people might disagree:

- The Bible teaches that humans were created higher than the animals, and that animals were given to humans for their use.
- Some religious people believe that money shouldn't be 'wasted' on caring for animals when it could be better spent relieving the suffering of humans.

*To get all 6 marks, you have to give your own opinion, back it up with good reasons, and balance it with other people's opinions. You won't get the marks if you just start ranting.*

4 a) Things that we're particularly good at, e.g. singing.
Many religious people believe that talents are gifts from God.

b) *It's not enough to just put a few words down for each reason — you need to develop each point for full marks.*

- Christianity, Judaism and Islam all teach that God created humans higher than the other animals, and that humans are created "in God's image".
- All three religions teach that, unlike animals, humans are created with a soul — a spiritual part that will continue to live after the body has died.

5 a) *This is a subject that people tend to feel quite strongly about. Whatever your opinion, make sure you give clear, rational arguments for holding it.*

Either: Yes. E.g. Because:

- Crops can be genetically engineered to produce higher yields. That way, we could produce enough food to feed everybody using less land.
- Crops can be genetically engineered to contain useful products not present in them naturally, e.g. extra nutrients.

Or: No. E.g. Because:

- Not everyone is convinced that genetically modified plants are safe to eat. We don't understand the science well enough to predict all possible effects.
- Christianity teaches that all creation belongs to God. By trying to create new organisms ourselves, we are 'playing God'.

b) Judaism —

- In Jewish teaching, there is a strong emphasis on having a family. God commanded the Jews to *"be fruitful and increase in number"*, so fertility treatment is generally encouraged if it's the only way for a couple to have children.
- Artificial insemination and in vitro fertilisation are allowed as long as the sperm comes from the husband.
- Artificial insemination using donor sperm is often not permitted, particularly by Orthodox Jews. Using another man's sperm is seen by some as a form of adultery.
- Egg donation is generally seen as okay, but the donor should ideally be a Jewish woman. According to Orthodox teachings, you're a Jew if your <u>mother</u> is a Jew, so this is important.

Islam —

- Scientific methods of conceiving a child are only permitted if all natural attempts have failed.
- Artificial insemination and in vitro fertilisation are permitted so long as the egg and sperm are from the couple.
- Using donated sperm is strictly forbidden by most Muslims, since it is seen as adultery. Some Muslims also worry about diseases being passed on from anonymous sperm donors.
- Some Muslims, particularly Shi'ites, accept egg donation if there's no other way for the couple to have a child.

*To get all 8 marks, you need to structure your answer sensibly and use good, clear English. Make sure you explain each of your points clearly, and don't waffle.*

c) (i) E.g. Yes, I agree with the statement.

- Christians have a duty to help and care for others.
- Donating your organs to save a life is an act of Christian love and charity.
- Christianity teaches that God will not need our bodies to be intact to resurrect us at Judgement Day, so there's no harm in removing organs from the body after death.

(ii) But some people may disagree with me, e.g. because

- Jews and Muslims believe that the human body is sacred, alive or dead, so it's forbidden to mutilate a body by removing organs.
- Some Orthodox Jews believe that the body will be resurrected intact at Judgement Day, so it should be buried intact.
- Some Muslims believe that all human organs belong to Allah, so we have no right to give them away.

*You have to refer to specific religious arguments in this question. If you haven't, your answer's only worth half marks.*

## Section Six — Peace and Justice

## Page 71 (Warm-up Questions)

1 An international organisation set up to promote peace, global cooperation and human rights.

2 E.g. religion, defence, tribalism, honour, economics

3 a) The only intended outcome of a war should be the just cause that it's being fought for, i.e. the just cause shouldn't be an excuse to achieve an unjust goal.

b) Any harm caused by fighting the war mustn't be as bad as the harm it's trying to prevent. / The military advantage gained by an attack must outweigh any harm caused to civilians.

c) War should target combatants only, and not civilians.

4 One of, e.g. in self-defence, to prevent an attack on their country, to prevent a murder.

5 Taking advantage of a weaker person or group of people.

6 Christianity, Judaism and Islam all teach that, e.g. it's a sin to attack someone else without cause / it's important to protect the weak and free the oppressed / everyone will answer on Judgement Day for harming, or failing to protect, an innocent.

7 Before Yom Kippur, Jews seek forgiveness from anyone they feel they've hurt during the year, then on Yom Kippur itself, they seek God's forgiveness for their sins.

## Page 72 (Exam Questions)

2 a) Attacking someone without provocation.

b) E.g. Pax Christi is a Roman Catholic peace organisation. They campaign worldwide for human rights, disarmament, reconciliation, the protection of civilians in conflict zones and peaceful conflict resolution.

*You could have written about any suitable organisation, e.g. the Jewish Peace Fellowship or Muslim Peace Fellowship.*

c) *You need to give clear reasons for this question, so don't just waffle on about peace being good.*

(i) E.g. Yes, I agree with the statement.

- Christianity, Judaism and Islam all teach that peace is the ideal state for all human beings.
- Jesus taught that people should love and forgive their enemies, and turn the other cheek. If everyone behaved in this way, there would be no more war.
- Jesus said that *"all who draw the sword will die by the sword"*, encouraging people to find peaceful solutions to problems.

(ii) But some others may disagree with me, e.g. because

- Over the centuries there have been many 'holy wars' fought in the name of religion, e.g. the Christian Crusades of the 11th, 12th and 13th centuries.
- Negotiations through international organisations like the UN are a better way to achieve lasting world peace.
- Many religious people believe that war is justified sometimes.

3 a) An obligatory war is a war fought in self-defence, one fought to prevent invasion of your country (a pre-emptive strike or the defence of a neighbour) or a war commanded by God. Jews are obliged to fight these wars.

*The question says 'briefly' and it's only worth 3 marks — so you don't have to go into loads of detail.*

b) Lesser jihad means 'striving' against an external enemy, e.g. in a war. Jihad must only be fought a last resort, in the name of Allah and according to his will.

c) *This question is asking you to explain, not just describe. Make sure you get plenty of details in and give reasons for each rule.*

There are five rules for declaring a 'just war':

- It must be declared by a proper authority. This is to make sure the other conditions have been thought about — the war isn't being fought on a whim.
- There must be a just cause. The Roman Catholic definition of a just cause is preventing damage that would be *"lasting, grave and certain"*. This usually means preventing the deaths of innocent people.

- All other ways of resolving the conflict must have been tried and have failed. This rule (and the 'just cause' rule) are because violence of any kind seems to go against Jesus's teachings.
- A war must have a reasonable chance of success. Fighting a war that you have no chance of winning is considered to be a waste of lives.
- The damage caused by fighting the war must be less than the damage you were trying to prevent. Otherwise, fighting the war would only make things worse.

4 *There are lots of religious issues that can cause family conflict. Here are some of the more common problems.*

- Society, particularly in the UK, is becoming increasingly secular (non-religious), so older generations are likely to be more religious than younger generations. Conflict can be sparked if a younger member of a devout family chooses not to take part in traditional worship or follow religious laws.
- Religious teachings are traditionally very strict when it comes to sex. If a member of a devout family breaks sexual laws, e.g. has sex outside marriage, uses contraception, has homosexual sex, this can cause serious conflicts.
- Mixed-religion relationships can be difficult, particularly if one or both families is strongly religious. There is often conflict over which religion children should be raised in.
- Social traditions, e.g. arranged marriages, can be linked to religion. If a member of a family breaks with tradition, this can be seen as turning away from their religion.

*All these issues have been from the point of view of a less religious individual in a more religious family, but of course conflicts can be triggered the other way round, too.*

5 a) Either: Yes. E.g. Because:

- If we don't forgive other people when they do something wrong, we can't expect God to forgive us for our sins.
- Being unforgiving can lead to bitterness and hatred, so people should forgive for their own happiness and peace of mind.

Or: No. E.g. Because:

- If you keep forgiving people when they do something wrong, they may never learn to do the right thing.
- Some evils, e.g. mass murder, are so bad that they should never be forgiven. Forgiving them would be an insult to the people they harmed.

b) *The teachings of Christianity, Judaism and Islam are broadly similar, but there are differences. Make sure you get in some points that are specific to the religion you've chosen.*

Christianity —

- Christians believe that Jesus died on the cross to atone for human sins, so that God might forgive us.
- Jesus taught that if people forgive the sins of others, God will forgive their sins: *"if you forgive men when they sin against you, your heavenly Father will also forgive you".*
- Jesus taught that people shouldn't seek revenge for wrongs, but should love and forgive their enemies.
- Christians believe that reconciliation — coming together and making peace — is important between people, and between each Christian and God.
- They believe that, for reconciliation to happen, people have to be genuinely sorry for the things they've done wrong, and genuinely forgiving of other people's wrongs.

Judaism —

- Jews believe that God is forgiving and merciful, and that he expects people to be forgiving and merciful towards each other.
- Judaism teaches that you should always seek forgiveness and try to make amends if you do something wrong.
- Jews are obliged to forgive other people if they apologise. The medieval rabbi Maimonides said, *"It is forbidden to be obdurate... one should forgive with a sincere mind and a willing spirit."*
- Jews believe that you can only be forgiven by the one you have injured, so God can only forgive a sin against God, not against another person.
- Yom Kippur is the Jewish Day of Atonement. Before Yom Kippur a Jew should be reconciled with other people. They seek forgiveness from anyone they feel they've hurt during the year and forgive others in return.
- On Yom Kippur, Jews seek God's forgiveness for the sins they have committed that year.

Islam —

- Muslims believe that Allah is forgiving and merciful, and that he expects people to be forgiving and merciful towards each other.
- Islam teaches that you should always seek forgiveness and try to make amends if you do something wrong.
- Muslims believe that wrongs should be forgiven if the offender is genuinely sorry and tries to make amends.
- Although the Qur'an allows retribution for injuries, it encourages people to forgive instead, *"whoever pardons and makes reconciliation — his reward is [due] from Allah."*
- Muslims try to follow the example of the Prophet Muhammad (as recorded in the Hadith), who was willing to forgive people who had wronged him.
- According to the Qur'an, Allah will forgive nearly any sin if the sinner is repentant, but will not forgive idolatry.

## Page 78 (Warm-up Questions)

1 a) Breaking a religious law.

b) The Muslim religious law code.

2 E.g. deterrence, protecting the innocent, reform, rehabilitation, retribution.

3 For capital punishment, e.g. the risk of death might act as a better deterrent than prison / if you execute a murderer, it's impossible for them to kill again / the Bible says *"if anyone takes the life of a human being, he must be put to death."*

Against capital punishment, e.g. many murders are committed in the heat of the moment, so the murderer isn't considering the consequences / execution doesn't allow for reform / there have been cases of innocent people being executed / the Bible and Qur'an encourage mercy.

4 Two of, e.g. drugs can affect people's judgement or make people feel invincible, which can make them more likely to take risks / some addicts stop caring about other aspects of their lives and forget their responsibilities / some addicts turn to crime to fund their habit.

5 Three of, e.g. excess alcohol can cause liver disease, brain damage and heart failure / mixing alcohol with other drugs can kill / smoking cannabis can cause lung diseases / taking cannabis can trigger psychological problems in vulnerable people / hallucinogens can cause permanent psychological damage / overdoses can kill / sharing needles can spread diseases like HIV.

## Page 79 (Exam Questions)

2 a) The idea of each person getting what they deserve, and of maintaining what's right.

b) *This question is about obeying laws, not just being a good person. Make sure your answers are specific enough.*

(i) E.g. Yes, I agree with the statement.

- Christians, Jews and Muslims all believe that God has commanded them to obey the laws of the land they're living in, e.g. in Romans, it says *"it is necessary to submit to the authorities".*
- Most crimes hurt someone and so they break religious laws and displease God. Most religious people believe that it's important to please God, and that any sins will be punished in the afterlife.

(ii) But some others may disagree with me, e.g. because

- They believe it is more important to follow religious teachings than the laws of the land. So if religious law and state law conflict, they feel it's better to commit a crime than a sin.
- Justice is very important to most religious people. So if they feel a law is unfair or cruel, they may believe it is their duty to make a stand against it.

3 a) Either: Yes. E.g. Because:

- If a punishment is bad enough in some way (e.g. expensive, embarrassing, restrictive, painful) it will put people off committing the crime.
- If criminals endure hardships as punishment, they'll be less likely to repeat their crimes, as they won't want to be punished again.

Or: No. E.g. Because:

- Lots of crimes are committed every day, even though people know what the punishment is. This shows that the threat of punishment isn't a very good deterrent.
- Lots of crimes are committed on the spur of the moment, or when the person is drunk or has taken drugs, so they're not thinking about the consequences.

b) *For these long discussion questions, you need to structure your answer carefully, use good English and get in some appropriate technical terms along the way.*

E.g. I agree with the statement because:

- Nobody is inherently bad. With help, most offenders are able to reform themselves.
- The Bible says that we should be merciful. Jesus said, *"be merciful, just as your Father is merciful"*. It shows mercy towards an offender to help them change their ways and guide them to do what's right.
- By learning a trade or improving their education, former criminals can make a useful contribution to society when they leave prison. Just locking a person up is a waste of their God-given talents.
- People aren't usually kept locked up forever, so offenders will be released eventually. Proper rehabilitation helps prevent people reoffending when they're released from prison.

However, some people may disagree because, e.g.

- They believe that the primary aim of punishment is retribution. Punishment should make a person 'pay' for the harm they've caused to other people. The Bible says, *"If anyone injures his neighbour... eye for eye, tooth for tooth. As he has injured the other, so he is to be injured."*
- Some offenders are very dangerous to the rest of society, e.g. rapists and murderers. Some people believe these offenders should never be released back into society.
- Some people think that punishment needs to act as a deterrent. If the punishment isn't seen to be harsh enough, e.g. if offenders are given counselling and training rather than being made to suffer, then there's no deterrent.
- Rehabilitation schemes can be very expensive. Some people argue that this money could be better spent on law-abiding citizens.

*Don't forget to give your own opinion somewhere in your answer — it's best to put it either right at the beginning or right at the end.*

4 *Remember, this is a question about Christian views — so it's not enough to write about general non-religious reasons.*

Some Christians support the use of capital punishment because

- The Old Testament identifies some crimes that should carry the death sentence, e.g. *"If anyone takes the life of a human being, he must be put to death."* This may be considered a clear instruction from God.
- If you execute a murderer, it's impossible for them to kill again. Some Christians argue that this justifies taking a life, because it protects the lives of innocents.

Other Christians do not support capital punishment because:

- In the Sermon on the Mount, Jesus taught that we should set aside "eye for eye" punishment in favour of mercy. He said that it is better to forgive offenders — so many Christians believe that punishment should give people the opportunity to reform.
- There have been cases where someone has been proved innocent after having been executed. Some Christians believe that it's better to give lesser punishments to the guilty rather than risk killing an innocent person.

5 a) A compulsion to keep doing something, even if you know it's harming you.

b) *If you really don't have a strong opinion on this sort of thing, just pick one that you know you can back up.*

Either: Yes. E.g. Because:

- The drugs that are currently banned are harmful. Most are addictive, and can impair people's judgement (making them more likely to take risks). They can cause serious psychological and physical damage and an overdose can kill you.
- Illegal drugs are a way of escaping the realities of life. This makes them socially damaging, as addicts are likely to forget their responsibilities.

Or: No. E.g. Because:

- Current drugs laws are inconsistent. Tobacco is as harmful and addictive as many illegal drugs, so either it should be banned too, or some other drugs should be legalised.
- People still take drugs, even though they're illegal — but they buy them from potentially dangerous criminals and can never be sure exactly what they're buying. Legalising and controlling drug sales would make it safer for users and could help to reduce the social problems associated with addiction.

c) (i) E.g. Yes, I agree with the statement.

- Alcohol can be very harmful to your body. Christians, Jews and Muslims all believe that your body is a gift from God and so it shouldn't be abused — St Paul wrote *"your body is a temple of the Holy Spirit"*.
- In Proverbs 31, it says that alcohol can make you forget your responsibilities. Abstentionist Christians think this makes it unwise to drink alcohol, in case you forget your duties to God.
- Alcohol is forbidden in Islam — it is seen as a weapon of Shaytan. Under the influence of alcohol, people are more likely to do stupid things, and to stop thinking about serving Allah.

(ii) But some others may disagree with me, e.g. because

- Moderationist Christians believe that alcohol is part of God's creation. As such, they argue that it is a gift to be enjoyed in moderation.
- Jesus and the Apostles drank wine at the Last Supper, and wine has been used as part of Holy Communion since then. Drinking the Communion wine is an important part of worship for many Christians.
- Alcohol is permitted in Judaism, although drinking to excess is disapproved of.

*For top marks on this question, you have to develop some of your points. That could mean adding details, giving examples or quoting from scripture.*

## Section Seven — Religion and Revelation

### Page 90 (Warm-up Questions)

1 A transcendent God is outside the world and doesn't act directly in human history.

2 Two of, e.g. Judaism, Islam, Christianity (although Christians believe in the Trinity).

3 An experience that reveals a god's presence.

4 a) E.g. Torah (or Tenakh) and Talmud

b) Two of, e.g. Qur'an, Hadith, Sunnah

5 a) Christians believe that Jesus *was* God, so God revealed himself fully in the person of Jesus.

b) Muslims believe that Allah revealed the Qur'an, word for word, to Muhammad through the Angel Jibril.

c) Jews believe that God revealed himself to Abraham and made a covenant with him which forms the basis of Judaism. Abraham agreed to devote himself and his descendants to God, and in return God promised never to abandon them.

## Page 91 (Exam Questions)

2 a) A divine person with whom you can have a conversation/relationship.

b) Judaism, e.g.

- God is omnipotent, omnipresent and omniscient.
- God is totally good and totally perfect.
- There's only one God.
- He made the Universe and everything in it.
- His energy sustains the Universe.
- He is the lawgiver and judge. Through the Torah, he gave his people rules by which to live a good life. God will judge all people based on how well those rules have been followed.
- He is merciful and will save his people from sin and suffering.

Islam, e.g.

- There's only one God — Allah is one. He is the Supreme Being and has no equal.
- He made the Universe and everything in it.
- He is loving and compassionate.
- He is the creator and judge of all humans, and knows everything they do.
- Allah is both immanent and transcendent.
- Allah's message was delivered by the prophets.

*Most of these points aren't developed — so you'd need to make sure you put lots of them down or develop some of them further.*

3 a) One in which religion and government are kept completely separate. Or: A society in which religion plays no official role.

b) E.g. No, I disagree with the statement.

- Even in a secular society, religions can provide community traditions, e.g. festivals like Easter, Christmas and Hanukkah.
- Religion provides believers with an authority on how they should behave. It will still guide their actions in a secular society, making them more likely to live moral lives and obey state laws.
- Religion is a key part of followers' identities. It will always have immense value to them.

However, some people may disagree with me because, e.g.

- In a secular society, religious views won't be taken into account when deciding public policy.
- Secular societies have their own laws and moral codes that are completely separate from religious faith. Some people think this makes religion unnecessary.

*When you've finished answering a question, read back over it and check you didn't forget any bits, such as referring to a religion.*

4 a)
- Some Christians believe that Jesus performed miracles to show God's power, and to demonstrate the importance of faith.
- Other Christians believe that miracles in religious texts should be interpreted symbolically, rather than literally.
- Some Christians believe that miracles still happen, e.g. healing at Lourdes.

*This question is asking for specific Christian beliefs. So make sure you give them, or you won't get the 3 marks on offer.*

b) Jews:

- The Torah is considered holy by all Jews.
- Jews believe that it tells them how to live.
- Orthodox Jews believe that the Torah is of divine origin, and the laws are to be followed to the letter.
- Progressive Jews believe that the Torah is merely people's interpretation of the word of God.
- Progressive Jews consider the Torah's moral commandments binding (although open to interpretation), but the ritual laws can be adapted or abandoned in response to changes in society.

*Religious Studies isn't a black and white subject — Examiners are really keen to see that you understand that followers of a faith don't all think exactly the same thing. Religions aren't like the Borg — they don't have a hive mind.*

Muslims:

- Muslims believe that the Qur'an records the exact words of Allah as they were revealed to the Prophet Muhammad.
- Muslims believe that the Qur'an is a complete record of all the revelations Allah made to the Prophet Muhammad.
- Muslims believe that the Qur'an is a complete guide to Islamic life. It tells them what they must believe, and how they must live, in order to get to Paradise.
- It's only the Qur'an if it's written in Arabic. Translations are only 'interpretations'.

5 a) Two of, e.g. a career, such as a teacher, or nurse. A life dedicated to God/Allah as a monk/nun/priest/rabbi/imam. Marriage and having children. For Jews, keeping the covenant made with God. For Muslims, the Greater Jihad.

b)(i) E.g. No, I disagree with this statement.

- Non-religious people can feel equally drawn to do something worthwhile with their lives, e.g. help people by nursing them.
- Non-religious people can believe that they have talents they should use for the good of humanity, even though they don't feel that the talents are God-given.

(ii) Some people might disagree with me because, e.g.

- Some Christians believe that vocations are meant to be challenging and something that you need God's help to do. You wouldn't be able do it without a belief in God.
- Jews/Muslims believe that their vocation is to serve God/Allah as the Torah/Qur'an says they should. Non-religious people wouldn't have this purpose.

*If you agree with the statement, then you'd swap the reasons to part i) and part ii) over. It can be tricky to think of reasons why anyone would disagree with you — but I bet someone out there would.*

## Section Eight — Worship and Symbolism

## Page 103 (Warm-up Questions)

1 a) E.g. cross and fish (icthys).

b) Two of, e.g. star/shield of David, menorah, Lion of Judah.

2 The adhan (call to prayer) is called from this tower.

3 a) The main part of a church where the congregation sits.

b) The ark that holds the scrolls of the Torah.

c) A niche that shows the direction of Makkah.

4 Some Christians (e.g. Roman Catholics and Orthodox Christians) believe that saints can join in our prayers to God to make them more effective. This is called intercession. Other Christians believe that Jesus is the only mediator between us and God, so we don't need the help of saints. Some Christians think that we shouldn't pray to saints because no-one does in the Bible (and it could be seen as idolatry).

5 a) Christians pray both in church and in private, at any time. There are no set times for prayer.

b) In Judaism, daily prayers happen at three set times a day. At these times, men will try to attend the synagogue and become part of a minyan. Women are expected to pray at home. There are also prayers said at home, e.g before and after meals, first thing in the morning, last thing at night, etc.

c) In Islam, daily prayers happen five times a day. For men, prayer should ideally take place in a mosque. If this isn't possible, a prayer mat can be used to make a prayer place. Women are expected to pray at home. Extra prayers (du'a) can be said anywhere and at any time.

6 The Kashrut lays down certain statutes to test Jews' obedience and to mark them out as different from other nations. These rules include the humane slaughter of animals.

7 A period of deep sorrow for someone who has died.

## Page 104 (Exam Questions)

2 a) E.g. Church: nave and altar.
Synagogue: Aron Kodesh (the Ark) and Bimeh/Almemar.
Islam: minbar and the mihrab.

b) E.g. large, grand buildings symbolise importance; shape of a cross to symbolise Christ's sacrificial death; dome symbolises nearness of Heaven/Universe.

*Don't forget to say what the architectural features symbolise — that's what the question is asking you to do.*

3 a) Paintings, representing saints, that are often found in Orthodox Christian churches to help believers pray.

*Make sure your definition is a good one. "Pictures of saints" would only get you 1 mark here.*

b) E.g. to represent the presence of saints/as a focus for prayer, to offer God the highest expression of worship, to create a sense of awe.

c) E.g. three from: hymns, readings, sermon, prayers, Holy Communion/Mass.

*"List", "Name" or "State" questions are easy ways to pick up marks. Don't spend ages explaining stuff — it's a waste of time.*

4 a) E.g. two from: to say goodbye to the dead, to remember/celebrate their lives, to comfort the bereaved.

b) Christianity:

- Verses from John 11, e.g. "Whoever lives and believes in me will never die" are often read.
- The priest often gives a short sermon about Christian belief in life after death. This may comfort the bereaved.
- The life of the person who has died is talked about to remember and celebrate them.
- There are prayers for the bereaved.
- A Roman Catholic funeral includes Holy Communion (the 'Requiem Mass'). The purpose of a Requiem Mass is to pray for the soul of the dead person.
- There's another short service at the graveside or crematorium. It doesn't matter whether the body's buried or cremated — Christians believe that at the Resurrection they will have new 'spiritual bodies', not their old ones.

Judaism:

- The dead person must be buried (not cremated) as soon as possible, preferably within 24 hours.
- The body is ritually bathed and wrapped in a plain linen shroud, before being placed in a plain, unpolished, wooden coffin — in death rich and poor are equal.
- At the funeral service in the synagogue, psalms are read and a prayer is said praising God for giving life and for taking it away.
- The rabbi might make a short speech about the life of the deceased to remember and celebrate them.
- The first week after the funeral is called shiva (seven). The immediate family stay at home and are visited by relatives and friends who pray with them three times a day and offer comfort. They do not cut their hair, shave, listen to music or have sex. The men recite a prayer called the kaddish.

Islam:

- After a person has died, the body is washed, as a sign of respect. The body is then wrapped in a clean white shroud.
- Funeral (Janazah) prayers are said, praying that the dead person may be judged mercifully and gain a place in Paradise.
- The body is buried in a simple grave, lying on its right side with the face towards Makkah.
- A period of mourning is kept for three days, finishing with Qur'an reading and prayers for the dead person. Some Muslims do this after 40 days as well.

*Wherever possible, explain the reasons why these rituals take place. Many of them will symbolise some crucial aspect of belief.*

5 a)
- Some religions teach that certain foods shouldn't be eaten. E.g. in Judaism and Islam, only certain animals may be eaten, and these must contain no blood and must be slaughtered with a single cut to the throat.
- Some religious people feel it is wrong to harm animals if it isn't necessary, so they may choose a vegetarian/vegan diet.
- Some people eat certain things to celebrate religious festivals, or to symbolise religious ideas, e.g. Easter eggs and Challot.

*If a question just asks about "religious believers" in general, you can talk about any faiths. If you're a religious believer, you can use examples from your own faith.*

b) Christians:

- Some Christian traditions teach that fasting is not necessary, so many Christians don't fast.
- Some Christians believe that fasting can bring you closer to God, since it helps you to concentrate on spiritual rather than physical things.
- Some Christians fast during Lent to commemorate the 40 days and nights of Jesus's fasting in the wilderness. Roman Catholics are obliged to fast on Ash Wednesday and Good Friday (although this doesn't mean going without food entirely).
- Roman Catholics should fast for an hour before Holy Communion.

Jews:

- In Judaism, food is associated with happiness, so fasting shows grief or repentance. Fasting is often considered an act of atonement for sin.
- Jews fast and pray for 25 hours during Yom Kippur, the Day of Atonement. On Yom Kippur, Jews should refrain altogether from eating or drinking — not even water.
- Jews believe that fasting can bring you closer to God, since it helps you to concentrate on spiritual rather than physical things.

Muslims:

- Fasting during Ramadan is one of a Muslim's most important obligations — it is one of the Five Pillars of Islam. Muslims fast between sunrise and sunset during the month of Ramadan.
- The fast includes no food, no drink, no smoking and no sex.
- Fasting is supposed to help Muslims understand hunger, and make them more willing to help others.
- Fasting is an act of total obedience to Allah — it shows publicly that Allah matters more than physical needs.

*This is a 6 mark question — so you need to get in plenty of detail and some specialist terms. E.g. don't just say that Jews fast at festivals, write about a specific festival.*

6 a) Prayer is an attempt to contact God, often in the form of a conversation.

b) They might agree because, e.g.

- Private prayer is communication with God. During prayer we develop a relationship with God and hear what He is saying.
- It is a time when we are focusing completely on God and are not distracted by other things. This deepens faith.

They might disagree because, e.g.

- Prayer is just one part of worship. There are other, equally important parts, such as reading the Bible.
- Whether believers live their lives according to God's wishes, e.g. showing kindness and compassion, is just as important as prayer.

# Section Nine — Roman Catholic Christianity

## Page 111 (Warm-up Questions)

1 Jesus is the Christ/Messiah. In the Incarnation, God became fully human in the form of Jesus. Jesus was born of a virgin. Jesus's death on the cross won his people forgiveness of sin. Jesus rose from the dead and is alive today. After the resurrection, Jesus ascended into heaven.

2 The split in the Christian Church that resulted in Eastern and Western Christianity.

3 Two of, e.g. transubstantiation of the Mass, the Immaculate Conception of Mary, the authority of the Pope / Magisterium, the sacrament of reconciliation.

4 The belief that Mary, mother of Jesus, was born without the flaws of original sin.

5 a) Cardinals are the highest rank of bishops beneath the Pope. They act as the Pope's advisors and elect the Pope's successor.

b) Deacons are the lowest rank of ordained clergy. They may carry out some of the offices of a priest, but may not celebrate Mass, hear confession or anoint the sick.

6 Roman Catholics believe that the teachings of the Church should be followed as well as the teachings of the Bible. Roman Catholics believe in the Apostolic Tradition — a body of teachings and ritual practices handed down through the early Church from the apostles. These teachings and practices don't appear in the Bible. They also believe in the Magisterium — the Holy Spirit given authority of the Pope and his bishops to teach correctly on all matters of faith and morals.

## Page 112 (Exam Questions)

2 a) Christ is seen as a sacrifice on behalf of humanity *(1 mark)*, just as lambs were sacrificed to God in the Jewish temple *(1 mark)*.

b) Christians believe that through his suffering and death, Jesus won forgiveness for the sins of all people. They believe that Jesus was without sin, but that God placed all the sins of the world on him at his crucifixion. Christianity teaches that his sacrifice saved humanity from eternal damnation, and meant that we could have eternal life with God.

*You'd get the full 3 marks for showing you understand this really well by developing your answer.*

3 a) The ascension is when Jesus ascended into Heaven after the resurrection.

b)
- God is one, but He exists in three forms — the Father, the Son and the Holy Spirit.
- God the Father is often considered the God of the Old Testament. Many Christian traditions teach that God the Father will be our Judge after death.
- Jesus is God the Son. He is the incarnation of God in human form, and God sending Jesus down to us shows how much he loves the world.
- Jesus is believed to be the Christ or Messiah ('anointed one') prophesied by Isaiah in the Old Testament.
- Jesus provides a model for Christian behaviour in obedience to God the Father.
- The Holy Spirit is the presence of God in the world. The Holy Spirit is believed to guide the Church and individual Christians.

*Don't forget — for questions worth this many marks, you'll be expected to write your answer using good English. And you need to organise it well too.*

4 a) Laity refers to all the non-ordained members of the Church.

b) E.g. two from: to lead Mass, hear confession, preach the Gospel, administer the sacraments of baptism, marriage and anointing the sick, offer support and guidance to the people of the parish.

c) (i) E.g. Yes, I agree with the statement, because:
- Celibacy allows priests to focus fully on their spiritual duties.
- The teachings of Paul say that *"It is good for a man not to marry"* and Jesus said that some *"have renounced marriage because of the kingdom of heaven"*.
- Church tradition is an authority for Roman Catholics. As priests have traditionally been required to be celibate, then this is right.
- The Magisterium says that priests should be celibate — this means that for Roman Catholics it is the right choice and shouldn't be questioned.

(ii) Others may disagree with me because, e.g.
- In recent years there has been a fall in the number of men wanting to become priests. Some Catholics blame this on the celibacy rule, and believe that it is important for the future of the Church that it be relaxed.
- Protestants argue that celibacy is not stated as a qualification for priesthood in the Bible.
- Some have argued that celibacy is too difficult for many and so becomes a distraction rather than an aid to spiritual life.

*To get full marks on this one, make sure you back your opinion up with good reasons. Then put just as much effort into thinking of reasons why people might disagree with you.*

5 a)
- She gave birth to Jesus.
- She is also seen as the model for Christian living, because she cooperated fully with God's will.
- Roman Catholicism teaches that she was born without original sin, so she wasn't born with the flaws of other humans.

b)
- The authority of the Church is absolute on matters of faith and morals. It's the supreme authority.
- The Apostolic Succession is what makes a Church.
- The Church is the means to salvation.
- The mission of the Church is to expand the community of Christian believers and to help care for those who are already part of the community.
- St Paul taught that the Church was the "Body of Christ" on Earth, with Christ as its head.
- The Church is holy/sacred/belonging to God.

*Remember the difference — 'the Church' is the community of believers, whereas 'a church' is a place of worship.*

## Page 121 (Warm-up Questions)

1 Baptism, confirmation, reconciliation, eucharist, ordination, marriage, anointing the sick.

2 a) The second part of the Mass, consisting of readings from scripture, a short sermon, and recitation of the Nicene Creed or Apostles' Creed.

b) The Roman Catholic belief in the transformation of the communion bread and wine into the body and blood of Christ.

3 The first day of Lent. Roman Catholics put ash on their foreheads to show that they are sorry for their sins. / They fast.

4 Atonement

5 Jesus told his followers to do their praying, giving to charity and fasting quietly for God alone, not in public to impress other people. He said that those 'displaying religion' have already had their reward in the effect it has on their audience, but those who do good things in secret will be rewarded by God.

6 Worship only God (*You shall have no other gods before me. You shall not bow down before idols.*) Respect the name of the Lord (*You shall not misuse the name of the Lord.*) Observe the Sabbath and keep it holy.

7 The vows of poverty, chastity and obedience taken by members of religious orders.

## Page 122 (Exam Questions)

2 a) Lent is the 40 days before Easter. / Lent commemorates the 40 days and nights of Jesus's fasting in the wilderness.

*There's a lot you could say about Lent. But this question is only worth 2 marks so you don't need to write down everything you know.*

b) (i) E.g. Yes, I agree with the statement because:
- Lent is a sombre time for Roman Catholics when the focus of worship is on the suffering of Jesus. Giving something up helps us to identify with Jesus's suffering.
- Giving something up is good for developing our self-control. Self-control is important for Christians.
- Giving something up for Lent can be an act of penance for sin.
- Money or time saved by giving something up for Lent can be donated to charity. It is a Christian's duty to help those less fortunate than themselves.

(ii) But others might disagree, because, e.g.
- Lent used to be kept very strictly and involved everyone giving up all rich food. If the tradition has been watered down so much, it can't be very important, and Christians should be able to choose what to do.
- It can be better to add something, e.g. attending extra Masses, or being especially kind to others.

3 a) • Penitential Rite: a confession of sin and a request for God's mercy and forgiveness in the form of a prayer.

• Liturgy of the Word: readings from scripture, usually including a section from one of the Gospels, followed by a homily (a short sermon based on the readings). This is followed by a recitation of either the Nicene Creed or the Apostles' Creed.

• Liturgy of the Eucharist: the point at which Catholics believe that the bread and wine are transformed into the body and blood of Christ.

• Rite of Communion: Everyone says the Lord's Prayer, followed by the sign of peace, where everyone shakes hands or hugs those around them. Then the congregation come forward to receive the bread and wine.

*To get the 6 marks, you need to show that you understand each feature — don't just list them.*

b) • Most see Holy Communion as largely commemorative — it reminds worshippers of the Last Supper and Jesus's sacrifice. However, many believe that there is a 'real presence' of Christ in the bread and wine.

• Roman Catholics believe that the bread and wine actually become the body and blood of Christ, by the power of the Holy Spirit. It is through this that Jesus takes up residence in his people.

• Quakers and the Salvation Army don't celebrate the Eucharist or any other sacraments, seeing them as unnecessary or inessential symbols for the inward acceptance of God's grace.

4 a) The life lived by members of a religious order who devote themselves to prayer and study.

b) E.g. The Passage is a Roman Catholic organisation set up to help the homeless.

• The Passage runs a hostel in London for homeless people, with priority given to the most vulnerable.

• It also offers medical care, skills training and advice to help homeless people get jobs and build new lives for themselves.

5 a) They might use them to help pray and meditate on the sufferings of Christ, particularly during Lent.

b) E.g. Yes, I agree with the statement, because:

• Confirmation happens around the age of seven, when a person is old enough to understand its meaning. Infants who are baptised do not have any understanding.

• Those about to be confirmed have to show that they understand their faith — usually by attending a course of religious instruction.

• In the Roman Catholic Church, only confirmed Church members can receive the Eucharist. Baptism isn't enough to allow you to receive the Eucharist.

Others may disagree with me because:

• It is baptism that marks a person's official entry into the Church.

• Baptism cleanses the person from original sin.

• They're both sacraments and so are equally important.

*AQA exam questions often ask you to give reasons why something is more or less important than something else. For example, you might get asked if Pentecost is more important than Advent, or if the Sermon on the Mount is more important than the Apostles' Creed.*

## Section Ten — St Mark's Gospel

### Page 134 (Warm-up Questions)

1 a) A follower of Jesus. (This can refer to just his followers in the Bible or to all Christians.)

b) A gift dedicated to God (and so not usable for anything else).

2 A rich man asked Jesus what he had to do to get into Heaven. Jesus said that he must follow the Ten Commandments and give all his wealth to the poor. Jesus said that it was *"easier for a camel to go through the eye of a needle than for a rich man to enter the kingdom of God"*.

3 A Jewish group who studied the Law and were dedicated to keeping the Jewish faith alive.

4 E.g. Jesus entering Jerusalem in the manner of a king (The Triumphal Entry – Mark 11:1-11), Jesus clearing the Temple courtyard of traders (The Cleansing of the Temple – Mark 11:15-18), Jesus arguing over the source of his authority (The Authority of Jesus Questioned – Mark 11:27-33).

5 Four of, e.g. Judas, *"the chief priests and teachers of the law"* (Pharisees, Sadducees, scribes, Temple elders, etc.), the Sanhedrin, Pontius Pilate, the crowd outside Pilate's court, Jesus himself.

6 As Jesus came out of the water, the heavens were torn open and the Spirit descended on Jesus *"like a dove"*. A voice from heaven declared *"You are my Son, whom I love"*.

7 Healing miracles, two of e.g. healing the paralysed man, healing the man with the shrivelled hand, raising Jairus's daughter from the dead, exorcising Legion.

Nature miracles, two of e.g. calming the storm, feeding the five thousand, walking on water.

### Page 135 (Exam Questions)

2 a) The rulership of God in people's lives / the total acceptance of God in someone's heart (or the final Kingdom after Judgement Day).

b) Jesus taught that true greatness in the eyes of God comes from serving others *"If anyone wants to be first, he must be the very last, and the servant of all."* Putting yourself last like this involves a great deal of self-sacrifice (putting other people's needs before your own).

*This is a three-mark question, so make sure you get down some details. It's worth learning some quotes for your Mark's Gospel exam.*

c) • Jesus didn't choose to call well-educated, religious experts to follow him. Instead he called common fishermen to learn from him and serve God. This shows that everyone is welcome in the kingdom of God.

• Jesus also called Levi, who was a sinner. Modern Christians take this to mean that it doesn't matter how much you have sinned in the past. Anyone who repents and follows Jesus is welcome.

• When Jesus sent out his disciples to preach, he sent them out with no provisions or money. The disciples trusted fully in God to provide for them during their mission (through the charity of others). Many Christians believe they should be prepared to do the same.

• The sending out also carries a message to modern Christians about charity. They should be among the people who would welcome the disciples, rather than those who would turn them away.

*Make sure you answer the question. It's not just asking you to describe the calling and the sending out, but to explain why modern Christians think they're important.*

3 a) Either: Yes. E.g. Because:

• Keeping the Sabbath is one of the 10 Commandments, and it is important for Christians to follow the Commandments.

• The Sabbath is a day entirely dedicated to God. It is important for Christians to forget about worldly things for one day a week to focus on serving God.

Or: No. E.g. Because:

• Jesus set an example of not always keeping Sabbath laws when he healed the man with the shrivelled hand (Mark 3:1-6).

• Jesus justified working on the Sabbath on the grounds that human need and doing good are more important than the letter of religious law. He said *"the Sabbath was made for man, not man for the Sabbath"*.

b) (i) E.g. Yes, I agree with the statement, because:

• Jesus set an example of challenging authority when he cleansed the Temple of *"money changers"* and *"those selling doves"* on his entry into Jerusalem. He challenged what he saw as impiety, and other Christians should be prepared to do the same.

• When Jesus healed the man with the shrivelled hand (Mark 3:1-6), he argued that doing good is more important than obeying rules.

ii) Others may disagree with me because:

- According to Mark, Jesus said that you should always pay taxes to the state, *"Give to Caesar what is Caesar's"*. Some people argue that this means Christians should always obey state authorities.
- Elsewhere in the Bible, e.g. St Paul's letter to the Romans, Christians are instructed to obey the law.
- When Jesus was arrested, he went peacefully and didn't challenge his capture. This suggest that Christians should be willing to submit to the authorities.

*The question says "In your answer you should refer to Christianity", so not all your reasons have to come from Mark's Gospel.*

4 a) The garden where Jesus prayed before his arrest.

b) *This stuff is pretty central to Christianity, so make sure you know it inside out.*

- Christians believe that when Jesus was on the cross, God placed on him all the sins of the world.
- Through Jesus's suffering and death, these sins were atoned for.
- Christians believe that this sacrifice was necessary for Jesus's followers to be forgiven their sins and gain a place in heaven.
- Jesus's resurrection was the fulfilment of his prophecies and demonstrated Jesus's divinity.
- According to the last verses of Mark's Gospel, Jesus was resurrected in the flesh, not as a spirit. This showed his power over death.

5 a) A synagogue ruler whose daughter was brought back to life by Jesus.

*These definitions are worth 2 marks, so make sure you give a full definition.*

b) (i) E.g. Yes, I agree with the statement, because:

- At Jesus's baptism and again at the transfiguration, a voice from heaven declared Jesus to be his son, e.g. at the baptism, *"You are my Son, whom I love; with you I am well pleased"*.
- In the story of Legion, the demons called Jesus *"Son of the Most High God"*.
- Jesus confirmed that he was the son of God at his trial before the Sanhedrin.
- Jesus performed many miracles that showed he had the power of God.
- Jesus rose from the dead, demonstrating his divinity.
- The Christian Creeds state that Jesus is the Son of God.

(ii) Others may disagree with me because, e.g.

- According to Mark's Gospel, Jesus showed normal human emotions when he prayed at Gethsemane and as he hung on the cross.
- Not everyone trusts the evidence of Mark's Gospel because he was not a first-hand witness of the events he described.
- If there is no God, he could not have been the son of God.

*There are plenty of reasons you could give here, but you don't have to write about them all to get the marks. Remember each part is only worth three marks, so don't waste time writing full page essays.*

## Practice Exam Papers

## Paper 1 — Religion and Life

*Remember, there are 4 marks available for correct spelling, punctuation and grammar in this paper.*

1 a) Not being sure (or believing that it's impossible to know) whether there's a god or not. *(2 marks)*

*You get 1 mark for a partially correct answer, e.g. 'Someone who isn't sure about religion.'*

b) E.g. No, because:

- Our existence is a test to see if we are fit for Heaven *(1 mark)*. It wouldn't be a test if we didn't have free will, and free will is what causes suffering *(1 mark)*.
- God has a plan and we can't know what it is *(1 mark)*. We have to trust that God's plan is good and not expect to understand his reasoning *(1 mark)*.

Or, yes because, e.g.

- According to the scriptures, God is good *(1 mark)*. A good God wouldn't let people suffer, so the God described in the scriptures can't exist *(1 mark)*.
- According to the scriptures, God is all-powerful *(1 mark)*. If he isn't powerful enough to prevent suffering, then he can't be the God described in the scriptures. *(1 mark)*.

*You get 1 mark for a brief reason, and 2 marks for a developed reason. You don't get any marks if you didn't say 'Yes' or 'No' to the question though.*

c)
- The Universe as we know it works on the principle of 'cause and effect' — everything that happens is caused by something else. If you trace this chain of cause and effect back in time, you eventually reach a starting point — an uncaused cause or 'First Cause'. Some people argue that this 'First Cause' must have been God.
- Some people believe that the intricate workings of the Universe/life cannot have come about by random chance. There must have been some kind of designer — and this designer must have been God.
- Examples of design arguments are Isaac Newton's thumb theory (because every thumbprint is intricate and unique, there must be a God) and William Paley's watchmaker theory (you would not think an intricate watch you found was made by chance — so why believe the world was).

*(These points are worth 4 marks each.)*

*This is a question where you get extra marks for how well you write your answer. You get 2 marks for a well-written reason and 4 marks for a well-written developed reason, up to a total of 8. The question asks about causation and design, though, so you only get full marks if you've written about both.*

d) (i) E.g. No, I disagree with this statement.

- A scientist can still believe in God if they don't take the Bible literally. For example, if they view the Creation story as symbolic, or as a parable describing evolution.
- We don't know the reason why the Universe exists, or what happens to us after we die. There is no scientific evidence for the truth about these things, so a scientist may believe they're to do with God.

*You get 3 marks for two developed reasons (both the above are developed), or for three brief reasons, or for one really well developed reason.*

(ii) But some people may disagree with me because, e.g.

- Some Orthodox Jews and some Christians take the Bible literally, and believe it to be the Word of God and so an accurate account of creation. This isn't consistent with scientific theories.
- There is no scientific evidence for the existence of God, and the existence of God is untestable. So there is no reason for a scientist to believe that God exists.

*As for part (i), you get 3 marks for two developed reasons, for three brief reasons, or for one really well developed reason.*

*BUT — if you didn't mention a religion, the most you can get is 3 marks for parts (i) and (ii) together.*

2 a) Immortal means that something will never die *(1 mark)*.

b) Any two from, e.g. It is immortal. It is separate from the physical body. It is the part that is judged on Judgement Day.
*1 mark for each, up to a maximum of 2.*

c) Christian beliefs about Heaven, e.g.

- It's a place of great beauty and serenity, a paradise where you'll spend eternity with God.
- To go there, you need to have believed in Jesus, have followed his teachings and have lived a good life.
- Many Christians see Heaven as a state of mind. In Heaven you'll be happy, and know God.

Jewish beliefs about Gan Eden, e.g.

- Some Jews see Gan Eden as a physical place of lavish banquets and warm sunshine.
- Other Jews have a more spiritual view of Gan Eden — as a closeness to God.

- Most Jews believe that only those who have led blameless lives go straight to Gan Eden when they die. (Most souls are first purified in Gehinnom.)

Muslim beliefs about Paradise, e.g.

- Paradise is a place of peace, happiness and beauty, described in the Qur'an as 'gardens of delight'.
- Obedience to Allah is the key to earning a place in Paradise.
- Most souls will only be judged and find a place in Paradise at Judgement Day. (Most Muslims believe that only martyrs go straight to Paradise when they die.)

*1 mark for each point, up to a maximum of 3.*

d) Many Christians give to charity because:

- Christians believe they have a duty to care for other people. The Bible contains many passages encouraging charity, e.g. *"The man with two tunics should share with him who has none, and the one who has food should do the same."*

  *"If anyone has material possessions and sees his brother in need but has no pity on him, how can the love of God be in him? ...let us not love with words or tongue but with actions and in truth."* "*Love your neighbour as yourself.*"
- The Bible suggests that being charitable in life will reap great rewards after death. E.g. *"Go, sell everything you have and give to the poor, and you will have treasure in heaven."*
- Giving to charity is a way of demonstrating Christian love and compassion.

Many Jews give to charity because:

- Jewish teaching says: *"If there is a poor man among your brothers in any of the towns of the land... do not be hardhearted or tightfisted toward your poor brother."*
- All Jews are expected to contribute 10% of their wealth to help the poor — this is called Tzedakah.
- Judaism teaches that all wealth belongs to God. Not giving to the poor deprives them of what they're owed.

Many Muslims give to charity because:

- Muslims believe that possessions ultimately belong to Allah.
- Islam teaches that you should act responsibly and help those in need.
- Zakah is one of the Five Pillars of Islam — 2.5% of your yearly savings should be given to the needy. It's a practical ways of showing obedience to Allah. (Showing obedience is what a good Muslim must do and will hopefully result in a positive judgement on Judgement Day.)

*Give yourself 1 mark for a well-written brief reason, and 1 mark for each well-written development of the reason, up to a maximum of 6 marks. You should have used relevant specialist terms correctly too, e.g. Zakah.*

e) E.g. I disagree with this statement.

- Sometimes it is compassionate to take a life, e.g. in the case of euthanasia, to allow a very ill person to die with dignity. Or in the case of abortion, to protect the mother's health, or if the child will be born with serious health problems.
- Christianity places great emphasis on showing compassion and relieving suffering.
- Some Christians argue that death can be a blessing in these circumstances.
- All humans are born with free will, so people should have the right to choose to end their own life.

But other people may argue that:

- Christianity, Judaism and Islam teach that all life is God's creation, and is therefore sacred.
- Only God should choose when life starts or ends. If we do that we are playing God/interfering in God's plan.
- Euthanasia is only wrong if it involves actively doing something to cause death, (e.g. giving someone a fatal overdose), but not if it involves just taking away measures to keep the person alive, (e.g. a life support machine).

*You only get full marks if you:*
- *Give your opinion clearly (1 mark).*
- *Give two really clear, well developed reasons for it (4 marks).*
- *Give two different viewpoints, with reasons (5 marks).*
- *Use really good English, correct spelling and specialist terms (2 marks).*

*If you don't talk about a specific religion, or if you didn't give other points of view, you can only get a maximum of 6 marks.*

3 a) Not taking part in sexual activities *(2 marks).*

*You get 1 mark for a partially correct answer, e.g. never getting married.*

b) E.g. No, I don't agree:

- Religious teachings say that the only proper context for sex is within marriage.
- Sex has a special status and shouldn't be treated casually.
- Self-control and sexual restraint are important.

Or: Yes, I do agree:

- The scriptures were written when contraception was unreliable. This has now changed, so their teachings are out of date.
- Sexual frustration is a bad reason to get married and so sex before marriage is good.
- Sex before marriage gives people a chance to explore their sexuality.

*You get 1 mark for a brief reason, and 2 marks for a developed reason. You need to state your opinion clearly though — or you won't get any marks.*

c) Christianity:

- The Roman Catholic Church teaches that humans have an obligation to 'be fruitful and increase in number'. It teaches that preventing conception is against 'natural law' and that the use of any artificial contraception is a grave sin. *(This reason is worth 4 marks.)*
- Many Protestant Christians are in favour of the use of contraception because it lets parents plan their family in a responsible way.
- Some Christians believe that barrier methods of contraception (e.g. condoms) should be encouraged, since they can reduce the spread of diseases like AIDS.
- Many Christians believe that decisions on moral issues like contraception should be a question of individual conscience. *(These reasons are worth 2 marks each.)*

Judaism:

- Orthodox Judaism generally opposes the use of contraception, since a child is a gift from God. Contraception interferes with God's plans to bless couples with children.
- Most Orthodox Jews will accept contraception if pregnancy could be physically or psychologically harmful to the mother or an existing child, since the life of a living person is considered more valuable than the potential life of an unconceived child.
- Many Reform Jews approve of the use of contraception for family planning. They believe that traditional teachings should be reinterpreted in the light of modern society, and that many issues are best left to the conscience of each individual. *(These reasons are worth 4 marks each.)*
- Some Jews believe that barrier methods of contraception (e.g. condoms) should be encouraged, since they can reduce the spread of diseases like AIDS. *(This reason is worth 2 marks.)*

Islam:

- The Qur'an encourages procreation, and Muslims believe that conception is the will of Allah, *"...He gives to whom He wills female [children], and He gives to whom He wills males ...and He renders whom He wills barren..."* So contraception is often seen as unwelcome.
- Some Muslims agree with contraception if it'll help prevent suffering. E.g. if there's a threat to the mother's health, if there is a greater than average chance of the child being born with disabilities, or if the family is too poor to raise a child. *(These reasons are worth 4 marks each.)*

*This is a question where you get extra marks for how well you write your answer. You get 2 marks for a well-written reason and 4 marks for a well-written developed reason, up to a total of 8. The question asks about different attitudes, so if you've only written about one attitude, you can only score a maximum of 4 marks.*

d) (i) E.g. No, I disagree with this statement.

- Marriage is out of date. People can have relationships that are just as committed and stable if they cohabit. Children will not be disadvantaged in such a family.
- Many children are brought up just as successfully in happy single-parent families.
- Same-sex couples can provide a child with as much love as a married couple.

*You get 3 marks for two developed reasons (the first reason above is developed), or for three brief reasons, or for one really well developed reason.*

(ii) But some people may disagree with me because, e.g.

- Marriage is a long-term commitment, which provides a stable home for raising children.
- It's important for children to grow up with a role model of each sex. E.g. they will have someone of their own sex to observe, and will see how they relate to someone of the opposite sex.
- Christianity/Islam/Judaism teaches that the only proper context for sex is within marriage.

*As for part (i), you get 3 marks for two developed reasons, for three brief reasons, or for one really well developed reason.*

*BUT — if you didn't mention a religion, the most you can get is 3 marks for parts (i) and (ii) together.*

4 a) The idea that everyone is of equal worth and should be treated with the same level of respect. *(2 marks)*

*You get 1 mark for a partially correct answer,*

b) They may view men and women as equal because, e.g.

- Men and women have an equal obligation to Allah in terms of prayer, fasting, pilgrimage and charity.
- Women were found among Jesus's early followers and he treated them equally.
- In Galatians, St Paul writes, *"There is neither... male nor female, for you are all one in Christ Jesus."*
- The role of men and women in religious texts reflected the society of the time, and shouldn't be used as a rule for today.

Or believe that men and women should have different roles because, e.g.

- Religious texts suggest this is the way things should be.

  *"I do not permit a woman to teach or to have authority over a man; she must be silent."*

  "*Men are in charge of women by [right of] what Allah has given one over the other and what they spend [for maintenance] from their wealth...*"
- God did create two different sexes, so he can't have wanted us all to be identical.
- In worship, men and women traditionally take on different roles.

*Give yourself 1 mark for each religious fact or development of a religious fact, up to a maximum of 4 marks.*

c)
- A Christian would be likely to agree. Christianity teaches that Jesus is the only path to God. Christians believe that only those who follow Jesus will receive everlasting life with God.
- Most Jews and Muslims also feel that there is only one true faith. However, they see that there are similarities between the faiths and believe that God might judge righteous people of other faiths positively.

*You should have put two reasons down. Give yourself 1 mark for each, and another mark for each that you've developed, up to a maximum of 4 marks.*

d) Two from:

Christianity:

- Christianity teaches that everyone was created equal by God, and so discrimination is wrong. In the Parable of the Good Samaritan, one man came to the aid of another who was suffering, even though the men were from enemy tribes.
- Many other Bible verses show the Christian attitude to discrimination and equality, e.g. *"...there is no Greek or Jew... barbarian, Scythian, slave or free, but Christ is all, and is in all."*
- The 'Golden Rule' of Christianity is to *"do to others what you would have them do to you"*. So if a Christian wouldn't want to be discriminated against, he or she shouldn't discriminate against others.

Judaism:

- The Book of Genesis suggests that all of humanity comes from the same source and is, therefore, equal before God.
- Other messages against discrimination are "*When an alien lives with you in your land, do not mistreat him... Love him as yourself...*" and "*Do not abhor an Edomite, for he is your brother. Do not abhor an Egyptian...*"
- Scriptures show that God does not want the Jews to turn their backs on non-Jews, but to be *"a light for the Gentiles"*.
- The story of Ruth promotes racial harmony: Ruth (a Moabite) is very loyal to her Israelite mother-in-law, and becomes devoted to God. This bloodline eventually produces King David. The message is that good things happen to those who are nice to people from other lands.

Islam:

- Islam teaches that all people were created by Allah, and were created equal (although not the same). He intended humanity to be created with differences. But this just means we're all individuals.
- Muslims all over the world are united through the ummah — the community of Islam. This promotes racial harmony, as no one is excluded or discriminated against.
- Hajj demonstrates equality. Those on pilgrimage all wear simple white garments, showing everyone's equal before Allah — wealth, status and colour don't matter.
- The fact that all Muslims should pray five times a day at set times, and face Makkah whilst doing so, also demonstrates unity and equality.

*For each religion, give yourself 1 mark for each teaching, up to a maximum of 3 marks — there are 6 marks on offer altogether.*

e) E.g. No, I don't agree.

- Religious people are just as likely as non-religious people to be concerned about the potential problems caused by immigrants, e.g. taking jobs from local people and placing a strain on the country's resources.
- If the immigrants follow a different religious tradition from the religious person, this could cause tension.

Other people might agree because, e.g.

- Christianity and Judaism teach that it is important to welcome strangers, *"When an alien lives with you in your land, do not mistreat him... Love him as yourself..."*
- Christianity, Judaism and Islam all contain anti-discriminatory teachings. (Most of the reasons given for part (d) of this question could be used here.)
- Christianity, Judaism and Islam teach that all human beings should be treated fairly and humanely.
- Christianity, Judaism and Islam teach the importance of charity, and of caring for other people, e.g. *"let us not love with words or tongue but with actions and in truth"*.

*There are 8 marks available here. You should have put down four, well-written, developed reasons. But to get full marks, make sure you've given specific religious teachings from two or more named religions. If you've only included one religion, only give yourself up to 6 marks. If you didn't mention any specific religious teaching, then 2 marks is the most you can have.*

## Paper 2: Ethics and Society

*Remember, there are 4 marks available for correct spelling, punctuation and grammar in this paper.*

1 a) The moral, legal and political rights that ought to apply to every human being on Earth.

*Give yourself 2 marks for a full definition or 1 mark for a partial one.*

b) E.g. Yes, I do, because:

- The Government sets laws and public policies. It is up to them to set laws to protect human rights and to punish people for infringing the human rights of others.

- Governments decide how taxes are spent, and how much is collected. Governments need to choose policies that protect people's human rights, e.g. universal access to healthcare.

Or, no I don't, because, e.g.

- Christianity teaches that all humans should be treated with dignity and respect. Therefore, it is up to everyone to help uphold human rights.
- Charities do a lot to protect human rights, e.g. Amnesty International and Liberty. They sometimes challenge the decisions of the Government.

*You get 1 mark for a brief reason, and 2 marks for a developed reason — and you should have put down two reasons.*

c) • Believers can look to sacred texts (e.g. the Bible, the Qur'an or the Torah and Talmud) for moral guidance.

- Religious people may also look at the lives and actions of teachers/prophets like Jesus and Muhammad to guide them along the right path. E.g. Jesus treated people equally well, regardless of race or gender.
- They can look to their conscience. Some believers argue that this is the voice of God, so it should be listened to and trusted.
- Believers can look to the teachings of religious leaders.
- For Roman Catholics, the teachings of the Magisterium are as important as the teachings of sacred texts. The Pope is considered infallible on matters of morals.

*This is a question where you get extra marks for how well you write your answer. You get 2 marks for a well-written point and 4 marks for a well-written developed point, up to a total of 8.*

d) (i) E.g. No, I disagree with this statement.

- Breaking the law is always wrong, and laws are made to protect people. Breaking the law will mean someone gets hurt somewhere. E.g. stealing something to help someone will hurt the person you stole from.
- If everyone broke the law whenever they thought it was right to, there would be no order, and society would be in chaos.

*You get 3 marks for two developed reasons (both the above are developed), or for three brief reasons, or for one really well developed reason.*

(ii) But some people may disagree with me because, e.g.

- The Christian principle of situation ethics means you should do whatever is the most loving. If this means breaking a law, then so be it.
- Some religious believers feel that religious laws are more important than civil laws. Therefore, if these conflict, then the civil law should be broken rather than religious law.

*As for part (i), you get 3 marks for two developed reasons, for three brief reasons, or for one really well developed reason.*

*BUT — if you didn't mention a religion, the most you can get is 3 marks for parts (i) and (ii) together.*

2 a) Protecting and preserving things, particularly natural resources *(1 mark)*.

b) E.g. recycling, reducing energy use *(1 mark for each)*.

c) • Some Christians believe that animals don't have souls. This means that God created us as superior to them, so it's okay for us to make use of them.

- Christianity teaches that we should treat animals with kindness, but that they can be used to benefit mankind (as long as their suffering is considered).
- But some Christians think that it's always wrong to cause suffering to animals whatever the benefits will be to us.

*Give yourself a mark for each clear point you make — up to a maximum of 3 marks.*

d) Christianity/Judaism/Islam:

- Christians/Jews/Muslims believe that the Earth is God's/Allah's creation.
- God/Allah gave us the Earth, but expects us to care for it — this idea is called 'stewardship', e.g. *"The Lord God took the man and put him in the Garden of Eden, to work it and take care of it."* Genesis 2:15
- Christians/Jews/Muslims believe that we should try to balance taking care of the Earth with providing for humankind.
- Christianity/Judaism/Islam teaches that everything is interdependent (i.e. everything depends on everything else), so driving species of animal or plant to extinction, or harming the planet, eventually ends up harming us.

Also for Judaism:

- Jews also believe that as custodians, they're responsible for making the world better — this concept is called Tikkun Olam.

Also for Islam:

- Muslims believe they have been appointed khalifah (vice-regents or trustees) of the Earth. This is the idea that they should take responsibility for the world in Allah's name.
- At the Day of Judgement questions will be asked of us. We will be required to answer for any ill-treatment of the planet and its resources.
- The Earth is seen as being a product of the love of Allah, so we should treat it with love.

*Give yourself 1 mark for each point you made and for each development of that point — up to a maximum of 6 marks.*

e) E.g. I disagree with this statement.

- Genetic engineering will make it easier to feed everyone on the planet. This will help those less fortunate than ourselves, which is important in Christianity, Judaism and Islam.
- Genetic engineering also helps us treat diseases. This is the compassionate thing to do, and Christianity emphasises the importance of this.
- People have been using genetic engineering in a more basic form for years — e.g. selecting the best cattle to breed from. This wasn't considered wrong.

But other people may argue that:

- Genetic engineering may lead to cloning and some Christians aren't convinced that clones would have souls.
- Some religious people see genetic engineering as 'playing God'. They believe God created all organisms, and by trying to create more ourselves, we are trying to step into his shoes.
- There are practical problems, e.g. reduction of biodiversity and a reduced gene pool.
- There are a lot of unknowns — e.g. we don't know if genetically modified food is safe to eat. Using genetic engineering is too risky.

*You only get full marks if you:*
- *Give your opinion clearly (1 mark).*
- *Give two really clear, well developed reasons for it (4 marks).*
- *Give two different viewpoints, with reasons (5 marks).*
- *Use really good English, correct spelling and specialist terms (2 marks).*

*If you don't talk about a specific religion, or you don't give other points of view, you can only get a maximum of 6 marks.*

3 a) Infertility is the inability to conceive a child.
*Give yourself 2 marks for a full definition similar to this one, or 1 mark for a partial one.*

b) E.g. Yes I do, because

- Animal testing is an important step in developing new medicines. Even if it isn't perfect, it still gives useful information.
- The book of Genesis tells us that God gave humans dominion over animals. This means that we can use them how we choose.

or, no, I don't because, e.g

- Animals react differently from humans to many medicines. Therefore, suffering caused during animal testing is often pointless.
- Drugs shouldn't be tested on animals routinely. Animals should only be used as a last resort, after it has been shown that there are no alternatives.

*You get 1 mark for a brief reason, and 2 marks for a developed reason — and you should have put down two reasons.*

c) Some Christians agree with organ donation because, e.g.

- Christians have a duty to help and care for others.
- Donating your organs (before or after death) to save a life is an act of Christian love and charity.
- Most Christians believe God won't need their bodies to be intact to resurrect them at Judgement Day, so there's no harm in donating organs after death.

But some Christians disagree with organ donation because, e.g.

- The human body is sacred and so shouldn't be tampered with after death.
- Family members can feel pressurised to allow a loved-one's organs to be donated.
- Transplants could encourage the harvesting and sale of organs from developing countries.

*This is a question where you get extra marks for how well you write your answer. You get 2 marks for a well-written reason and 4 marks for a well-written developed reason, up to a total of 8. The question asks about different attitudes, so if you've only written about one attitude, you can only score a maximum of 4 marks.*

d) (i) E.g. No, I disagree with this statement.

- All forms of IVF create 'spare' embryos that are thrown away. Many people, including most Roman Catholics, argue that life begins at fertilisation, and that even an embryo has rights.
- Only fertility treatments which don't involve another person should be used, e.g. AIH. Other methods, such as AID shouldn't be allowed, as this is a form of adultery, which Christians believe is forbidden by the Ten Commandments.

*You get 3 marks for two developed reasons (these two reasons are developed), or for three brief reasons, or for one really well developed reason.*

(ii) Some people may disagree with me because, e.g.

- It should be up to individual people to choose whether they use medical help to have a child. Everyone should have the right to procreate, whatever their circumstances are.
- Christianity sees children as blessings from God. It shouldn't matter how they were conceived.
- It doesn't matter which type of fertility treatment is used. A child's parents are the people who love the child and who bring it up. It doesn't matter where the sperm and egg come from.

*As for part (i), you get 3 marks for two developed reasons, for three brief reasons, or for one really well developed reason.*

*BUT — if you didn't mention a religion, the most you can get is 3 marks for parts (i) and (ii) together.*

4 a) A pacifist is someone who believes that physical violence is always wrong *(1 mark)*.

b) Christian: E.g. two from:

- God is always ready to forgive us.
- God's forgiveness can only come when we repent of our sins.
- We should always be willing to forgive others.

Jewish: E.g. two from:

- You should always seek forgiveness and make atonement for any wrongs you've committed.
- You can only be forgiven by the one you've injured — so God can only forgive a sin against God, not another person.
- When asked by an offender for forgiveness, one should forgive with a sincere mind and a willing spirit.

Muslim: E.g. two from:

- The Qur'an encourages Muslims to forgive instead of seeking retribution.
- Injuries should be forgiven if the offender is sorry and tries to make amends.
- According to the Qur'an, the only sin Allah will not forgive is idolatry.

*1 mark for each belief — up to a maximum of 2 marks.*

c)
- Christians believe that justice is very important, since we are all equal in the eyes of God.
- God demands justice. This is shown by the fact that Jesus suffered on the cross to pay for our sins.
- Jesus taught that judgement and punishment belong to God: *"Do not judge, or you too will be judged. For in the same way you judge others, you will be judged, and with the measure you use, it will be measured to you."*

*1 mark for each belief, or development of a belief — up to a maximum of 3 marks.*

d) Some religious people are in favour of capital punishment because:

- The risk of death is sometimes believed to act as a better deterrent than a prison sentence.
- If you execute a murderer, it's impossible for them to kill again, so it protects the innocent.
- The Torah/Old Testement is very clear that capital punishment should be allowed: *"If anyone takes the life of a human being, he must be put to death."*
- The Qur'an also clearly states that murderers that can be punished by death, but encourages the family of the victim to accept compensation instead.

Other religious people are against capital punishment because:

- Most Christians (and Jews too) are in favour of mercy. Jesus said that we should set aside *'an eye for an eye'*, in the name of love and forgiveness.
- A lot of murders are committed in the heat of the moment, so many murderers won't be thinking about the consequences so it's not an effective deterrent.
- Execution doesn't give the offender the chance to reform.
- There have been cases where someone has been proved innocent after having been executed.

*Don't forget, religious people won't just have religious reasons for an opinion — they're likely to have moral viewpoints too.*
*Give yourself a mark for each point you made — up to a maximum of 6 marks. Also, make sure you gave some religious arguments for capital punishment, and some against.*

e) E.g. I disagree with this statement.

- War is sometimes necessary to protect innocent people.
- Christians believe that war is sometimes necessary to bring about peace. They have a concept of a just war. This is one that is declared by a proper authority, is defensive, preventing damage that would be "*lasting, grave and certain*", is a last resort, has a reasonable chance of success, and is proportional.
- Jews believe that some wars are obligatory. These are wars fought in self-defence, pre-emptive strikes in order to avoid being attacked, wars to help neighbouring countries (so that your own country is not invaded), or wars commanded by God.
- Muslims believe that war is sometimes necessary. There are strict rules for military jihad, which is similar to the Christian idea of a just war.

But other people may argue that:

- War and physical violence are wrong under any circumstances. All disputes should be resolved peacefully.
- Innocent people are always hurt in wars. The Golden Rule of Christianity is to treat others as you'd like to be treated.
- All violence goes against Jesus's teachings to love your enemy and 'turn the other cheek'.
- The Bible also says: *"Put your sword back in its place... for all who draw the sword will die by the sword."*

*You only get full marks if you:*
- *Give your opinion clearly (1 mark).*
- *Give two really clear, well developed reasons for it (4 marks).*
- *Give two different viewpoints, with reasons (5 marks).*
- *Use really good English, correct spelling and specialist terms (2 marks).*

*If you don't talk about a specific religion, or you don't give other points of view, you can only get a maximum of 6 marks.*

## Paper 3 — Philosophy of Religion

*Remember, there are 4 marks available for correct spelling, punctuation and grammar in this paper.*

1 a) When God reveals his presence to us (or reveals a truth about the world or how we should behave) *(1 mark)*.

b) Christianity: E.g.

- There's only one God.
- God is omnipotent (all-powerful).
- God is omnipresent (everywhere).
- God is omniscient (all-knowing).
- God is perfect and totally good.
- God made the Universe and everything in it.
- God exists in three 'persons' — the Father, the Son and the Holy Spirit (the idea of the Trinity).

For Jewish and Muslim beliefs, see the answers to p91, Q2b.

*This one is straightforward — you don't have to explain anything. Just write down two beliefs, and you'll get 1 mark for each.*

c)
- The Trinity is the idea that God exists in three 'persons' — the Father, the Son and the Holy Spirit.
- God the Father might be described as the transcendent part of God.
- God the Son might be described as the immanent and personal part.
- The Holy Spirit might be described as the immanent yet impersonal part.

*The examiners will be impressed if you use specialist religious terms — but make sure you use them correctly. Give yourself 1 mark for each belief, and 1 mark for each development of a belief, up to a maximum of 3 marks.*

d) E.g. for all three religions:

- God/Allah is believed to have revealed Himself through the scriptures. Many religious followers believe these to be the word of God/Allah.
- A person might feel the presence of God in an answered prayer, e.g. if an ill person they pray for is cured, or if they are filled with a sense of inner peace or wonder.
- In meditation, a believer clears their mind of distractions and focuses on God. Meditation can result in visions or voices as the believer draws closer to God.
- Believers may think that God reveals his presence continually through numinous experiences. These are experiences that inspire awe and wonder, where someone can feel God's presence, e.g. a beautiful sunset, a wild sea or a butterfly's wing might convince you there must be a creator.
- God/Allah is believed to have revealed himself by speaking through the prophets.

Also:

- Christians believe that God revealed himself fully in the person of Jesus.
- Christians and Jews believe that miracles showed God's power and presence.

*Your answer to this question needs to have "range and depth". That means you need to give several different types of revelation, and then develop at least some of them more fully. Give yourself 1 mark for each type of revelation, e.g. scriptures, up to a maximum of 4 marks. Then give yourself 1 mark for each development — 6 marks is the maximum for the whole question.*

e) E.g. Yes. I believe that God/Allah can be found outside scripture:

- Miracles happen today, not just in the scriptures, e.g. healing at Lourdes.
- Some people experience religious ecstasy — ranging from singing, dancing, shaking or crying during worship to 'speaking in tongues' (unknown languages), having visions or prophesying (speaking a message from God).
- God can be found through prayer or meditation. Someone may feel God's presence or hear his voice this way.
- God's presence is often sensed through numinous experiences.

Other people may disagree because, e.g.:

- Religious ecstasy, and experiencing God through prayer cannot be proven. It is likely to be a product of people's imaginations.
- Many Christians believe that we don't live in a time of miracles any more — so called 'miracles' today have a scientific explanation. You need to look to the scriptures to learn about God's power.
- Scriptures are the only place where everyone can learn the same truths about God/Allah, and the only way to truly get to know him.
- They believe he doesn't exist, so can't be found anywhere.

*You only get full marks if you:*

- *Give your opinion clearly (1 mark).*
- *Give two really clear, well developed reasons for it (4 marks).*
- *Give two different viewpoints, with reasons (5 marks).*
- *Use really good English, correct spelling and specialist terms (2 marks).*

*If you don't talk about a specific religion, or you don't give other points of view, you can only get a maximum of 6 marks.*

2 a) Symbolism is when visible things are used to represent beliefs *(1 mark)*.

b) Christians use icons to represent the presence of saints *(1 mark)* and as a means to help them to pray *(1 mark)*.

c) Christian:

- There are no strict rules on the representation of religious figures.
- Jesus is often represented on the cross to remind people of his suffering.
- Frescoes and stained glass windows often depict bibical stories and feature the characters of these stories.
- Pictures and statues of saints are used to represent their presence.

Jewish:

- Jews never try to picture God. This is because no one knows what he looks like and it is considered idolatry (banned by the 10 Commandments).
- No other images or statues of people are allowed in the synagogue, as they're made in the image of God. This is also to avoid idolatry.

Muslim:

- No one is allowed to draw Muhammad or Allah.
- To avoid idolatry, no pictures of any living things are allowed in the mosque.
- The names of Allah and Muhammad are instead written in richly coloured calligraphy.

*Give yourself 1 mark for each belief, and 1 mark for each development of a belief, up to a maximum of 3 marks.*

d) Church, e.g.:

- Altar: the most important place in the church — a table which holds the items for the Communion service.
- Font: this is used to hold water (or 'holy water') for baptism.
- Lectern: this supports the Bible, and its important position in the building shows the Bible's key role in belief.

Synagogue, e.g.:

- Aron Kodesh (the Ark): this is the most important item of furniture, since it holds the Torah. It is a large cupboard or alcove, with doors or a screen, set on the wall facing Jerusalem.
- Ner Tamid (Perpetual Light): above the ark is a light which never goes out. It represents the menorah which was always kept alight in the Temple.
- Bimah or Almemar: a raised platform with a reading desk, from which the Torah is read.

Mosque:

- Minaret: a tall tower from where the muezzin calls the adhan (call to prayer).
- Dome: represents the universe.

- Mihrab: a special niche that shows the direction in which Makkah lies. This is the direction in which Muslims should pray.

  *Give yourself 1 mark for each feature (up to a maximum of 3 marks), and 1 mark for explaining what each is for (up to a maximum of 3 marks again).*

e) E.g. Yes. I agree with this statement.

- A Christian's deeds and actions are more important than what their church looks like.
- Many Christians hold services in their homes, some because Christianity is prohibited in their country — others as they believe it is more like the simpler worship described in the New Testament. This type of worship is just as valid.
- Prayer, hymns and Bible readings are the key elements of Christian worship. These can be done in any sort of building.

Other people may disagree because, e.g.

- Many Christians consider decorating churches elaborately as an expression of worship.
- Many of the visual features of a church, e.g. cross, icons, statues, symbolise religious ideas rather than being just decorative. It is important to keep these ideas in mind during worship.
- Some Christians believe that it is important to have a plain church, so that they are not distracted from God.

*You only get full marks if you:*
- *Give your opinion clearly (1 mark).*
- *Give two really clear, well developed reasons for it (4 marks).*
- *Give two different viewpoints, with reasons (5 marks).*
- *Use really good English, correct spelling and specialist terms (2 marks).*

*If you don't talk about Christianity, or you don't give other points of view, you can only get a maximum of 6 marks.*

3 a) Worship is the religious person's way of expressing their love of and devotion to *(1 mark)* a god or gods *(1 mark)*.

b)
- Someone with a religious faith may feel that the deceased person has moved on to eternal life in, e.g. Heaven, Gan Eden or al'Jannah.
- They might believe that they're going to be reunited with the deceased person after they die, which would be a comfort to them.
- They may pray to God for strength to help them through the difficult time.

*There are 4 marks available here. Give yourself 1 mark for each point, and 1 mark for each elaboration or example.*

c)
- A Christian believer might agree because Christianity teaches that at the Resurrection, everyone will have new spiritual bodies, not their old ones. It is the soul that is judged and lives on, so it doesn't matter what happens to the physical body after death.
- Other religious believers, e.g. Jews, might disagree. They're taught that the physical body will be resurrected one day. Therefore, it shouldn't be cremated, or cut up after death.

*You get 1 mark for a brief reason, and 2 marks for a developed reason. You should have put down two reasons — that's what the question said to do (it's really important to read the question carefully so you know what it's asking you to do).*

d) Christianity:

- For Christians, Sunday is the Sabbath — so most churches have their main service on a Sunday morning.
- In Roman Catholic, Orthodox, and most Anglican churches it will be structured and liturgical.
- Methodists and other nonconformists have structured but non-liturgical services, e.g. following the 'hymn sandwich' pattern, where the service consists of hymns alternating with things like readings, prayers and a sermon.
- Roman Catholic and Orthodox Sunday services always include the Eucharist (also known as Holy Communion or Mass). Anglican churches usually include the Eucharist.
- Pentecostals, House Churches and other independent Christian fellowships may have spontaneous, often charismatic worship.
- Some Christians hold church services in their own homes. Some do this because Christianity is prohibited in their country — others as they believe it's more like the simpler worship described in the New Testament.
- Many Christians worship informally at home (not just on Sundays). This can be anything from saying Grace before a meal to singing worship songs with family and friends.

Judaism:

- Prescribed daily prayers happen at three special times — in the morning, afternoon and evening.
- At these times, men will try to attend the synagogue and become part of a minyan — a group of at least ten men, which is the minimum needed for a service. Women (traditionally because of their domestic commitments) are trusted to pray at home.
- The main service of the week takes place on Saturday morning. The rabbi will read from the Torah and give a sermon. Also, seven men are called up to read or recite a blessing, and an eighth reads a portion from the books of the Prophets.
- As well as the normal daily prayers, there are also special prayers for getting up, going to bed, before and after eating, etc.
- During worship, Jewish men will often wear special clothing, e.g. a prayer shawl, a kippah, tefillin (or phylacteries).

Islam:

- Muslims should pray five times a day — at sunrise, early afternoon, late afternoon, after sunset, and late at night.
- Wudu (washing exposed parts of the body three times before prayer) is important, so that a Muslim is pure and clean when approaching Allah.
- Muslims face Makkah when they pray.
- There is a set ritual for prayer — each unit of prayer is known as a rak'ah. Each rak'ah involves standing, then kneeling, then putting your forehead to the ground as a sign of submission.
- If several Muslims are praying in one place, then they all do the ritual together as a sign of unity.
- Friday prayers are called Salat-al-Jum'ah — it's a community occasion, and at least 40 people should be praying together.

*You don't need to put all of these points down to get the marks. Remember — the more you develop each point, the fewer different points you need to give. For each religion, give yourself 1 mark for each point or development of a point, up to a maximum of 3 marks — there are 6 marks on offer altogether.*

e) E.g. No, I disagree, because:

- Laws about what should be eaten are set down in some religions. E.g. the Kashrut (Jewish food laws) are statutes laid down by God to test Jews' obedience, and to mark them out as different from other nations. To ignore them would be ignoring God's instructions.
- Obedience to Allah is what is required of Muslims. The Qur'an says that certain foods, such as pork, aren't allowed, and since the Qur'an is the word of Allah, it would be disobedient not to follow the food laws.
- Fasting is an important feature of many religions. This is believed to help you focus on spiritual rather than physical matters.
- Food plays a symbolic part in certain religious festivals, e.g. the Jewish Pesach (Passover) feast.

However, some people may agree with the statement, because:

- Food laws laid out in religious scriptures are out of date, like many of the teachings. We should interpret them in light of today's culture — e.g we now use different farming and slaughtering methods.
- It is more important to look after the body that God gave us by eating a healthy diet. We now know more about nutrition than we did when the scriptures were written.

*There are 8 marks available here. You should have put down four, well-written, developed reasons. But to get full marks, make sure you've given specific religious teachings from two or more named religions. If you've only included one religion, only give yourself up to 6 marks. If you didn't mention any specific religious teaching, then 2 marks is the most you can have.*

## Paper 4 — Roman Catholic Christianity

*Remember, there are 4 marks available for correct spelling, punctuation and grammar in this paper.*

1 a) The final week of Lent / the week before Easter / the week commemorating Jesus's final week on Earth *(2 marks)*.

b)
- The Eucharist is the most important part of Mass and the altar is where the bread and wine are consecrated and transubstantiation is believed to occur.
- The altar represents the table at the Last Supper. It is where Jesus's sacrifice is recalled and re-enacted.

*1 mark for each simple point, and 1 mark for each development, up to a maximum of 4 marks.*

c) E.g. No, I don't agree, because:
- Easter is the most important time of year for all Christians as it celebrates Jesus's victory over death.
- Roman Catholics should focus on God everyday, not just on religious festivals. They should consider each day as a sacred celebration of Jesus's life.

Other people might disagree with me because:
- Christmas celebrates the Incarnation — when God came to Earth in human form.
- In today's secular society, Christmas has much more prominence than any other festival. Christians have been influenced by this and so Christmas has taken on more importance than other festivals.

*1 mark for each simple point, and 1 mark for each development, up to a maximum of 6 marks.*

2 a) The Incarnation was the act by which God became a human being *(1 mark)*.

b) Two from: the Bible, Church tradition, the Pope, the Magisterium *(1 mark for each)*.

c)
- The world must be a good thing in itself, since God chose to create it.
- All life is created by God, and so is sacred.
- Since God is the Creator, the world belongs to him, and it is our duty to take care of it for him — this is the idea of stewardship.

*1 mark for each simple point, and 1 mark for each development, up to a maximum of 3 marks.*

d)
- Different beliefs about the Holy Spirit separated the Roman Catholic Church from the Orthodox Church. Roman Catholics believe that the Holy Spirit descended from God the Father and God the Son, whereas the Orthodox Christians believe that the Holy Spirit is the product of God the Father alone.
- The Roman Catholic belief in the importance of Apostolic Succession (that current bishops were ordained by earlier bishops going back in an unbroken chain to the Apostles) separates the Roman Catholic Church from Protestant denominations. Apostolic Succession is what Roman Catholics believe gives the Pope and his bishops their authority.
- The Roman Catholic belief in Apostolic Tradition also separates the Roman Catholic Church from Protestant denominations. Apostolic Tradition is a body of teachings and practices that Catholics believe was passed to the Church directly from the apostles, e.g. belief in the Immaculate Conception. Protestants base all their teachings on the Bible.
- The Roman Catholic belief in the transubstantiation of the Mass separates the Roman Catholic Church from Protestant denominations. Protestants do not believe that the bread and wine become the body and blood of Christ during the Eucharist.

*1 mark for each simple point, and 1 mark for each development, up to a maximum of 6 marks.*

e) No, I don't agree with the statement because:
- The Pope only has authority for Roman Catholics.
- The Pope has no specialist knowledge on most issues, e.g. abortion. We should listen to people with specialist knowledge, e.g. doctors.
- If the Pope's opinion is listened to, then the opinions of other religious leaders should be given equal weight.
- Society should be secular, and religious views shouldn't be considered when deciding public policy.

But other people may disagree with me because:
- Roman Catholics believe that the Pope is able to speak infallibly on matters of faith and morals.
- The Pope has special authority because he is a direct successor of St Peter — 'the first Pope' who was chosen by Jesus.
- If the Pope's teachings on morals are correct, they must be correct for non-Catholics as well as for Catholics.
- We should listen to everyone's opinion in case they make a really good point that hasn't been thought of before.

*You only get full marks if you:*
- *Give your opinion clearly (1 mark).*
- *Give two really clear, well developed reasons for it (4 marks).*
- *Give two different viewpoints, with reasons (5 marks).*
- *Use really good English, correct spelling and specialist terms (2 marks).*

*If you don't mention Roman Catholic Christianity, or you don't give other points of view, you can only get a maximum of 6 marks.*

3 a) E.g. two from: It's a sacrament, and is therefore a vehicle of God's grace; through it, the Holy Spirit renews the person's faith and strength; it links the person's suffering to that of Christ and allows their sins to be forgiven *(1 mark for each point)*.

b)
- Reconciliation through confession is how Roman Catholics obtain forgiveness for their sins.
- Confession is where a believer admits to a priest any sinful things that they've done. To prepare for this, a believer must think seriously about the sins they've committed.
- The priest will give a penance (a certain number of prayers to be said, or an action to be done) and will then pronounce absolution (God's forgiveness).

*1 mark for each simple point, and 1 mark for each development, up to a maximum of 4 marks.*

c) E.g. No, I disagree, because:
- The Eucharist is the most important sacrament. It is through this that Roman Catholics believe that they are taking in the body and blood of Christ, and that this is how Jesus takes up residence in them.
- Confirmation is more important because the person is old enough to understand the vows they are making. The vows are only made on their behalf at baptism.
- Reconciliation is vital for Catholics, because if they die unreconciled they believe they'll go to Hell.

However, some people may agree with the statement, because:
- Baptism marks a person's entry into the Church and washes away original sin.
- Roman Catholics believe that baptism is necessary to enter the Kingdom of God.

*1 mark for each simple point, and 1 mark for each development, up to a maximum of 5 marks. You get the 6th mark for using good written communication.*

4 a)
- They'll understand that it's wrong to even think angry thoughts about someone, or to think lustful thoughts about someone they shouldn't, e.g. someone else's spouse. They'll then be able to seek reconciliation for their sins (or try to avoid these sins).
- They may not tell people about their good deeds, but do them secretly in expectation of a reward from God.
- They may concentrate more on spiritual things and helping others, rather than on material riches.
- They may try to judge others less and forgive their failings.

*1 mark for each simple point, and 1 mark for each development, up to a maximum of 3 marks.*

b) Some local churches demonstrate their love for others by getting involved in campaigns on social issues, e.g. by raising money to help the poor and underprivileged, or encouraging people to buy Fair Trade products. They may also visit the sick and offer consolation to the bereaved.

*1 mark for each simple point, and 1 mark for each development or example, up to a maximum of 3 marks.*

c) E.g. No, I disagree, because:

- Christianity teaches that it is the duty of Christians to relieve poverty. E.g. the Catechism of the Roman Catholic Church says, "*Rich nations have a grave moral responsibility towards those which are unable to ensure the means of their development by themselves...*" This encourages Christians to help the poor.
- There are Christian charities, such as The Passage and Church Action on Poverty which help the poor.
- Members of apostolic orders devote their lives to helping less fortunate people, including the poor.

However, some people may agree with the statement, because:

- Christianity has limited power to help the poor. It is governments that should change their policies.
- Some Churches are very wealthy organisations. They could donate all their wealth to help the poor if they were serious about tackling poverty.

*It's always good to refer to specific teachings, or to give specific examples (like the names of the charities). 1 mark for each simple point, and 1 mark for each development, up to a maximum of 5 marks. You get the 6th mark for using good written communication.*

d) (i) Poverty — Members have no personal possessions. These are given to the community or the poor.

Chastity — Members abstain from sexual relationships to better focus on a life of prayer.

Obedience — Members follow the rules of the community, and promise to obey superiors in the order.

*1 mark for each vow mentioned, and 1 mark for each explanation of a vow, up to a maximum of 6 marks.*

(ii) Yes, I agree with the statement, because:

- Those in contemplative orders remove themselves from the world. They don't do anything to physically help people who are suffering, which is a key teaching of Christianity.
- Even though many religious orders make things to sell to fund the community, this doesn't help others, it is purely selfish.
- They could commit to a life of worship by joining an apostolic order. Members of these orders also dedicate time to prayer and study — but fit it around their work 'in the world'.

However, some people may disagree with the statement, because:

- Jesus said that loving God was the most important commandment — loving others came second.
- Members of contemplative orders are doing what they choose to with their lives. Therefore, they're not wasting them, as the contemplative life must make them happy.

*1 mark for each simple point, and 1 mark for each development, up to a maximum of 5 marks. You get the 6th mark for using good written communication. However, if you didn't mention Christianity, you can only get up to 3 marks.*

## Paper 5: St Mark's Gospel

*Remember, there are 4 marks available for correct spelling, punctuation and grammar in this paper.*

1 a) The brothers James and John — two of Jesus's earliest disciples.

*Give yourself 2 marks for a full definition similar to this one, or 1 mark for a partial one.*

b) E.g. Yes, I do, because:

- It was sinners like Levi who most needed to hear Jesus's teachings. Jesus said *"It is not the healthy who need a doctor, but the sick. I have not come to call the righteous, but sinners."*
- It showed that whatever your background, and however much you've sinned, anyone who repents and follows Jesus is welcome.

Or, no, I disagree, because:

- Levi was a tax collector for the Romans. He betrayed his people by working for the occupiers, so Jesus shouldn't have had anything to do with him.
- The Pharisees didn't approve of Jesus spending time with 'sinners' like Levi, so this led to conflict.

*You get 1 mark for a brief reason, and 2 marks for a developed reason — and you should have put down two reasons.*

c)

- Jesus taught that a believer's true family is his fellow Christians, not his blood relations.
- When his family came to see him while he was teaching, he said *"Who are my mother and my brothers?"* He pointed to those sat listening to him and said *"Here are my mother and my brothers!"*
- Some Christians interpret this as Jesus rejecting his physical family in favour of his spiritual family — and that he was telling his followers to do the same.
- Many modern Christians are uncomfortable with these ideas, and feel that you should love and respect your family whatever their beliefs.

*This is a question where you get extra marks for how well you write your answer. You get 2 marks for a well-written reason and 4 marks for a well-written developed reason, up to a total of 8.*

d) (i) E.g. Yes, I agree with this statement.

- In Mark's account, the disciples sometimes seemed to lack understanding. For example, Jesus had to explain the Parable of the Sower to them, saying *"Don't you understand this parable? How then will you understand any parable?"*
- Peter, James and John failed Jesus three times at Gethsemane. Each time when he went to pray, Jesus asked them to watch with him, but each time they fell asleep.

*You get 3 marks for two developed reasons (both the above are developed), or for three brief reasons, or for one really well developed reason.*

(ii) Some people may disagree with me because, e.g.

- The disciples did Jesus's work by travelling around teaching and spreading the gospel — both during Jesus's life and after his death and resurrection.
- Mark records that the disciples successfully drove demons from people and healed them in Jesus's name, *"They drove out many demons and anointed many sick people with oil and healed them."*

*As for part (i), you get 3 marks for two developed reasons, for three brief reasons, or for one really well developed reason.*

*BUT — if you didn't refer to Christianity, the most you can get is 3 marks for parts (i) and (ii) together.*

2 a) A group of priests who ran the Temple in Jerusalem *(1 mark)*.

b) Laws on food and washing *(1 mark)* that prevented anything spiritually 'unclean' entering a Jew's body *(1 mark)*.

c)

- Jesus saw the faith of the man and his friends and so forgave the paralysed man his sins.
- The Jewish teachers of the law believed that only God could forgive sins, so they thought this was blasphemy.

*Give yourself a mark for each clear point you make — and an extra mark for a development.*

d)

- Jesus argued with the Jews over working on the Sabbath. One of the 10 Commandments forbids work on the Sabbath, but Jesus healed a man's hand and allowed his followers to pick grain to eat. Jesus justified this on the grounds that human need and doing good should come before the letter of religious law. Many modern Christians try to follow this example, e.g. by using Situation Ethics.
- Jesus disagreed with the Jews over the importance of ritual cleanliness. He argued that *"What comes out of a man is what makes him 'unclean'... out of men's hearts come evil thoughts, sexual immorality, theft, murder..."*. For modern Christians, this means that just taking part in rituals such as Holy Communion isn't enough to make them good people in the eyes of God.

*Give yourself 1 mark for each point you made and for each development of that point — up to a maximum of 6 marks.*

e) I agree with this statement.

- According to Mark's account, Jesus was pleased with what she did, saying *"Leave her alone... She has done a beautiful thing to me."* If Jesus approved her action, it can't have been wrong.
- Anointing with perfumed oils was part of the preparation of a body for burial. According to Mark, Jesus felt that she was preparing him for his coming death and burial, *"She poured perfume on my body beforehand to prepare for my burial."*
- It may have been an act of worship. By anointing Jesus with perfume, the woman at Bethany may have been expressing her faith in Jesus as the Messiah or 'anointed one'.

- Anointing with perfumed oils was part of the ceremony to crown a new King of Israel. She may have been recognising Jesus's kingship.
- Whatever her reason was, it was her perfume, so it was up to her what she did with it.

But other people may argue that:

- The perfume was very expensive. Jesus's disciples argued that it could have been sold for *"more than a year's wages and the money given to the poor"*. Her action may be considered very wasteful.
- Jesus had taught before about the importance of giving to the poor, *"sell everything you have and give to the poor, and you will have treasure in Heaven"*, so it seems inconsistent of him to approve of her wastefulness.

*You only get full marks if you:*

- *Give your opinion clearly (1 mark).*
- *Give two really clear, well developed reasons for it (4 marks).*
- *Give two different viewpoints, with reasons (5 marks).*
- *Use really good English, correct spelling and specialist terms (2 marks).*

*If you don't talk about Christianity, or you don't give other points of view, you can only get a maximum of 6 marks.*

3 a) The supreme Jewish council (who tried Jesus for blasphemy).
*Give yourself 2 marks for a full definition similar to this one, or 1 mark for a partial one.*

b) E.g. Yes, I do because:

- Judas chose to betray God in return for money. This is entirely selfish and immoral.
- Whether or not you believe that Jesus was the Son of God, Judas's betrayal sent a good man to his death.

or no, I don't because, e.g.

- Christianity teaches that Jesus's death on the cross was necessary for the salvation of mankind. If Judas hadn't betrayed Jesus, he wouldn't have been arrested and crucified.
- Since Jesus's betrayal, arrest, trial and crucifixion were destined to happen, it was Judas's destiny to betray Jesus. He couldn't have chosen not to.

*You get 1 mark for a brief reason, and 2 marks for a developed reason — and you should have put down two reasons.*

c)
- During the Last Supper, Jesus broke bread with his disciples and said, *"Take it; this is my body."* He then passed around a cup of wine saying *"This is my blood of the covenant, which is poured out for many"*.
- This part of the Last Supper is the origin of the central Christian act of worship — the Eucharist/Holy Communion/Lord's Supper.
- Many Christians believe that by re-enacting the Last Supper, they receive the saving power of Jesus into themselves — Jesus is believed to be present in the bread and wine.
- Drinking the wine during the Holy Communion service also reminds Christians of the new *"covenant"* that God made with his people through the death of Jesus.

*This is a question where you get extra marks for how well you write your answer. You get 2 marks for a well-written reason and 4 marks for a well-written developed reason, up to a total of 8.*

d) (i) E.g. Yes, I agree with this statement.

- As the Roman governor, Pontius Pilate had the power to overrule the Sanhedrin. He could have found Jesus innocent.
- Pilate had the authority to choose Jesus's sentence, and he chose death by crucifixion. He could have passed a lesser sentence, e.g. banishment.
- Mark writes that it was traditional to release a Jewish prisoner to mark passover. Pilate could have chosen to release Jesus — he didn't have to do what the crowd said.

*You get 3 marks for two developed reasons (all the above are developed), or for three brief reasons, or for one really well developed reason.*

(ii) Some people may disagree with me because, e.g.

- The priests who plotted with Judas to have Jesus arrested were responsible for his death.
- The Sanhedrin, and the people who testified falsely in court were responsible for Jesus's death.
- Jesus refused to defend himself in front of Pilate, so Pilate had to find him guilty — Jesus was responsible for his own death.
- The crowd was responsible. They had been stirred up to call for Barrabas, and Mark writes that Pilate didn't want to make them angry by releasing someone else: *"Wanting to satisfy the crowd, Pilate released Barrabas to them"*.
- Jesus was destined to die to atone for human sin, so God was responsible for Jesus's death.

*As for part (i), you get 3 marks for two developed reasons, for three brief reasons, or for one really well developed reason.*

*BUT — if you didn't refer to Christianity, the most you can get is 3 marks for parts (i) and (ii) together.*

4 a) An event in which Jesus's appearance changed miraculously, making his clothes 'dazzling white'.
*Give yourself 2 marks for a full definition similar to this one, or 1 mark for a partial one.*

b) E.g. Yes, I do, because:

- Jesus fulfilled many of the Old Testament prophecies about the Messiah during his life on Earth, for example, in the Triumphal Entry into Jerusalem.
- Jesus's miracles showed that he had the power of God, so he must have been God's chosen, or 'anointed one'.

Or, no, I disagree, because:

- Jesus was just an ordinary person. He showed normal human emotions while he was praying at Gethsemane — he was *"overwhelmed with sorrow"*.
- He didn't fulfil all the prophecies about the Messiah from the Old Testament, e.g. he didn't usher in the 'messianic age', so he can't have been the Messiah.

*You get 1 mark for a brief reason, and 2 marks for a developed reason — and you should have put down two reasons.*

c)
- Peter's confession is the first time that one of Jesus's disciples had openly declared Jesus to be the Christ.
- In Mark's account, Jesus just tells Peter and the other disciples to keep his identity a secret. But in Matthew's account, Jesus responds to Peter's confession by giving him the *"keys to the kingdom of heaven."*
- According to Matthew, Jesus said *"I tell you that you are Peter, and on this rock I will build my church"*. For Roman Catholics, this marks the founding of their Church.
- In the passage, Jesus goes on to give Peter authority on earth: *"whatever you bind on earth will be bound in heaven, and whatever you loose on earth will be loosed in heaven"*. Roman Catholics believe that this authority has been passed down from Peter through a continuous line of Popes to the present day.

*This is a question where you get extra marks for how well you write your answer. You get 2 marks for a well-written reason and 4 marks for a well-written developed reason, up to a total of 8.*

d) (i) E.g. Yes, I agree with this statement.

- Mark recorded the event in his gospel. If you accept the truth of the Bible, you should accept the truth of the account.
- Jesus was the Son of God, so he had the power to perform miracles like the feeding of the 5000.

*You get 3 marks for two developed reasons (both the above are developed), or for three brief reasons, or for one really well developed reason.*

(ii) Some people may disagree with me because, e.g.

- It is physically impossible to turn five loaves and two fishes into enough food to feed 5000 people, so it couldn't have happened.
- Mark's account of the feeding of the 5000 should be viewed symbolically, not literally. It can be seen to represent God providing for those who have trust and faith in him.

*As for part (i), you get 3 marks for two developed reasons, for three brief reasons, or for one really well developed reason.*

*BUT — if you didn't refer to Christianity, the most you can get is 3 marks for parts (i) and (ii) together.*

# Glossary

The **purple** definitions are only for those studying **Christianity** or **St Mark's Gospel**. The **blue** ones are for **Judaism** only. The **green** ones are for **Islam** only. The **red** ones are for everyone.

| | |
|---|---|
| **abortion** | Removing a foetus from the womb before it is able to survive, ending the pregnancy. |
| **absolution** | Forgiveness of sins granted by God through a priest, following confession and penance. |
| **addiction** | A compulsion to keep doing something, even if you know it's harming you. |
| **adultery** | A married person having sex with someone who isn't their husband or wife. |
| **aggression** | In war, this means attacking someone without provocation. |
| **agnosticism** | A belief that it's impossible to know whether or not there's a god. Not knowing if God exists. |
| **akhirah** | The concept of life after death. This is a key Islamic belief. |
| **al'Jannah** | The afterlife paradise — described as 'gardens of delight' in the Qur'an. |
| **apostolic** | A belief that the Church was founded by, and receives its authority from, Jesus's Apostles. |
| **assisted suicide** | Ending your own life with the help of someone else, e.g. asking for a fatal dose of pills. |
| **atheism** | A complete denial of the existence of a god. |
| **atonement** | Reconciliation with God. This often refers to Jesus's sacrifice on the cross to pay for our sin. |
| **barzakh** | The "cold sleep" that the soul enters after death while it waits for the Day of Judgement. |
| **bereavement** | The loss of someone close to you through their death. |
| **bullying** | Intimidating, frightening and controlling people who are weaker than you. |
| **capital punishment** | The death penalty as punishment for a crime. |
| **catechism** | A series of statements laying down the official teachings of the Roman Catholic Church. |
| **catholic** | Universal. Used to describe the community of all Christian believers. |
| **celibacy** | Not taking part in any sexual activities. |
| **chrism** | The blessed oil used in the sacraments of confirmation and ordination. |
| **civil partnership** | The joining of a same-sex couple with the same rights and responsibilities as in a civil marriage. |
| **cloning** | Creating children who are genetically identical to one parent. |
| **cohabitation** | Living together in a sexual relationship without being married. |
| **community cohesion** | The bonds holding a community together, e.g. shared values, shared culture. |
| **conscience** | An inner feeling of what's right and what's wrong. |
| **confession** | Acknowledging something. In the case of Peter at Caesarea Philippi, acknowledging faith. |
| **conservation** | Protecting and preserving resources, particularly natural resources. |
| **conversion** | When someone's life is first changed by becoming a follower of a faith. |
| **corban** | A gift dedicated to God (and so not usable for anything else). |
| **creed** | Statement of religious beliefs. |
| **cremation** | The burning of dead bodies. |
| **Decalogue** | The Ten Commandments, as listed in Exodus 20. |
| **deterrence** | The idea that potential punishment will put people off (or deter them from) committing a crime. |
| **discrimination** | Treating different people, or groups of people, differently (usually unfairly). |
| **disciples** | Followers of Jesus. This can refer to just his followers in the Bible or to all Christians. |
| **displaying religion** | Making a show of good deeds or religious observance to impress other people. |
| **Elijah** | The Old Testament prophet who is prophesied to return before the Messiah. |
| **ethnic minority** | A group of people who have a different ethnic background from most of the population. |
| **euthanasia** | Ending someone's life to relieve their suffering, especially from an incurable, painful illness. |
| **evangelical counsels** | The three vows taken by members of religious orders — poverty, chastity and obedience. |
| **exploitation** | Taking advantage of a weaker person or group of people. |
| **fasting** | Not eating and/or drinking for a set time. Used in religion for atonement or to focus the mind. |
| **free will** | The ability to choose how to behave. All three religions believe humans have free will. |

# Glossary

| | |
|---|---|
| **Gemilut Hasadim** | Kind and compassionate actions towards those in need. |
| **Gethsemane** | The garden where Jesus prayed before his arrest. |
| **Golgotha** | The 'place of the skull' where Jesus was crucified. |
| **Hadith** | Islamic scripture containing a collection of things the Prophet Muhammad said. |
| **holy orders** | Ordination to a deacon, priest or bishop. |
| **Holy Week** | The last week of Lent, lasting from Palm Sunday until the day before Easter Sunday. |
| **humanity** | Either the human race or the caring nature of humans towards each other. |
| **human dignity** | The idea that all human life is valuable and everyone has the right to be treated with respect. |
| **human rights** | The moral, legal and political rights that every human being on Earth is entitled to. |
| **icon** | Paintings of religious figures, used in the Orthodox Christian tradition to help believers pray. |
| **immortality of the soul** | The belief that the soul of a person lives on after the death of the body |
| **Islamophobia** | Fear and/or hatred of all Muslims. |
| **Jairus** | A synagogue ruler whose daughter was brought back to life by Jesus. |
| **justice** | The idea of each person getting what they deserve, and maintaining what's right. |
| **ketubah** | The marriage contract, which sets out the couple's rights and responsibilities. |
| **kiddushin** | Betrothal — the first part of the marriage ceremony. |
| **Incarnation** | The act by which Christians believe God became human, in the form of Jesus. |
| **the kingdom** | The rulership of God in people's lives. |
| **laity** | All non-ordained members of the Church — those who aren't bishops, priests or deacons. |
| **the Law** | The Jewish laws of the Torah, handed down by God. |
| **Lent** | The 40-day period before Easter spent remembering Christ's 40 days of fasting in the desert. |
| **Levi** | A tax collector who was called to be one of Jesus's disciples. |
| **literalism** | The belief that everything in religious scripture is literally true. |
| **liturgy of the word** | The second part of Mass. Bible readings, a short sermon and a recitation of the creed. |
| **Magisterium** | The ability and authority of the Pope and bishops to teach on matters of faith and morals. |
| **mahr** | A dowry paid by a groom to the bride when they get married. |
| **meditation** | A form of religious discipline that involves clearing the mind of distractions. |
| **miracle** | An event believed to be the work of God, that can't be explained by the laws of science. |
| **moral evil** | Suffering caused by human beings, e.g. war, murder, rape, torture. |
| **mourning** | A period of deep sorrow for someone who has died. |
| **natural evil** | Suffering caused by the world we live in, e.g. disease, floods, earthquakes, hurricanes. |
| **natural resource** | Anything found naturally that's useful to humans, e.g. metals, oil, fertile land, etc. |
| **near-death experience** | A vision experienced by someone close to death, usually an 'out-of-body' experience. |
| **nuclear family** | A family made up of a mother, a father and their children living together. |
| **numinous experience** | An experience that inspires awe and wonder, in which someone can feel God's presence. |
| **omni-benevolence** | Showing unlimited love and compassion. |
| **omnipotence** | Having unlimited power — all things are possible. |
| **omniscience** | Knowing everything — in the past, present and future. |
| **Oral Torah** | Jewish teachings passed down orally and recorded in the Talmud. |
| **ordination** | The sacrament of holy orders, by which someone is made a deacon, priest or bishop. |
| **pacifism** | The idea that war and physical violence are wrong under any circumstances. |
| **papacy** | The office of the Pope. |
| **paranormal** | Things that science can't explain, which are thought to have spiritual causes, e.g. ghosts. |
| **Peter's denial** | Peter denying that he knew Jesus after Jesus's trial by the Sanhedrin. |

# Glossary

| | |
|---|---|
| **Pharisees** | A Jewish group who studied the Law and were dedicated to keeping the Jewish faith alive. |
| **Pontius Pilate** | The Roman governor of Judea who sentenced Jesus to death. |
| **prayer** | An attempt to contact God, often in the form of a conversation. |
| **prejudice** | Judging something or someone with no good reason, or without full knowledge of a situation. |
| **pressure group** | An organisation that tries to influence government policy on particular issues, e.g. Greenpeace. |
| **procreation** | Having children. |
| **promiscuity** | Having many sexual partners. |
| **racism** | Discrimination against people of other races — often based on unfair stereotypes. |
| **reconciliation** | Returning to harmony and friendship after conflict. |
| **reform** | The idea that punishment should aim to change criminals so that they won't reoffend. |
| **rehabilitation** | Preparing someone for a return to a normal life. |
| **religious freedom** | The freedom to openly practise or teach a religion, change religion or not follow a religion at all. |
| **religious pluralism** | Accepting that more than one religious view is valid, and that all faiths have the same right to exist. |
| **religious symbol** | An object that represents aspects of religious belief. |
| **reincarnation** | The rebirth of a soul in a new body after death. |
| **resurrection** | Being brought back to life after death. This could be the resurrection of the body or the soul. |
| **revelation** | An experience that reveals a god's presence. |
| **ritual cleanliness** | Laws on food and washing that prevented anything spiritually 'unclean' entering a Jew's body. |
| **the Rosary** | A string of beads used by Catholics, and the set of prayers that goes with them. |
| **the Sabbath** | The Jewish day of rest (Saturday). |
| **Sadaqah** | Aid given in addition to the compulsory Zakah, e.g. money or an act of compassion. |
| **Sadducees** | A group of priests who ran the Temple in Jerusalem and believed in sticking rigidly to the Torah. |
| **sacrament** | A ceremony, or outward sign, of the direct communication of God's saving grace. |
| **Sanhedrin** | The supreme Jewish council, who tried Jesus for blasphemy. |
| **Sawm** | The Muslim obligation to fast during daylight hours through the month of Ramadan. |
| **scribes** | Religious lawyers who made copies of the Torah, and so knew it very well. |
| **Sermon on the Mount** | A summary of Jesus's teachings on how to live a Christian life — Matthew 5-7. |
| **sexism** | Discrimination based on someone's gender (male or female). |
| **the Siddur** | The Jewish prayer book, which gives details of set prayers for specific times. |
| **sin** | An act that breaks a religious law, i.e. when God's teaching is disobeyed. |
| **Situation Ethics** | A Christian ethical principle based on the idea that we should always do the most loving thing. |
| **Sons of Zebedee** | The brothers John and James, two of the first disciples to be called. |
| **stewardship** | Taking care of the Earth as custodians of creation, so it can be passed on to the next generation. |
| **surrogacy** | When a woman bears a child for another woman. |
| **tawhid** | Belief in the oneness and incomparability of Allah. |
| **Tikkun Olam** | The belief that Jews should 'mend the world', e.g. by caring for the environment and the poor. |
| **transfiguration** | An event in which Jesus's appearance changed miraculously, making his clothes 'dazzling white'. |
| **transubstantiation** | Transformation of the Eucharistic bread and wine into the flesh and blood of Christ. |
| **true greatness** | Jesus's teaching that greatness in the eyes of God comes from serving others. |
| **Tzedakah** | The practice of giving 10% of your wealth to the poor. |
| **United Nations** | An international organisation set up to promote peace, global cooperation and human rights. |
| **usury** | Charging high rates of interest on a loan. |
| **wudu** | The ritual washing of exposed parts of the body three times before prayer in Islam. |
| **Zakah** | A Pillar of Islam — all Muslims must donate 2.5% of their yearly savings to the poor. |

# Index

# Index